Ronald Russell has been active in the world of
waterways for many years. He was founder-Chairman
of the Cambridge Branch of the Inland Waterways
Association and chairman of the 1973 National Rally
of Boats. At present he is keeper of the photographic
archives of the Railway & Canal Historical Society.

Lost Canals And Waterways of Britain

RONALD RUSSELL

SPHERE BOOKS LIMITED
30-32 Gray's Inn Road, London WC1X 8JL

First published in Great Britain by
David & Charles 1971
Revised edition published 1982
Copyright © Ronald Russell 1982
Published by Sphere Books Ltd 1983

This book is an expanded and updated version of
Lost Canals of England and Wales by Ronald Russell
first published by David & Charles in 1971

Set in Bembo

Reproduced, printed and bound in Great Britain by
Hazell Watson & Viney Ltd, Aylesbury, Bucks.

CONTENTS

INTRODUCTION

This book is a guide to the exploration, by car or bicycle and on foot, of more than a hundred abandoned canals and derelict river navigations. It is not much concerned with boats or with the economic history of inland waterways except where a few details provide useful background information. The directions are based on the Ordnance Survey 1:50,000 maps, known as the Land-ranger Series, although for a thorough study of a waterway the 2½in (1:25,000) sheets are preferable. Otherwise all you need, apart from a means of transport, are a pair of stout shoes or wellingtons, some sense of direction and an eye for a gradient. Do please remember that many abandoned canals run through pri-vate property and that whatever may have happened to the right of navigation there is no automatic right of trespass.

Each section mostly corresponds with a volume in the Canals of the British Isles Series, edited by Charles Hadfield. There are also sectional maps, titles of helpful books and articles and a list of local canal societies or trusts. To contact any of these groups write to the Inland Waterways Association, 114 Regent's Park Road, London NW1 8UQ, for the name and address of the current secretary.

In 1971 my *Lost Canals of England and Wales* was published. This gave details of over eighty canals and branches lost to navi-gation. Now I am trying to bring the account up to date and to extend the coverage by including Scottish canals and some of the old river navigations. The earlier descriptions have been revised in the light of recent events and it is a pleasure to omit some of the gloomier observations on restoration prospects—on the Thames & Severn Canal, for instance—and to pay tribute to the efforts of the British Waterways Board, and the thousands of voluntary workers of the restoration societies and the Waterways Recovery Group. When in 1962 the Forth & Clyde Canal was closed it was, according to a local newspaper, 'with no protest and very little regret'. Now any threat to an existing waterway is met with the fiercest resistance and obstacles to restoration are confronted with a determination to overcome them whatever the difficulties.

Restoration, however, is not the subject of this book, which I would rather see as the sharing of a personal pleasure. Tracing lost canals has led me into intriguing corners of countryside and towns which otherwise I might never have found. The aqueduct over the River Rea, Oxenhall Tunnel, Sleaford Navigation Wharf, Belan Locks, the Combe Hay flight—these and other fascinating relics of the busy Canal Age, disused, derelict or crumbling away, make their own eloquent comment on the passing of time.

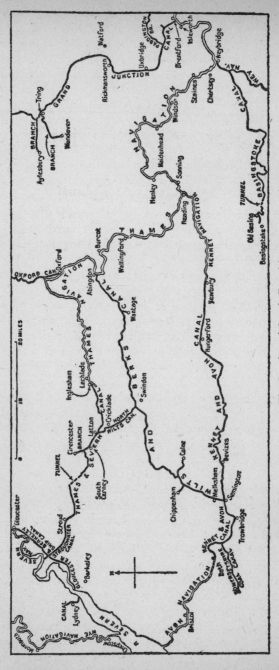

The South and South-East (1)

1

THE SOUTH AND SOUTH-EAST

The Somersetshire Coal Canal

There is an odd remoteness about the countryside south of Bath. It is a region of steep hills, small streams and narrow valleys; the hedges are tall and the roads narrow and winding. It is easy to lose your sense of direction and easy, too, to lose track of the Somersetshire Coal Canal, whose two branches straggle across the area from Paulton and Radstock north-eastward to a junction at Midford and thence to the Kennet & Avon by Dundas Aqueduct beside the A36 road from Warminster to Bath. Dundas Aqueduct, half-way between Claverton and Limpley Stoke, is readily accessible; there is a convenient lay-by on the east side of the main road and a path takes you down to the basin. Here was the junction with the Somersetshire Coal Canal; the towpath bridge has gone, but you can see the line of the canal in the garden of the adjacent cottage, once the lock cottage, with the coping stones of the lock visible in the garden. This junction with the Kennet & Avon was made in 1801, although the SCC was not open throughout until four years later.

The Coal Canal was promoted by Somersetshire mine-owners worried about competition from South Wales and the Forest of Dean and the heavy cost of carriage to Bath. They employed John Rennie, then working on the Kennet & Avon, to make a survey, and among the other engineers involved in the planning were William Jessop, Robert Whitworth and John Sutcliffe. William Smith, later to become famous as a pioneering geologist, was the canal company's own surveyor. The plan that emerged was for a canal with two lines, each serving an area of the coalfield with the mines connected to the canal by tramroad. The line from the K & A to Paulton, a distance of 10½ miles, was completed as planned—or rather as amended; the Midford-

Radstock line was a different matter, as we shall see.

After you have inspected the site of the junction, note the Viaduct Hotel marking the point where the main road crossed the canal. There is a bridge over the canal line close by. Take the Monkton Combe road and continue towards Midford; the canal lies between this road and the Midford Brook at the bottom of the valley. Look out for William Smith's cottage, which cost him his job with the canal company as he bought it for himself while on company business. There is a plaque on the cottage wall commemorating the 'father of English geology'. Next to the cottage there used to be a tucking-mill, but this disappeared many years ago.

Midford has no fewer than three disused and decaying railway viaducts. The main road here is the B3110, which crossed the canal between the Hope and Anchor and a house now called The Moorings but once known as Canal Cottage. Behind this house there was a weigh-house, built in about 1830, a construction of some style and dignity. Boats—the conventional canal narrow boats—were floated into a lock and on to a cradle. Six pillars of Bath stone supported a handsome pointed roof inside which was the cradle's operating machinery. With the boat ensconced, the water was let out and the weight of the boat then recorded. The weigh-house was demolished some years ago and a private house built on the site; the culvert through which excess water was run off into the brook below is in the adjoining garden.

Opposite the Hope and Anchor, beside a bus-stop, you can

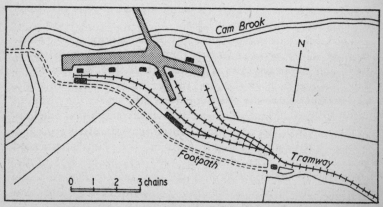

Midford Basin (Radstock arm), Somersetshire Coal Canal

find a footpath. This leads alongside the bed of the canal, now a beautifully cultivated garden. Part of the old bridge survives in this garden, with the date 1800 visible on the coping stone. Follow the path through the nettles to the end of the garden and beyond. The line of the canal is clear. In about 100yd it widens out as a branch joins it from your left. A few steps along is the Midford Aqueduct which took the Radstock line over the Cam Brook. This is 66ft long, with 3 arches over the brook. On the western side most of the facing stone has crumbled away; the eastern side is in comparatively good condition and the lettering on the plaque 'MIDFORD AQUAEDUCT ERECTED 1803 R. TYLER' is legible through binoculars. Some of the coping stones are displaced, but the grooves formed by the chafing of wire-cored ropes are still clear on one of them. Across the aqueduct is the site of the basin where the wagons of the Radstock Tramway offloaded into the canal boats.

Back on the north side of the aqueduct you can continue along the canal bed to a dramatically isolated accommodation bridge. A few yards further on, the line is cut across by an embankment of the Camerton–Limpley Stoke Railway. From the top, you can see the canal continuing westward, soon to coincide with the railway for about $\frac{3}{4}$ mile.

The next point to make for is Combe Hay—not the village in the first instance, but the flight of locks. The SCC was a two-level canal and it was the connecting of the two levels that caused its promoters the greatest concern and expense. Following a country-wide tour of canal inspection by committee members and an examination of a model of Robert Weldon's 'caisson lock' which had been successfully tested on the Shropshire Canal, the committee authorised the construction of a caisson lock at Rowley Bottom, near Combe Hay. This device involved the construction of a masonry chamber, like an enormous enclosed well, in which a watertight wooden box—the caisson—was suspended. This box had a door at each end which lined up with corresponding doors at the top and bottom of the chamber. The box was large enough to take a full-length loaded narrow boat, which was floated into it and then, the doors being closed, raised or lowered to the desired level. Water could be added to or drawn off from the box to enable it to ascend or descend as required. This fearsome machine came to grief on its first trial in February 1798 but was repaired and was operated several times later in the year, some

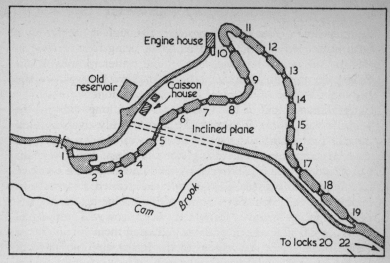

Plan of Combe Hay locks

gentlemen being brave enough to accompany the boat. Further trials took place in the following year, one series being watched with great interest (but no personal involvement) by the Prince of Wales; however, the costs were mounting and, as it seemed that four caisson locks would be needed to overcome the gradient, the committee's enthusiasm waned. Called in to advise, Benjamin Outram pronounced against the caisson lock and the disappointed Weldon, who had supervised the trials himself, departed. If you want to find out more about the caisson lock, Kenneth Clew's *The Somersetshire Coal Canal and Railways* contains two contemporary descriptions of it and a plan. Excavations have so far not revealed its precise site, although the evidence points to somewhere near Lock 5 of the Combe Hay flight.

In his report, Outram proposed the construction of an inclined plane and, despite some bizarre counter-proposals, including one for a 'geometrical lock', it was this that was next built. For conveyance on the incline the coal was carried in boxes, offloaded from the boats by crane at the top, lowered three at a time into wagons on the incline and transferred into boats again at the lower level. (Nearly all the SCC traffic was, of course, downwards.) To obviate a cutting, three locks were built in the canal at the foot of the slope. The inclined plane descended from a point close to the west side of Caisson House, with the later Lock 5 on its line. It was brought into use in November 1801, completing the main line of the canal. However, although it operated for four years it did not solve the problem, being found both inefficient and time-consuming. Six months after its completion the canal company obtained a new act enabling locks to be built and a special lock fund was set up to raise the money.

By 1806, 19 locks had been built, each 75ft long and 7ft 3½in wide, falling 5ft 9in. With the 3 locks previously constructed at the foot of the incline, the flight lifted the canal 154ft. You find them by continuing towards Combe Hay from Midford. You pass a turning to South Stoke and then look out for the entrance to a field on the north side of the road, crossed by a railway bridge. On the other side of the road is a blue-painted house. Note the footpath sign into the field, where you will find several of the locks close to the perimeter. Following them takes you in a semi-circular sweep until they straighten out alongside a track leading up through trees, with the railway embankment on the other side with which the track soon coincides. At the top of the track you find yourself on a bridge over the canal with the locks continuing in a field on one side and Caisson House, which antedates the canal but became a handsome residence for its engineers, on the other. A milepost near the house shows 4 miles from the Kennet & Avon. In the grounds of the house you can find the overgrown site of the engine-house, near Lock 10, installed to pump water up the flight, the upper canal basin and part of the inclined plane, but if you wish to see them you should first obtain permission from the owner. Some of the lower locks of the flight have been cleared of the trees and other growth; the lock chambers are in remarkably good condition, especially when you remember that the canal was closed in 1898.

Now carry on to Combe Hay. The canal looped north of the village; a few hundred yards on the west side is a short tunnel with rubbish tips on either approach. This was originally a canal tunnel but was adapted for the Camerton-Limpley Stoke Railway, opened in 1907 with much of its line built on the canal bed. This line was closed in 1951, raised from the dead the following year for the filming of *The Titfield Thunderbolt*, and finally destroyed in 1958 when the track was lifted.

Continue towards Dunkerton. In a lay-by on the Bath-Radstock A367 road, just north of where you will cross it, are the remains of the bridge which took this road over the canal. From here you may see the earth aqueduct on which the canal was carried over a valley to the north-west. The canal line continues on the north side of the Dunkerton-Camerton road and is not difficult to trace. A milepost lurks in the undergrowth. Note the Jolly Collier Inn at Camerton, recently enlarged. This used to be a popular boatmen's halt, with the canal running at the back of the building.

At Radstock the road crossed the canal just to the north of the cross-roads. From here, either try walking along the canal line to Paulton Basin, or drive on towards Paulton and turn off northwards along a lane leading to Hanham House. The lane becomes a track which you can follow downwards, past the remains of Paulton Ironworks with the spoil heaps of Paulton Colliery on your left. You cross the brook and come to the clearly defined outlines of two basins. The first one, with a ruinous bridge that once spanned the entrance to a dry dock for boat repair, served the colliery and foundry; the basin to the west was the terminus of the canal. It was fed from the little brook, and the channel and a stone culvert can be found. The ruins of the wharfinger's house are nearby.

Of the Radstock arm of the canal there is little left to be seen. The canal had been cut from a basin at Radstock, on the south side of the Waldegrave Arms, to Twinhoe. From there a tram-road 1 mile long took the coal to Midford, where it was loaded on to boats again for the remainder of its journey. There was never enough money to build locks at Twinhoe, and the arm, as it was originally constructed, was little used. The engineer John Hodgkinson was called in to advise and recommended building a tramway on the towpath of the canal. This the company did: the line was opened in 1815 and proved generally successful. It eradicated the canal apart from a short stretch at Wellow where part of a 405ft tunnel survives in a farmyard on the opposite side of the road to the church. The north portal could be found, bricked up, in a field behind the church, below the spire as you look up towards the higher ground. In 1871 the Radstock Tramway was sold to the Somerset & Dorset Railway; this line was closed in 1967.

In its time the Somersetshire Coal Canal was a profitable undertaking, carrying well over 100,000 tons of coal a year in the 1830s and 40s, and paying healthy dividends. In the mid-nineteenth century it served between twenty and thirty pits, building up the prosperity of the Somerset coalfield and contributing greatly to the trade of the Kennet & Avon and Wilts & Berks

Canals which carried Somerset coal across the country. It continued to make profits until 1890, when it was overwhelmed by railway competition. Despite the fact that railway lines were laid over much of its course—and where else could they be laid in this difficult countryside?—there are many relics that can still be found. It seems unlikely—I am cautious here in view of what has happened elsewhere—that a Somersetshire Coal Canal Restoration Society would ever meet with much support or success; but a preservation society, to ensure the retention of the locks, Midford Aqueduct, Paulton Basin and the other remains, would have an important role to play. The Somersetshire Coal Canal created much wealth for the country and deserves better than neglect.

OS sheets 172, 183

The Stroudwater and the Thames & Severn Canals

In the southern half of England there were once three cross-country inland waterway routes. The greatest of these, the Kennet & Avon, is now well on the way to full restoration. The least of them, the Wilts & Berks, is never likely to be restored, although some isolated stretches are being preserved and improved. For the third route, the Stroudwater, Thames & Severn, the prospects in the last few years have brightened considerably. When the Kennet & Avon is reopened, the line from the Severn to the Thames will share with the Montgomeryshire Canal the foremost position in the list of ambitious, valuable and popular restoration schemes.

The Stroudwater Canal and the Thames & Severn were quite distinct undertakings. The growth of industries in the Stroud Valley, particularly woollen mills, directed interest to the provision of water transport. A canal 8 miles long with 12 wide locks was completed in 1779, connecting Stroud with the Severn at Framilode. Coal from Staffordshire and the Forest of Dean was carried to Stroud and wool was exported. The canal prospered, trade increasing still more when the Gloucester & Berkeley Canal was opened in 1820 enabling boats to bypass the trickier reaches of the Severn and, with its later extension to Sharpness, easing the access to and from Bristol and South Wales.

A few shareholders of the Stroudwater were among the promoters of the Thames & Severn, opened from Stroud to the

Thames near Lechlade in 1789. The first of the southern cross-country routes was now complete with the two canals meeting at Wallbridge, near the centre of Stroud, although the canal companies remained independent. The Thames & Severn, however, never equalled the prosperity of its neighbour. Much of the workmanship, especially in the long tunnel at Sapperton, was faulty and the summit level suffered from both water shortage and leaks. The Upper Thames was a poor navigation which traders using London wished to avoid. Moreover, the Severn trows which used the Stroudwater could navigate only as far as Brimscombe on the Thames & Severn as the locks to the east were too narrow for them. Hence goods had to be transhipped at Brimscombe Port, an operation regarded by many traders as a waste of time and money.

The last recorded through voyage on the Thames & Severn was made in 1911. Many attempts to keep the canal going had been made in the previous decades, but all had failed. The Chalford–Stroud section, the last to be navigated, was abandoned in 1933. The Stroudwater Canal continued for a few more years, commercial traffic ending in 1941, and the waterway being legally abandoned, despite opposition in Parliament and from voluntary bodies, in 1954. Then in 1972 the Stroudwater Canal Society was founded, later to become the Stroudwater, Thames & Severn Canal Trust; decay was halted and the outlook began to change. Now as you visit the inland waterways connection between the Severn and the Thames you will see evidence of the efforts of voluntary working-parties and job-creation schemes. Restoration throughout is no longer an idle dream.

The junction of the Stroudwater with the Severn is filled in, although part of the length between Saul Junction on the Gloucester & Sharpness and Framilode village is used for fishing. Saul Junction lies about 2 miles west of the A38; a turning west at Whitminster, 7 miles south of Gloucester, takes you across the Stroudwater and you can walk beside it to the junction. This part of the canal is used for moorings. South of Whitminster much of the canal has vanished under the motorway interchange. East of the interchange, from Chippenham Platt to Stroud the canal runs close to the southern side of the A4096. A short stretch has been filled in and you will find a few culverts, but generally the waterway is in reasonable condition with some original bridges—Nutshell Bridge, south of Stonehouse, is a good example. The canal is popular with fishermen. Some of the lock chambers are sound enough, although the upper gates have been replaced by weirs.

The final stretch of the Stroudwater Canal in Stroud itself is culverted. Wallbridge Junction is on the south side of the town centre, accessible from the A46 south of the railway bridge. There are the chambers of the two Wallbridge locks of the Thames & Severn and the Stroudwater company headquarters building by the site of the basin. From here you can follow the towpath of the Thames & Severn for 8½ miles to the west portal of Sapperton Tunnel; a few diversions are necessary but present no problem. On the walk you will see results of the work of the canal trust; a lock and some bridges have been repaired and parts of the channel dredged. Much of the immediate landscape is not inviting, consisting of the backsides of garages and factories of no architectural merit. The A419 Stroud-Cirencester road accompanies the canal as far as Chalford.

Whether walking or travelling by car you should make time to stop at Brimscombe, midway between Stroud and Chalford. South of the main road is the Ship Inn, an old canalside pub; a few yards eastward is the site of Brimscombe Port, the centre of the canal's trading activities. The basin, 700ft long, was filled in and the large and elegant three-storey warehouse, long transit shed, forge, barge-weighing machine and manager's office were demolished in 1966 to make way for Benson's factory which now occupies the site. Two only of the old buildings survive near the factory entrance; one was a wharfinger's cottage and the other a salt store. In the middle of the basin a coal store was built upon an island, for reasons of security. On one of the factory buildings there is a plaque commemorating the port with a stone bearing the date 1801 inset beside it. In the canal's working life a permanent staff of seventeen used to work at Brimscombe, which was by far the busiest of the twelve wharves on the waterway.

The towpath can be regained from a lane alongside the River Frome, never far from the canal between Stroud and Chalford. At the end of the port site was Bourne Lock, the last of those large enough to take the Severn trows. From here eastward, West-Country barges or narrow boats were the vessels used. About 2 miles further on you come to the first of the canal's five round-houses, built to accommodate the lock-keepers or 'watchmen'. They were three-storey dwellings, with a stable, living-room and bedroom in ascending order, providing good views along the canal in both directions. Their denizens, however, did not much like them—which is not altogether surprising—and no more were built after the first five. Several mill buildings and factories that were once served by the canal still survive in Chalford.

The main road swings southward away from the canal at Chalford; to continue by car you have to aim for Sapperton, either via the lower road through Chalford and across the hills through Oakridge or by turning north to Frampton Mansell. If you get lost, ask for the Daneway Inn; or you can follow the towpath past a succession of delightfully named locks: Bell, Red Lion, Golden Valley, Lower and Upper Baker's Mill, Lower and Upper Puck Mill, Lower and Upper Whitehall, Bathurst's Meadow and the three locks of Sickeridge Wood. This is the Golden Valley, with the wooded hills rising steeply on either side, luxuriant and beautiful.

At the top of the climb are the two Daneway locks—the upper lock now beneath the car park of the Daneway Inn. This was originally a house built for the canal company in 1784, which a few years later was converted into a pub called the Bricklayers' Arms. It was modernised and renamed in the late 1960s. Between the last two locks there were a basin, warehouse and coalyard and the company also made a road from here to Sapperton village for the conveyance of coal. A battle to prevent the bridge at Daneway from being rebuilt without navigational headroom has recently been won, so that restoration of the Golden Valley ascent remains a possibility.

From Daneway it is a short towpath walk to the west portal of Sapperton Tunnel, 3,817yd long. The Gothic-styled stonework is crumbling away, but full restoration is proposed. The problems of cutting the tunnel and of dealing with the many contractors including the 'vain, shifty and artfull' Charles Jones are graphically described in Humphrey Household's comprehensive study *The Thames & Severn Canal*. It is estimated that 200–300 men were employed in making the tunnel, many of them miners from the West Country and Derbyshire. They lodged in the Bricklayers' Arms and the New Inn (later the Tunnel House); some of them married local girls and several are buried in the parish churchyards of Sapperton and Coates.

Twenty-five shafts were sunk in the construction of the tunnel. Much of its length ran beneath Earl Bathurst's park and the spoil heaps were disguised by clumps of trees easily visible from the A419. The east portal is in Hailey Wood, accessible from the road between Coates and Tarlton. This road crosses a restored length of canal running through a wooded cutting. A track leads you across the portal and into the car park of the Tunnel House, originally a three-storey building but damaged by fire in 1952. The top floor, now lost, was used as a dormitory by the men working on the tunnel. The portal itself has been splendidly restored under the aegis of the canal trust.

From the bridge on the Coates-Tarlton road you can follow the towpath to the derelict Coates round-house. This is bleak, upland country, very different from the Golden Valley; here the canal water leaked away through the oolite, adding to the problems the canal company faced. The towpath leads you beneath a railway bridge and in 1½ miles to Thames Head Bridge on the A433 Cirencester-Tetbury road, built on the line of Akeman Street. Midway between the round-house and the bridge is the source of the Thames, although the statue that used to mark the spot has been removed to St John's Lock at Lechlade. 'The numerous little fountains rise in infantine playfulness, four to five inches in height, at the foot of some rising ground planted with trees or shrubs,' wrote W. G. Fearnside—although few people have seen more than a few dry stones. The canal is embanked above the source. Thames Head Bridge is now in a lay-by off the A433, with a plaque affixed to the eastern parapet.

A short distance along the canal eastward is a group of buildings, the site of Thames Head Pumping Station. Soon after the canal opened and the shortage of water on the summit became apparent, the canal company built a windpump with six sails to lift water from the springs and watercourses below. In 1792 the windpump was replaced by a steam-engine designed by Boulton & Watt; this served the canal for 52 years until, at last worn out, it was dismantled. A Cornish beam-engine was installed in its place, able to raise 3 million gallons of water every 24 hours. It was removed for scrap-iron in the 1940s and the engine-house was demolished. Near the dwelling house and outbuildings is the well, over 60ft deep, and the conduits through which water was fed to the canal can also be found.

The canal straggles eastward; the Smerril Aqueduct used to take it across the Cirencester-Kemble road and you can see the abutments. Siddington Upper Lock marks the end of the summit level and begins the descent of 129ft to the Thames. The short branch to Cirencester left the main line at Upper Siddington, but very little of it can now be traced. At Siddington four locks were built very close together; a house now stands on the site of the lowest. The towpath is a right of way from Siddington to South Cerney, where the three locks have been filled in; you can see the coping stones of Cerney Upper in the garden of the former lock cottage. From South Cerney to Latton the canal is intact. Access from the A419 Cirencester–Swindon road is from the Spine Road at a stretch of dual carriageway about midway between Cirencester and Cricklade. There is a tourist information lay-by beside the canal; walking northward you will come to the two Wildmoorway Locks and southward to the round-house and lock at Cerney Wick.

At Latton, west of the village, is the junction with the North Wilts, connecting the Thames & Severn with the Wilts & Berks Canal at Swindon. South of Latton the road crosses the canal; look for the Cricklade wharf house by the minor road to Kempsford. The canal swings north-eastward and now lies between the Kempsford road and the Thames. The third turning to the right, just past the road to Marston Meysey, leads to Marston Meysey round-house. On the south side of Kempsford there is a house built for the canal agent, with warehouses attached.

The last 3 miles from Kempsford to Inglesham run through open and deserted country, the only dwelling being the farm at Dudgrove. The double locks at Dudgrove no longer remain. From the north, the River Coln now approaches, to join the Thames alongside the canal at Inglesham. Access to the junction is from a lane leading south at Downington, ½ mile along the A417 west of Lechlade. Inglesham round-house is privately owned and in good condition, as is the chamber of Inglesham Lock. The canal company's wharves were not at Inglesham but on the north-west side of Halfpenny Bridge at Lechlade; there were two wharves, a dock with boat-houses, a warehouse and offices and stores.

Restoration of the Thames & Severn to navigable standards may involve cutting a new canal from Latton to the Thames, near Cricklade. It would also involve resiting several of the locks; one of the reasons why the canal's operation was beset with difficulties was that the locks were made with unequal falls. Nevertheless, the prospects are real; in a few years'—or decades'—time, it may again be possible to voyage from Stroud to the Thames by way of Sapperton Tunnel, and perhaps the two mighty rivers of the Thames and Severn may celebrate their remarriage beneath Lord Bathurst's woods.

OS sheets 162, 163

The Wilts & Berks Canal

Of the three east-west cross-country waterway routes in the southern half of England, the Wilts & Berks must have inspired the least confidence. Unlike those of the Kennet & Avon and the Thames & Severn, its locks could take only narrow boats; there were no tunnels or major aqueducts to shorten its line, which wandered across the two counties as if, at times, its surveyor had lost his sense of direction.

The history of this canal, like its engineering, lacks drama. The main line was opened in 1810 from Semington, on the Kennet & Avon, to Abingdon, on the Thames, 51 miles with 42 locks. Branches to Calne, Chippenham, Longcot and Wantage had been completed in the previous decade. Coal from Somerset was the main cargo, travelling eastward along the Somersetshire Coal Canal—another narrow-boat waterway—and the Kennet & Avon. There was little traffic in return, however, and boats often returned uneconomically light or empty. In 1819 a connection was made with the Thames & Severn by the 9 miles long North Wilts Canal; this brought some coal from the Forest of Dean and the Midlands and enabled craft off the Thames & Severn to bypass the difficult stretch of the Thames between Lechlade and Abingdon. The canal met mild financial success in the 1830s and 40s, but suffered from railway competition and the gradual closing down of the Somerset coalfield. In the 1870s it was losing money and in the next few years it was sold, leased and taken over, all to little avail. Abandonment was sought in 1897, although an act was not obtained until 1914 as local landowners wanted it kept for water supply. By 1906 all commercial traffic had ended and much of the canal was stagnant and smelly. Since 1977, however, what is left—and there is a good deal—has become the concern of the Wilts & Berks Canal Amenity Group, which hopes to preserve the remains and improve their condition wherever possible.

This is a long canal, but much of its course is shown on the OS maps and itineraries have been published in recent years, notably in L. J. Dalby's *The Wiltshire & Berkshire Canal*. Travelling from west to east, go first to Semington Bridge where the A350 crosses the Kennet & Avon 2 miles south of Melksham. The bridge that carried the K & A towpath over the entrance to the Wilts & Berks has been filled in but is discernible. The private house to the north of this spot was the toll-collector's house; in the garden is the site of the regulating lock. Continue to Melksham, looking out for a line of trees and hedges on the right, marking the line of the canal. Melksham Wharf was by Devizes Road; possibly some buildings may survive. At the Forest Road/Calne Road junction look for traces of a bridge that once crossed the canal.

From Melksham the line winds northward in the general direction of Chippenham, keeping on the east side of the Avon. You can try following it across the fields, noting the remains of Melksham Forest Lock and a small aqueduct over a stream near Forest Farm; or take the A350 and turn off to Lacock: the canal is ½ mile east of Lacock Abbey and accessible from two minor roads. The walker should be able to follow the canal to the A4, with some interesting minor structures to see. By car you carry on to Chippenham, where almost all of the 2 mile branch has vanished, including a short tunnel. A bus station has been built on the site of the basin. Leave Chippenham on the A4 Calne road to find the line of the canal 2 miles from the town centre; then on to Studley and turn left into the village and left again to the site of Stanley Abbey. In a few hundred yards look for the canal line past Stanley Abbey Farm; leave your car and follow the line north-eastward. In a few yards you will find a bridge that took the branch railway to Calne over the canal. A further 300yd brings you to Stanley Aqueduct over the Marden. One of the aqueduct's two 12ft arches partly collapsed in 1906 and the remaining structure is fragile. This insignificant-looking aqueduct, as L. J. Dalby remarks, was the largest engineering work of the Wilts & Berks. Follow the canal past the chambers of the two Stanley Locks: Bottom, with a fall of 9ft 2in, and Top, falling 7ft 11in. The Wilts & Berks locks were deeper than average, most of them measuring about 9ft, with two of the Pewsham locks (you may have noticed their remains near the junction with the Chippenham Branch) measuring just over 10ft. Soon after Stanley Top is the junction with the branch to Calne. This can be traced alongside the Marden to the site of another aqueduct over the river. To cross the river you may have to divert, returning to follow the branch around Conigre Farm and through the remains of the two Conigre locks. The branch once tunnelled beneath the A4; south of the road on the final stretch are the sites of three drawbridges and Calne Lock. Harris Ltd, of pork-pie fame, use the Calne Wharf site as a car park.

From Stanley Top to Dauntsey Lock is more than 6 miles, with access to the canal from only 4 minor roads. The B3102 heading north from Calne meets the A420 at Lyneham; turn left and Dauntsey Lock is 2 miles away. The lock itself has vanished, but the lock cottage, wharf house and other canal cottages are still there. Some of these buildings have recently been surveyed by the amenity group, whose members hope to clear a length of canal here.

Between Dauntsey Lock and Wootton Bassett the canal lies close to the railway line on its southern side, roughly parallel to the A420. There are 7 locks within $\frac{1}{2}$ mile on this section. A minor road on the left, $\frac{1}{2}$ mile east of Lyneham on the A420, takes you across the canal near Bowd's Farm. Here was the bottom lock, and you can examine the remains of the others by walking north-eastward along the canal. These locks raised the canal by about 60ft.

Like the railway, the canal keeps south of Wootton Bassett. There was a wharf at Templar's Firs; here the town council and the amenity group hope to establish a canal park. Further eastward is the site of Summit Lock: from Semington the canal has climbed through 24 locks, and now it descends through 18 to the Thames. The M4 cuts across the canal midway between Wootton Bassett and Swindon, and you may find it best to take the A420 into Swindon and retrace the canal from there.

Kingshill, on the south-west side of Swindon, is another place where the amenity group are working. A skew bridge, recently damaged, took a branch line over the canal near West Leaze. The canal is in water here and the intention is to make a water park in this area. Approaching the centre of Swindon the canal becomes a footpath; note rope marks beneath Cambria Bridge and the handsome Milton Road Bridge. Market Street was once Wharf Road—there are plenty of indications of the Wilts & Berks despite a massive rebuilding programme. Make for Canal Walk in the Brunel Shopping Centre and look for a milestone—not quite in its original position—near Regent Street. The Parade covers the junction with the North Wilts Canal; Fleming Way is built on the main line and the fire station covers the site of a wharf. Leave Swindon by the A420; beyond the town the canal is on the south side of the road but filled in for nearly 2 miles. Past Long-leaze Farm were the four Marston locks and the site of an aque-duct over the River Cole.

Approaching Shrivenham, turn south on to the B4000 for Shrivenham Arch Bridge, now cleared of a disgusting accumula-tion of rubbish by the amenity group. The Longcot Branch leaves the main line about 1½ miles further on, in the field east of the military college. You can reach the branch from the B4508 Shrivenham-Kingston Bagpuize road; the first turning left on this road brings you to the site of the basin. Unless you have unlimited time, it is best to cut south to the B4507 and make for Wantage. All the turnings northward off this road take you to the canal, which swings around Uffington and passes through West Challow and East Challow. In Wantage the site of the wharf is near the bottom of Mill Street with several of the early buildings, including the wharfinger's house. The junction with the main line is ¾ mile northward from the wharf, by the site of Grove Top Lock. On the south side of Grove by the first milestone from Wantage on the A338 there is a group of wharf cottages; Grove Common Lock was on the right of the main road.

Abingdon is now about 7 miles away and access by road to the canal again is difficult. A minor road through Grove Park crosses the canal near Neville's Farm and another road from East Hannay on the A338 to Steventon crosses at Cow Common. There are the remains of three locks in varying states of decay between these roads.

If you approach Abingdon by the A34 you will find the canal bed at Caldecott; look for signs of an embankment on the west side of the road. Opposite the embankment, Caldecott Road takes the line of the canal towards the Thames. On the riverside at the southern edge of Abingdon is a cast-iron bridge over the River Ock, erected by the canal company in 1824 and so in-scribed. To the south of the bridge is the site of the canal entrance and the basin is in the yard of a laundry. Here, on Friday 10 September 1810, 'a body of the Proprietors passed the last lock into the Thames amidst the loud huzzas of multitudes assembled to witness the spectacle'.

To explore the North Wilts Canal it is advisable to begin from the Thames & Severn Junction at Latton, near Cricklade, and travel southward to Swindon. In fact, an hour or two in the Cricklade area will reveal most of this canal's more interesting relics and as you approach Swindon there is less and less to see. Latton is just over a mile north-west of Cricklade on the A419 Cirencester–Swindon road. A private lane on the west side of the road leads to a basin, clearly visible, and the lock cottage. An aqueduct took the North Wilts over the Churn and another, about ⅓ mile further on, over the Thames. This used to have three arches; it has been replaced by a footbridge.

In Cricklade turn on to the B4040. West Mill Lane, running north, takes you to the canal and to the site of the north portal of Cricklade Tunnel, now buried. There was a wharf on this lane. On the opposite side of the B4040 look for a cutting and any trace of the south portal of the tunnel. Chelworth Wharf was nearby. Now move to the B4041 and, just under a mile from the centre of Cricklade, stop at a left fork. At this point the B-road crosses the canal; on your left is the River Key and, lurking in the roadside shrubbery, is the aqueduct that took the North Wilts over this Thames tributary. For about 3 miles the canal accompanies the minor road that forks off the B4041. South of Pry Farm the canal moves away eastward, soon to cross the River Ray by a three-arch aqueduct. Between here and Swindon may prove unrewarding as most of the remainder of the North Wilts is either filled in or inaccessible.

With a total of 67 miles the Wilts & Berks and its branches is the longest of our derelict canal navigations. Although there is nothing splendid to see, it is worth spending some time on your exploration, giving it at least two full days if that is possible. There is much more to discover than has been mentioned here and, away from the main roads, it is a pleasant, placid countryside that the old canal traverses.

OS sheets 164, 173, 174

Hampshire Waterways

The Avon
The navigations of Hampshire were no more commercially successful than those of neighbouring Sussex, despite their antiquity. Andrew Yarranton (of the Dick Brook and the Worcestershire

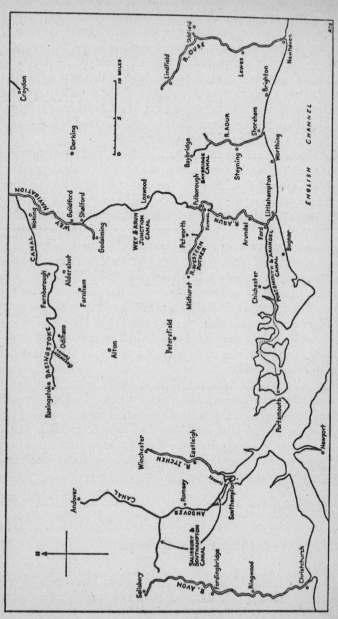

The South and South-East (2)

Stour) undertook a survey in 1664 and work started the following year. There is some evidence that barges navigated to Salisbury in the 1680s, but before the end of the century the works were either left incomplete or were damaged by floods. Further attempts were made to complete the navigation but by 1730 these were abandoned. A petition of 1772, seeking parliamentary leave to have obstructions in the river removed, says that 'navigating the said River was soon found to be attended with so many Difficulties and Inconveniences, that it did not answer the Purposes intended and is now wholly discontinued'.

The navigation cuts are shown on William Naish's map of Salisbury, 1751. There were ten in all, but not all of them can be traced today. The first cut was at Britford, south of Salisbury, on the west side of the A338. On the second turn to Britford, past Manor Farm, a brick bridge crosses the cut. Beside this bridge is a lock, the only one of the navigation's three pound-locks that can now be identified. It is estimated that it dates from the early eighteenth century; it may have replaced a flash-lock built earlier. The iron sluice-gates are nineteenth century and have nothing to do with the navigation.

Nothing conclusive has been found at the next cut at Downton, and the lines of the next two southward cannot be ascertained. The making of channels for water meadows has confused this issue—a look at the map will show how complex the Avon is. At Fordingbridge there is a significantly named place called the Horseport on the A338, where the road crosses the navigation cut; it has been suggested that there was a wharf where Victoria Cottages now stand. There were further cuts at Ellingham Church, Ringwood, Avon, Sopley and Winkton, all of which can be traced, although there is no firm proof of navigation structures.

It seems unlikely that the navigation ever had a towpath and the probability is that the barges were sailed when possible and hauled through the locks. Valuable evidence has been found in a deposition of 1737 in which inhabitants of Standlynch recalled the old navigation:

> Farmer Arnold ... Saith the navigation has begun about 45 years ago, and he remembers the barges navigating the river and coming through Standlynch where they were hauled through by windlass ...

The Christchurch–Salisbury voyage is estimated to have taken two days.

The Salisbury & Southampton Canal

A later attempt to provide water communication for Salisbury took the form of the Salisbury & Southampton Canal. This proved a disaster: it cost £90,000 for 13 miles of canal; the line was never completed and what there was of it operated for only 3 years. The plan involved 2 sections of canal linked by 9 miles of the Andover Canal. The Salisbury section was to run from Salisbury parallel to the Avon to Alderbury and thence eastward to Kimbridge on the Andover. The Southampton section left the Andover Canal at Redbridge and led into the docks, with a short branch to Northam. However, the Salisbury–Alderbury length was not made and the Southampton section was incomplete as the tunnel under the city centre seems never to have been navigable. The contractors were wasteful and incompetent; John Rennie, asked to survey the work in progress in 1799 and estimate the cost of completion, gave one reason why the canal was a failure:

> I must say ... that I never had through my hands a work where less attention seems to have been paid to the Proprietors' interest than has been here.

He was still asking for his own bill to be paid ten years later.

By 1807 traffic had ceased and the company met for the last time the following year. Much of the canal's line was used for railway construction, but enough is left to make exploration worth while. However, improvements in 1978 to the A36 Salisbury–Southampton road have obliterated the cutting on the summit level at Whaddon Common, by Alderbury. It is unlikely that any work took place between Alderbury and Salisbury, but Tunnel Hill at Alderbury may owe its name to a proposed tunnel on this section.

Only minor roads approach the canal between Alderbury and Kimbridge. You should find a bridge south of East Grimstead; it carries a farm track over the dry canal and is in a fair state of preservation. Turn eastward by the bridge to West Dean; beneath a footbridge on a farm track on the north side of the road are the remains of a lock. There were fifteen locks on the canal, but no complete lock chamber has survived; the sites of some of them are shown as fords on the 2½in (1:25,000) map. Continue through East Dean to Lockerley and look for substantial remains of a lock on the road from Lockerley to Holbury Wood. Along much of this length a stream now uses the canal bed. A mile from Lockerley you reach the B3084; follow this south for ½ mile, then turn east through Kimbridge to the Bear and Ragged Staff on the A3057. North-west of you is the junction of the Salisbury section with the Andover Canal. The line of the canal from the west is distinguishable by a line of scrub and trees leading into a field which obscures the actual site of the junction. Once the Salisbury & Southampton crossed the Test by an aqueduct. The Andover, on the east side of the Test, is now a wide ditch.

Very little is left of the Southampton section. It left the Andover by Test Lane, but this junction disappeared under railway building in 1864. Blocks of flats obscure it at the top of Redbridge Road. At Redbridge Station, the garden of the station-master's house incorporated a bit of canal. The entrance to West Marlands Tunnel was on the north side of the railway tunnel. As built, the canal tunnel was 580yd long, running beneath the present Civic Centre and Above Bar Street to emerge in the Hoglands. The Southampton & Dorchester Railway had wished to use this tunnel but found it unsafe and had to cut their own next to it; this caused part of the canal tunnel to collapse. More of it collapsed in 1975 and much of its length is now filled in.

From the Hoglands the Northam Branch headed east towards the coal depot on the Itchen, but there is no trace of it today. The main line continued south; look for Canal Walk and Lower Canal Walk and see if the mooring rings are still there at the top of a flight of steps. The line coincided with the ditch of the eastern wall of the old town and terminated at the river by the Gaol Tower.

The Andover Canal

To follow the Andover Canal, return to Redbridge where it entered the Test just above the old bridge, now disused but preserved on the north side of the present bridge. In Test Lane were the canal company's warehouses. This canal, with 24 locks in its 22 miles, lasted from 1794 to 1859, when it was bought by the Andover & Redbridge Railway. It was an unprofitable concern, like the other Hampshire inland waterways, and its history was unspectacular, as are its remains.

A footpath from Test Lane uses the line of the canal to Nursling, from where it swings to the east of Broadlands House making for Romsey. In Romsey it can be found by the cinema car park; a footpath takes you alongside it out of the town northward across the fields. From Romsey to Andover the A3057 accompanies the canal as it ascends the Test Valley. Much of it was built on by the railway, but you can seek traces in Horsebridge, where the railway diverged, and Stockbridge, where there used to be a wharf. Between Longstock and Fullerton the canal is preserved as a fishery. At Fullerton the railway took over again through Goodworth Clatford and Upper Clatford to Andover, where Henley's Garage was built on the site of the wharf.

OS sheets 184, 185, 195, 196

The Itchen Navigation

The villages of Old and New Alresford lie on and near the junction of the A31 and B3046, 7 miles east of Winchester. Between the villages is Old Alresford Pond, a reservoir originally of about 200 acres constructed by Godfrey de Lucy, Bishop of Winchester, towards the end of the twelfth century. Stand on what is left of its high embankment and you are looking at the first canal reservoir in England. The Bishop owned mills at Alresford and the reservoir was designed both to provide a head of water and to help make the Itchen navigable through Winchester to the sea. The Bishop also caused the river to be 'trenched' at his own cost and was granted the right to take tolls. The river seems to have been navigable until the mid-fifteenth century, but it is doubtful whether it was in a condition to be used regularly.

Trade on the Itchen recommenced in 1710 when the river was improved from Winchester to Woodmill; locks, lock cuts and a towing path were constructed. Ownership of the navigation changed hands several times and various improvements were made. By the end of the eighteenth century in the $10\frac{3}{8}$ miles length, there were 15 locks—3 of masonry and 12 turf-sided—2 single-gated locks and a tide-lock at Woodmill. Nearly 3 miles were composed of artificial cuts. Below Woodmill barges continued a further 2 miles along the estuary to Northam where the navigation's wharves and warehouses were built.

Even before the opening of the railway from Winchester to

Southampton in 1839 trade on the Itchen was in decline, partly owing to the effect of the new Basingstoke Canal and partly because cargoes down from Winchester were few and far between. Against railway competition receipts fell sharply. By 1862 there were only two barges and two employees of the navigation and the last boat-load of coal to Winchester was off-loaded in 1869. From 1841 the navigation was in the hands of the Bulpett family. William Bulpett managed it until his death in 1899 at the age of 92; it then passed to his nephew Charles. In 1911 a company calling itself the Itchen Navigation Ltd was registered with the intention of buying the navigation and re-opening it. Legal problems prevented action being taken and the company was wound up in 1925 without having traded at all. Shortly after that date Charles Bulpett emigrated to Kenya. The Acts of Parliament relating to the Itchen Navigation have not been repealed, but its present ownership is uncertain.

Blackbridge Wharf at the head of the navigation is in the grounds of Winchester College; the buildings include a ware-house, stables and the manager's dwelling. You can join the towpath at Wharf Bridge, off Domum Road, and walk for a mile to the site of the top lock, St Catherine's. There are traces of masonry and brickwork and a sluice has been constructed at the head of the lock. This part of the navigation is an artificial cut which continues beneath the crossing of the A33 and A333 to below Twyford Lane End Lock, of which evidence is still visible. The main river then flows in from the west. From here the towpath is walkable for almost 2 miles southward to just before the site of Malm Lock. On this stretch you pass the remains of Compton Lock and you will see several hatches used to control the water-levels in the navigation. The B3386 crosses the river by Shawford Mill; south of the bridge a weir with a plank bridge over it has been constructed on the site of a half-lock, Shawford Single Gates.

Between Malm Lock and the modern College Mead Bridge there is no access, but you can rejoin the towpath below the bridge opposite the point where the main river leaves the cut on the east side. Alternatively, you can approach the navigation from the minor road between Brambridge on the A335 and Otterbourne on the A33. To the north of Brambridge Bridge is a lock with a decaying brick chamber and to the south the site of Brambridge Single Gates—here the watercourse narrows and there are some brickwork remains. For about 400yd the river and the navigation flow side by side with the towpath between them. South of the point where they diverge the navigation is embanked, alongside the much larger railway embankment to the west.

At Allbrook the A335 crosses the tail of Allbrook Lock, the chamber of which is in better condition than those of the other locks, as it was built in the 1830s to replace a lock demolished when the railway crossing was made. Continuing southward, the river separates Eastleigh from Bishopstoke. From Stoke Bridge on the B3037 Eastleigh-Fair Oak road you can walk northward past the sites of Stoke and Withymead Locks, both of which have had weirs installed at the head. South of the bridge is the turf-sided Conegar Lock. Then a few hundred yards further on you come to the beginning of a 2½ mile length of dry—or damp—cut, with the main river away to the east. This cut runs along the eastern boundary of Southampton airport; it can be followed by footpath but there is no road access. There are four locks in varying states of dilapidation on this stretch. The cut rejoins the main river just above New Mans Bridge, which carries the A27 Southampton-Fareham road. Old Mans Bridge, now closed to traffic, was one of the early navigation bridges. The remaining ½ mile to the site of the sea-lock at Woodmill (now obliterated) runs through Riverside Park and is much used by canoeists and anglers. Here at Woodmill the towpath ended, but it is possible to walk along the tidal river to Cobden Bridge.

The Itchen Navigation footpath, which coincides with much of the original towpath, follows the navigation for all of its length apart from three diversions totalling about 1¼ miles. It is surprising how much survives of the navigation works and it is refreshing to note how little rubbish has been dumped in it. There are threats from the M3 motorway, scheduled to cross the Itchen. Although prospects for restoration are not exactly encouraging, destruction of parts of the navigation by this road would put such prospects beyond realisation. While dubious about the possibility of full restoration, the Southampton Canal Society, which surveyed the navigation in detail a few years ago, felt that clearance of the pounds and improvement of the weirs to give depth for canoeing and rowing would not be an impossible or especially costly task. There are no strong arguments for the use of powered craft on a waterway which never knew them, but the society would greatly like to see a horse-drawn barge operating on the waterway immediately south of Winchester with the two highest locks restored and reopened.

OS sheets 185, 196

The Wey & Arun Junction Canal and the Line to Portsmouth

Owing to the energies of the canal trust, the visitor to the Wey & Arun may see more activity along its line today than he would had he been able to tour the canal in the mid-nineteenth century. When Mr and Mrs Dashwood navigated the canal in 1867 they saw only two other boats and about three people: one of the boats, a steamer, had fouled her propeller and burst her boilers in the weeds, and the other had not begun its journey. In 1871 the canal was closed.

The Wey & Arun was the central link in an ambitious scheme to provide a water connection between London and Portsmouth. The Thames, the Wey, the Wey & Arun Junction Canal, the Arun Navigation and the Portsmouth & Arundel Canal were the components. Despite the powerful support of the wealthy and influential Lord Egremont, the scheme was, with very little qualification, a failure. Of the two canal links, the Wey & Arun opened in 1816 and the Portsmouth & Arundel in 1823. It was hoped that some 55,000 tons of goods would be carried annually. However, in the 116 miles of waterway there were 52 locks; the river navigations were chancy and the Wey & Arun was chronically short of water on the summit; and the through passage took 4 days and sometimes longer. In the first full year of operation only 3,650 tons were carried and that figure was never exceeded. Transport by coaster was cheaper and usually quicker. It was especially difficult to obtain cargoes for the journey to London and barges, too, often returned empty. For a couple of years, however, there was a monthly bullion run from Portsea to the Bank of England, the barges having an armed guard who slept on board. This ended in 1826; in that year Lord Egremont withdrew his support and the Portsmouth & Arundel Canal found itself in financial trouble. For the next few years a trickle of through traffic continued, but it dried up altogether in 1838. A little trade was maintained on the Wey & Arun, including the transporting

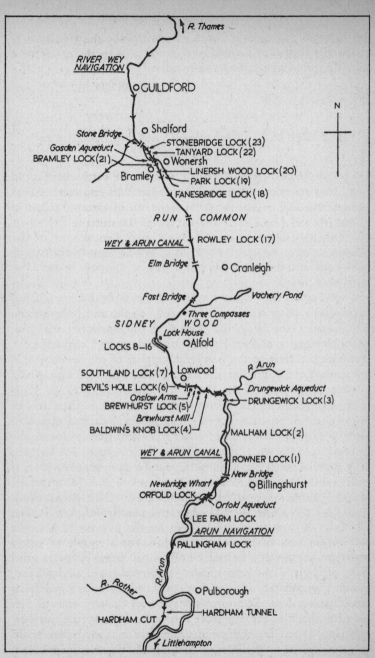

N

The Wey & Arun Junction Canal

of materials for railway construction. In 1865 the Horsham & Guildford Railway opened, running parallel to the canal for 6 miles and providing direct competition. With no prospect of a commercial future for the canal its shareholders lost heart and shortly the company went into liquidation.

Until a few years ago the Wey & Arun was very much a 'lost' waterway. From the Wey at Shalford it climbed slowly up to its summit to the south-west of Cranleigh, then descended more sharply to join the Arun Navigation at Newbridge. With no major aqueducts, no long tunnels, no massive earthworks it did not leave much mark on the countryside. Its engineering was modest; indeed, unlike the great majority of canals, its cost at completion was little more than the original estimate. Its line—it was cut shallower than most canals—seemed to wander uncertainly southward through Surrey into Sussex, almost getting lost in Sidney Wood. Now, however, you can obtain from the Wey & Arun Canal Trust a guide, *Wey—South Path*, which directs you to as much of the canal's route as you can trace by following legal public rights of way. This path links the two Countryside Commission paths, North Downs Way and South Downs Way, and the guide outlines the scenery:

Starting at a gap in the North Downs, the route passes through the Surrey hills, dense woodland in Sidney Wood, remote areas of the Weald, the lush water meadows of the upper Arun, over outcrops of greensand and through wild marsh areas to reach the high chalk land of the South Downs escarpment.

If you are walking the whole line, the guide is essential; even if you are relying mainly on a car, the guide will be of help.

Take the A281 south from Guildford for 2 miles to Shalford. The canal leaves the Wey Navigation at Stonebridge Wharf, to the west of the road which shortly crosses it; you can see the bricked-up arch of the bridge. Continue for Bramley but take a turning to your left past Gosden School. A bridge takes the road over the canal and the line of the Horsham-Guildford Railway, closed in 1965. You will find Gosden Aqueduct—or a good part of it—taking the canal across the Bramley Stream. A mile further on is Bramley where stretches of the canal have been cleared by the trust. Almost 2 miles south of Bramley a minor road forks off to the south-east. This crosses the track of the railway and leads on to Run Common where there is a good clear stretch of canal bed. Run Common Wharf was close to the road-crossing. Carry on towards Cranleigh; then, as you approach the town, turn west on to the B2130. In a mile you reach the site of Elmbridge Wharf. This is the summit level, although there is little trace of the 7 locks which lifted the canal here, 163ft above sea-level. Continue until you reach a cross-roads with the A281 and turn south. Look out for the canal on your left as it gradually approaches the road; there is an old brick bridge by the point of crossing. Alfold Crossways is a mile further on; here you leave the A281 and turn north-westward on to a minor road leading to an entrance to Dunsfold Airfield. It may be a good idea to stop at the Three Compasses Inn. Try to visualise the scene that day in September 1816 when the Earl of Egremont, the mayor and aldermen of Guildford and several shareholders of the canal company embarked on four barges to lead a procession of coal- and timber-laden barges on the maiden voyage to Guildford. Then the 200 navvies who had cheered them on their way turned to their roasted ox and 200 gallons of beer; the villagers of Alfold joined in, and a good time was had by all.

From the Three Compasses turn towards Dunsfold with the canal on your right. The road crosses the canal by an entrance to Sidney Wood; enter the wood by a bridlepath and you will soon pick up the canal and can walk along the towpath until you reach a large private house. This used to be the lock house and the main workshop of the canal company. Here the descent begins through 9 locks close together; the chambers were all destroyed some years ago. You have to divert around the garden of the old lock house but can then follow the canal along a bridlepath for 4 miles; try to find the lock sites in the first part of this stretch. The walk brings you conveniently to the Onslow Arms at Loxwood with a well-preserved lock near the pub. The trust owns the length of canal here and is restoring it. Should you not have time to walk through Sidney Wood you will have to return to Alfold Crossways and head south to Loxwood on the B2133.

Unless you are walking, access to the canal is difficult for the next few miles. From Loxwood it curls eastward through the stone-built Brewhurst Lock to the site of Drungewick Aqueduct, which used to take it over the Arun but was demolished in 1957. From here the canal closely follows the course of the river as it winds southward through water-meadows. The two southernmost locks, Malham and Rowner, have been restored by the trust.

The canal meets the Arun Navigation at Newbridge, close to the junction of the B2133 and A272. On the south side were the wharf and basin. Access from the road is no easier than it was before, but with the aid of the guide you can follow the navigation until it meets the main river south of Coldwaltham.

The Arun Navigation was made as the result of an act of 1785; it involved 2 lengths of canal, one between Newbridge and Pallingham, with 3 locks and an aqueduct, and the other cutting off a bend in the river through Pulborough, also with 3 locks and a 375yd tunnel at Hardham. Lord Egremont was chairman when the Wey & Arun Junction was being built. It operated with some success until the mid-1860s; the last regular traffic ended in 1888 and the navigation was officially closed in 1896. Today, very light craft may be able to reach Pallingham where the lock, now derelict, used to mark the head of tidal waters.

The area south-west of Pulborough is interesting. On the A283 is the six-arched Stopham Bridge, dating from 1423: there was a wharf on the south side and, further south, the junction with the Rother Navigation. And from the A29 between Pulborough and Coldwaltham you can find Hardham Tunnel; a grating covers the entrance of the south portal on the south side of the road. The Dashwoods passed through the 395yd tunnel in 1867, while their pony was walked over the top. Mr Dashwood described the passage:

> I punted the boat along by means of the boat-hook against the roof. In the middle it became quite dark, and we could only just guide ourselves by means of the bright outlet at the end. The roof was covered with stalactites and in places the water fell upon us from crevices above so that we had to try and steer clear of them where we heard their splashes on the water below. It took about ten minutes to pass through this subterranean passage . . .

but they had to wait another twenty minutes as the groom had got lost traversing the top! Today it is the natural river, not the navigation, that boats may use.

The final section of the London–Portsmouth route consisted of the Portsmouth & Arundel Canal. The Dashwoods, who had intended to use it, were informed by William Stanton, coal-merchant and superintendent of the Wey & Arun, to their dismay 'that this Canal no longer exists: in fact, there is now but small trace of it'. It had not, Stanton said, been used for eleven years, 'had been trodden in by cattle, filled-in in places, and was now quite dry'. In fact, the Portsmouth & Arundel was not officially abandoned until 1896, but virtually all barge traffic had ceased fifty years earlier.

The Portsmouth & Arundel left the River Arun at Ford, about midway between Arundel and Littlehampton. It rose through 2 locks and headed almost due west for $12\frac{3}{8}$ miles to meet the Chichester channel at Salterns Lock. From Hunston there was a branch to Chichester; the length between Salterns Lock and Chichester Basin, constructed to take larger vessels than the rest of the canal, is often known as the Chichester Canal—as painted by J. M. W. Turner. From Salterns westward the canal was a succession of dredged channels around the north of Thorney and Hayling Islands and across Langstone Harbour to Portsea. Here there were locks and a pumping station and a conventional canal to a basin about $2\frac{1}{2}$ miles west. The Portsea Canal was replaced in 1830 by a cut at Cosham enabling vessels to sail around the north of Portsea Island and into Portsmouth Harbour—a voyage which very few undertook.

The Ship & Anchor at Ford marks the entrance to the canal and a marina has been laid out on the junction. Bridge, locks and pumping station have long since disappeared. Then make for the Shoulder of Mutton and Cucumbers at Yapton; there is a length of canal and a brick bridge to the north of the pub and the village boasts a Canal Road. After that—well, the Ordnance Survey sheet shows the line of 'old canal' parallel to the coastline about 3 miles inland. It may be still visible along a farm track at Barnham, opposite the church, and at Lidsey Sewage Works on the A29. Recently, a Portsmouth & Arundel Canal Society has been formed and it may succeed in preserving surviving bits of canal bed from infilling. There were never any structures of signifi-cance between Ford and Salterns, however, except at either end, and you may prefer to make for Chichester. Here the canal is still in water and used for angling. Southgate Basin is on the south side of the city—ask for Basin Road. Some early buildings may be found at the basin, which is still its original size. From here you can follow the towpath to Hunston and thence to Salterns. Look for iron swivel-bridges; these are the original bridges, each named after one of the canal company's major shareholders.

There is little left of the Portsea Canal. Some of it is under Goldsmith Avenue and a hump in Ironbridge Lane indicates the previous existence of a bridge. If you want to find the lock, make for the headquarters of the Langstone Harbour Fishermen's Association. The mooring here is old canal and the remains of Portsea Lock are close at hand. There may still be traces of an embankment in a caravan site at the end of Locksway Road. Most of the line disappeared in railway development in the mid-nineteenth century.

Tracking down the Portsmouth & Arundel may not be a very rewarding experience—any more than the canal itself proved much of a reward to its shareholders. The London–Portsmouth line, however, was one of the most imaginative conceptions of the whole Canal Age, and for a few years it became a reality. It taxes our imaginations to appreciate that.

OS sheets 186, 196, 197

The Sussex River Navigations

The Western Rother
The Western Rother was made navigable on the initiative of Lord Egremont who employed local labour to make 8 locks and 2 miles of lock cuts in the total length of $11\frac{1}{4}$ miles from Midhurst to the Arun at Stopham. With coal as the chief import, and timber, corn, and 'Petworth marble', as the local limestone was known, as exports the navigation traded profitably for some fifty years and continued with some commercial carrying into the 1880s. Gradually thereafter the locks fell into decay, although the navigation was not legally abandoned until 1936, forty years after the abandonment of the Arun.

The terminal basin at Midhurst is still called The Wharf, south of the Market Square and opposite South Pond. At the end of the lane the Frazer Nash Works have been built on the site of the basin. Wharf and basin were built not on an artificial cut but on a tributary stream of the Rother; it is this stream which feeds South Pond, popular with ducks and one of the many attractive features of the lovely little town. There is a well-preserved navigation bridge incorporating a towpath just below the site of the basin, with the date 1794 inscribed on both parapets as well as various sets of initials. In a few yards the stream meets the Rother a few hundred yards south of Cowdray Castle.

There are traces of most, if not all, of the Rother's lock chambers, although some are on private territory and inaccessible. Others have been displaced by river authority works. Lodsbridge Lock, between Halfway Bridge on the A272 and the village of Selham, now lies in an estate belonging to Baron Evelyn de Rothschild and a large enclosed swimming pool has been built on top of the navigation cut. An old edition of the Ordnance Survey map will help you to trace the sites, but none of them is shown on the current issues.

At Coultershaw Bridge on the A285 south of Petworth an interesting development is taking place. A lock chamber can be seen immediately above the navigation bridge; below the adjacent river bridge the Rother is controlled by sluices and opens out into a sizeable pool. Here a water-wheel operated pump used to draw off water for the Petworth Estate; the remains of this pump were recently rediscovered and restoration by the Sussex Industrial Archaeology Society is in hand. South of the bridge is the coal wharf, supplied in turn by the navigation and the nearby railway, a branch of the Mid-Sussex line. Coultershaw was the wharf for Petworth. One of Lord Egremont's ideas was to link Petworth with Stonebridge Wharf near Guildford, with a branch canal to Horsham, and surveys of possible lines were made. Nothing came of this, but Lord Egremont did build a short Petworth Branch Canal, which was actually opened a year before the rest of the Rother Navigation. This branch left the river by the navigation cut above Stopham Lock, almost a mile below Coultershaw. It was $1\frac{1}{4}$ miles long, terminating at Haslingbourne Bridge, and had 2 locks. It was little used, as a few years later the road from Coultershaw to Petworth, which used to pass through Rotherbridge, was realigned to its present track and, although longer, proved more convenient for the movement of goods to and from the town. The Petworth Canal was to have been the first stage of Egremont's ambitious cross-country scheme. Part of its line to Haslingbourne may still be traced.

The lowest lock on the navigation is at Fittleworth, above Fittleworth Bridge on the B2138. The lock cut is above the bridge behind a fine three-storey mill, now used for storage. This was the toll-lock; tolls on the Rother were comparatively low as it was run rather as a utility than as a profit-making concern, but before railways came to the district it managed to earn about

£550 a year. A mile below Fittleworth the longest of the navigation cuts was made, crossed by a bridge in the grounds of Stopham House. For the entry to the Rother Navigation, follow the
public footpath sign on the south side of the A283 to the east of
Stopham Bridge on the Arun. This leads to a footbridge across
the Arun and from here you can see the cut, a shallow, straight
line, with poplars on its southern side. Rother and Arun join by
the pumping station a couple of hundred yards away.

OS sheet 197

The River Adur and the Baybridge Canal

Like other Sussex rivers the Adur was a natural navigation long
before the age of canals. It was improved from the outfall at
Shoreham to a wharf at Bines Bridge under an act of 1807; the
improvements did not include locks and the river remained a
tidal navigation. In 1825, the Baybridge Canal Company was
formed 'to make a navigable cut or canal from the River Adur at
or near Binesbridge ... to Baybridge'. What resulted was not a
canal but an improvement of the north-west arm of the river,
which was widened and dredged. Two locks were built, and a
wharf at Bay Bridge. The north-east arm of the Adur was also
navigable to Mockbridge, 2 miles north of Henfield on the A281.

The Baybridge Canal functioned for about thirty-five years. It
was abandoned in 1875, but it seems unlikely that it was used
after about 1861 when the Shoreham-Horsham railway line was
opened. The site of the basin is on the east side of Bay Bridge, on
the A24 1½ miles south of the junction with the A272, close to the
ruins of Knepp Castle. A stream flows down from Kneppmill
Pond to the Adur as it swings north. It may be advisable to
approach the river from the bridge on the B2135 as the double-
track main road is very busy, especially in the summer. The
wharf lay alongside the stream while the basin, in which it seems
as if boats could turn, was excavated off the river.

Take the turning to West Grinstead off the B2135 and make
for the church—which itself is well worth a visit and contains
memorials to the Burrell family, two of whom were among the
canal's promoters. A path through the churchyard takes you to a
footbridge over the river. Do not cross the river but walk alongside it to the west, and in about 300yd you come to a brick lock-
chamber, filled with debris but generally in good condition. The

gates have gone, but some of the iron fitments can be seen. You can walk to the site of the basin from here.

For the other lock, continue on the B2135 through Partridge Green and turn left for Lock Farm. You cross the river in ¾ mile. Walk downstream through a field towards the trees, where you will find the short lock-cut and brick lock-chamber with ivy trailing down it. Note some fine brickwork and remains of iron fitments. This is a lock for connoisseurs: remote, in a beautiful setting, quietly decaying—and not used as a rubbish tip.

Bines Bridge lies a mile south of Partridge Green. The wharf was on the downstream side to the east of the river and you may be able to distinguish it. For the site of Mockbridge Wharf you need to return to Partridge Green, turn right on the B2116 to the junction with the A281 and then turn right again, southward, for about ¾ mile. The wharf was downstream of the bridge on the northern side of the river and had two arms leading off, shaped like the letter F.

Below Bines Bridge and Mockbridge the Adur is embanked. On the lower reaches some trade in clay to cement works at Beeding and Shoreham continued until 1929. The full history of this little navigation, however, is still waiting to be written.

OS sheet 198

The Sussex Ouse
The Ouse was by far the longest of the Sussex river navigations. From Newhaven to the old head of navigation at Upper Ryelands Bridge the distance is 32 miles, with Lewes Bridge, 8 miles from Newhaven, marking the division between the lower and upper river. The lower river seems to have been navigable throughout the eighteenth century and probably earlier, and remains of a flash-lock have been found 8½ miles above Lewes. An act of 1790 enabled the upper river to be made fully navigable on the lines of a survey by William Jessop. It proved a troublesome business; shortage of money and difficulties with the contractors caused long delays in the work and not until 1812 was the navigation completed to Upper Ryelands Bridge, a few miles short of the intended terminus at Hammer Bridge. Jessop originally proposed the construction of 25 locks, but only 18 were built on the shortened navigation. Barges 45ft by 12ft, carrying up to 30 tons, were used on the river: many were built at a yard in Lewes.

Chalk, for the making of lime, and coal were the main cargoes on the river, with agricultural produce being carried downwards. A moderate trade was maintained until the London-Brighton Railway was opened in 1841; thereafter, with further development of the railway network, receipts decreased and the condition of the river deteriorated. Despite reducing tolls the navigation company could not compete with the railway and closed its books in 1859. Within two years the navigation above Lindfield became unusable and the last recorded trading voyage above Lewes took place in 1868. Below Lewes the river was commercially used into the 1920s and the tidal reaches can still be penetrated by small craft.

Although over 120 years have passed since the navigation fell into disuse, much evidence of the works can easily be found. In Lewes, Canal Bridge in the High Street divided the upper from the lower navigation, each of which was administered separately. Landham Wharf has been obliterated, but the coal wharf with several associated buildings still survives. On the north of the town you can pick up the towpath and follow it to the site of Hamsey Lock, which in fact marks the end of the tidal reach. Here a $\frac{1}{4}$ mile cut led off to chalk pits near Offham. The straight Hamsey Cut, nearly a mile long, bypassed a wide bend of the river; it is crossed midway by a navigation bridge taking the road from Hamsey village to a farm and the isolated church.

Following the river takes you through varied and comparatively unspoiled countryside with no settlement of any size between Lewes and Haywards Heath. Above Hamsey the next locks are at Barcombe, half-way between the A26 and Barcombe Cross. Amid a maze of waterways, many of which were created by the river authority to maintain water-levels, are the chambers of the two Barcombe Mill locks now adapted to fish ladders and in the care of the Ouse Angling Preservation Society. Pike's Bridge crosses between the two. A lane north from here leads to the site of another mill near the junction with the Iron River and the chamber of Oil Mills Lock. A short distance above is the Anchor Inn, dating from 1790, accessible from a turning eastward off the road between Barcombe Cross and Mount Pleasant.

There are few road bridges over the Ouse and exploring by car necessitates many lengthy detours. To find the site of Isfield Lock, now a weir, you have to return to Barcombe Cross and make for the A26, turning left and branching for Isfield in just over a mile.

A lane westward on the north side of the village leads to the river. Now you are on this side of the Ouse, continue northward from Isfield for 2½ miles towards Shortbridge, stopping by the second of two turnings to Uckfield. Follow a public footpath sign through a field on your left. On the right you will notice a raised track, grass-covered; this was an old roadway, and it leads you in a few hundred yards to Shortbridge Basin at the end of a canal-ised branch of the river just under a mile in length. This branch served Uckfield, about 1½ miles distant. You can follow the branch to the junction with the main river and the site of Sharp's Bridge Lock.

The next bridging point is at Sharpsbridge; between here and Goldbridge on the A272 it may prove impossible to walk along-side the river owing to impenetrable undergrowth. There was a lock on the north side of Gold Bridge and another where the road from Fletching to Fletching Common crosses the Ouse; this one is now a weir. North of Fletching Common is the site of Iron Gate Lock, now barely distinguishable.

Between 1793 and 1805 Sheffield Bridge (on the present A275) was the terminus of the navigation pending the raising of funds to complete the works. The first Lord Sheffield, the most powerful landowner on the navigation's route, had taken a major role in promoting and managing the undertaking but was suspected of being reluctant to have it extended beyond his own wharf by this bridge. It took strong efforts by the other proprietors, a new act, and the appointment of the geologist William Smith as engineer and a local man, Dymoke Wells, as contractor to force matters onward. From Sheffield Bridge to the next road-crossing at Freshfield Bridge the riverside scenery is especially attractive with the Bluebell Railway from Sheffield Park Station to Freshfield Halt on its northern side. Bacon Wish and Polebay Locks can be found on this stretch, but there are no road approaches.

At Freshfield Bridge the chamber of Freshfield Lock is on the opposite side of the road to the Sloop Inn, originally a bargemen's inn built at the beginning of the nineteenth century. Between Freshfield Lock and East Mascalls progress along the riverside may be impossible; in any event, there are few if any traces of the two locks at Henfield Wood and East Mascalls. The waterway is narrow and it seems an improbable navigation. It swings north-eastward of Lindfield, now a constituent of Hay-wards Heath. Pim's Lock is near Lindfield Bridge on the B2028 road to Turner's Hill. Pim was the owner of the adjacent Dean's Mill when the navigation was being made and this lock is one of three with stone chambers—all the other Ouse locks were built of brick. Upstream is the overgrown chamber of Fulling Mill Lock, while the third stone lock, Tester's, is about ½ mile below Lower Ryelands Bridge on the Haywards Heath-Ardingly road. The last lock from Lewes, Riverswood, is close to the point where the abandoned Horsted Keynes Branch Railway crossed the river.

The terminal basin is by Upper Ryelands Bridge on the Haywards Heath-Balcombe road, north of River's Wood and close to the Balcombe Viaduct. The basin is on the north bank of the river to the east of the bridge and you should find that its outline is still discernible. Despite the plans of the promoters, the navigation extended no further; searching for traces at the next two major crossings, Pilstye Bridge and Hammer Bridge, will (as I have found) prove fruitless.

OS sheet 198

Lost Navigations of London

London has something, but not a great deal, to offer to the searcher for the remains of lost navigations. Several tributaries of the Thames, some of which were navigable in part, lie beneath the built-up areas incorporated into the sewage or drainage systems of the capital, and evidence can be found of the existence of a handful of short canals. Relics and reminders occur sometimes unexpectedly; Tyburn water is piped across the District Line platforms at Baker Street and Victoria, and the Serpentine in Hyde Park is part of the River Westbourne.

The most important of the 'lost' navigable tributaries was the Fleet. Rising from springs in Hampstead and Highgate, the Fleet flowed into the City via Camden Town. It was certainly navigable in the twelfth century as there are references to its being used for the conveyance of stone for St Paul's Cathedral, and there are several mentions in historical records of goods being carried on the Fleet, and of its propensity for silting up. In 1670, following the Great Fire, an act provided for the deepening of the river from Holborn Bridge to the Thames and for the building of wharves on either side. This canalised length of about ½ mile was used for several decades, but it silted up continually and also proved too convenient a rubbish dump. In 1733 the section between Holborn Bridge and Fleet Bridge was arched over, the wharves became streets and the Fleet Market was opened on top of the river. The lowest section continued as a navigation until in 1766 it was covered in for the approaches to Blackfriars Bridge. In 1829 Farringdon Street replaced the Fleet Market. The river was an unhealthy sewer, carrying raw sewage down from its upper reaches until London's waste-disposal system was reorganised by Sir Joseph Bazalgette in the 1860s. Since then it has taken off storm water into the Thames.

To retrace the course of the canalised Fleet, make for the point where Holborn Viaduct crosses Farringdon Street. From the north the river, sometimes known as the Turnmill Brook, flowed down from Highgate Ponds; Holborn Bridge, made of Portland stone like the other three bridges over the canal, crossed where you are standing. Walk towards the Thames; there was a bridge at Fleet Lane and another—Fleet Bridge—where now is Ludgate Circus, with Fleet Street on your right. Carry on along New Bridge Street, noting Bridewell on your right; there was the last bridge here. Bridewell Dock, at the mouth of the Fleet, was filled in when Blackfriars Bridge was built. Nothing of the past history of the Fleet remains to be seen, but the water still rushes along under your feet.

To the west, other navigable waterways on the north side of the Thames included Hammersmith Creek and the Kensington and Grosvenor Canals. About a mile of the creek was at some time navigable, but in later years the head of navigation was King Street. The banks were lined with wharves and malt-houses and a little trade continued until 1930. The creek was filled in during 1936.

The Kensington Canal was a canalisation of a stream known as Counter's Creek, which ran from Kensal Green to Chelsea Creek on the Thames. An act in 1824 authorised the improvement of the lower $1\frac{3}{4}$ miles and a basin was built at Warwick Road close to the present Kensington (Olympia) Station. There was one lock near the entrance to the basin, the rest of the canal being tidal. The intention was to promote the trade of the growing township of Kensington and within a few years a proposal was made to link the canal with the Paddington arm of the Grand Junction. Railways were moving into the area by this time and in 1839 the West London Railway took over the canal and within a few years opened a line from Olympia Station. Later, the canal was transferred to the London & North Western Railway; the upper section between Warwick Road Basin and King's Road, Chelsea, was filled in and a railway line laid on it in 1863.

The remainder of the canal operated quite profitably for a number of years, despite the need for frequent dredging and the tendency of the banks to slip. The Gas, Light & Coke Company made much use of it and early this century a new dock was built by its entrance near Lots Road Power Station. Until 1959 it was usable to King's Road; then, following the British Transport Commission Act, it was blocked off above the gas works dock. The lowest few hundred yards of canal are still open, but by now the dock has probably been filled in.

The entrance to the Kensington Canal is off Chelsea Creek about midway between Battersea and Wandsworth Bridges. You may be able to trace its course up to King's Road. From there on, it has been obscured by the railway line, but try looking for the lock cottage from the railway bridge by the Warwick Road/ West Cromwell Road crossing, or ask for the headquarters of the Kensington Rifle Club—this is what it has become. The site of the basin is a little further on towards Kensington High Street behind a pair of wooden gates.

The basin of the Grosvenor Canal, another of London's short navigations developed from a tidal creek, lies under Victoria Station. The creek originally served the Chelsea Waterworks and was also used by sailing barges in the eighteenth century. With the surrounding land the creek was leased from the Grosvenor Estate; when the lease expired in 1823 the Earl of Grosvenor improved the creek into a navigable canal, $\frac{3}{4}$ mile long, with a terminal basin and a tide-lock. As a private undertaking the canal continued in trade, mostly importing coal, until the building of the station in 1859. For the next forty years or so the canal terminated at Eccleston Bridge; then a further stretch was absorbed by railway and Ebury Bridge became the terminus. In 1928 the lock was rebuilt, but the length of canal above it was shortened to only 163yd. This length is still in use by its owners, now Westminster City Council, for the removal of refuse by lighters. You will find the entrance on the east side of Chelsea Bridge. If you walk up Ebury Bridge Road and Buckingham Palace Road the line of the Grosvenor Canal is on your left, merging with the line of the railway at Ebury Bridge.

There are a few other traces of lost navigations on the north bank of London's Thames, including the Isle of Dogs Canal, opened in 1805 and closed in 1829 to become the South West India Dock, and the Romford Canal, planned to run from Romford to the Thames with 6 locks and a tunnel under the Barking-Upminster railway line. Some work on the Romford was done in 1877, but very little of the line was completed. The remains of a lock and a length of cut can be found on the north side of the A13, near Dagenham Road.

On the south side of the Thames there were two undertakings of some importance: the Grand Surrey and the Croydon Canals. The Grand Surrey—not quite so grand as it was originally proposed—was cut from the docks at Rotherhithe to Camberwell, a distance of just under 4 miles. It was opened in 1810 and a short branch to Peckham was added in 1826. As a canal it was no great success; the company came to concentrate more on the docks, turned itself into the Grand Surrey Docks & Canal Company and in 1864 merged with the Commercial Docks Company to develop the Surrey Docks. The canal continued to be used until after World War II; since then it has been closed and eliminated. The Surrey Docks shut in 1970 and the basin at Camberwell is now a park.

The Croydon Canal ascended by 26 locks from a junction with the Grand Surrey at New Cross through Penge and Norwood to a basin in Croydon, a distance of $9\frac{1}{4}$ miles. It competed directly with the Surrey Iron Railway, which had opened in 1803, six years before the canal, although as it happened there was not enough traffic to make either route especially profitable. Some enthusiasts saw the Croydon Canal as the first link in a line of communication between the Thames and the Channel, but with water having to be pumped up the 26 locks between the Grand Surrey and Forest Hill it proved difficult and expensive to maintain. For nearly thirty years canal and iron railway plodded along, their horses, one likes to think, neighing to each other across the fields. Then in the 1830s the London & Croydon Railway Company moved in, offering to buy the canal in order to build its line on the bed. After some bargaining the canal company sold for £42,250, a good price in the trading circumstances; navigation stopped in 1836, but before the canal was drained it overflowed, flooding 200 houses in Deptford. In 1839 the railway was opened. West Croydon Station was built on the canal basin; parts of the basin walls can be seen in the adjacent car park. The first bridge north was extended from a canal bridge. In Betts Park, Anerley, between Anerley Road and Weighton Road, a short stretch of the canal has been preserved as a rectangular ornamental lake with fountains along the middle. There is now a commemorative plaque. Another visible reminder is South Norwood Lake, constructed as a reservoir for the canal.

There may be more to be found: the alignment of roads, for example, is evidence of the sometime presence of the canal. However, exploring the heavily built-up area between New Cross and Croydon in search of the remains of a canal which was virtually obliterated over 140 years ago is an activity that will appeal to few. When the canal was opened, Croydon's population was 7,000; now it is 350,000 and bears little obvious evidence of its past. Its present prosperity owes little to the canal, however, which is remembered as much for the recreational facilities it provided. It evoked one of the pleasantest of recollections, from William Page, writing in 1880 and quoted by Charles Hadfield in *The Canals of South and South East England*:

> This Canal was a source of delight to the inhabitants, who derived much pleasure from it, whether they were angler, bather, skater, boatman or pedestrian ... Boats could be hired, and parties were made up to enjoy pleasant rows to Forest Hill, through a beautiful country, with scarcely a house to be seen on the journey ... The walk on the banks, or towing path, of the Canal from its terminus to Norwood or farther on could not be surpassed in the neighbourhood. Norwood and its grand woods were on one side, and wide, well-cultivated fields on the other. Nor was it a monotonous walk; the passing and repassing of loaded barges diversified it; parties in pleasure boats rowed on the canal surface; and patient anglers sat on the banks anxiously watching for a nibble.

It must be agreed that London's lost navigations are more interesting historically than they are topographically; there is little left to see, and, while pursuing the few remains, you are in constant danger from London's traffic. A voyage along the Regent's Canal or a stroll along its towpath is much more fun and you can compare the careful restoration that has taken place—in Camden, for instance—with the sad condition of the City Basin. For the waterways that have disappeared there are two good books to be read: Nicholas Barton's *Lost Rivers of London* and the relevant chapters of Martyn Denney's *London's Waterways*. There are also some interesting old photographs in Martyn Denney's *London and South East England* volume in the Historic Waterways Scenes Series.

OS sheets 176, 177

The Royal Military Canal

The only British waterway to be constructed solely as a defence work, the Royal Military Canal was dug between 1804 and 1806 as part of the preparations for an invasion by Napoleon. Equipped with a parapet and a military road, it formed a barrier against an enemy landing on the Romney or Welland Marshes; gunboats could be stationed along it and it was convenient for the movement of troops. With the canal built, only if the invading force landed in overwhelming numbers would it be necessary to flood the marshes.

However, by the time the canal was completed the threat of invasion had passed. The Government appointed commissioners, including the holders of many of the chief offices of state, to oversee the running of the canal on a commercial basis, keeping it in good order should it ever be needed for military reasons. Commercial traffic continued on the canal until 1909; sand and shingle, bricks, stone and timber were the principal cargoes carried. Tolls were also charged for the use of the military road and some income accrued from the sale of grass from the parapet and surrounding land.

The canal runs from Shorncliffe, to the east of Hythe, to Iden Lock on the Rother, a mile north-east of Rye. It takes the course of the Rother to Rye where it transfers to the Brede. From the Brede at Winchelsea a smaller canal was cut to Cliff End. The total length was 30 miles.

The Shorncliffe terminus is in the angle where the A259 Hythe–Folkestone road meets the Hythe coast road. Surplus water from the canal was led off here to the sea. The line runs behind the golf course and through Hythe centre; the terminus of the Romney, Hythe & Dymchurch Railway is beside the canal. You can hire a rowing-boat or a canoe for a paddle through Hythe Park. The canal is the setting for a Venetian fête on alternate years, with fireworks and assorted merriment.

Leaving the town the canal heads westward, the marsh country on the left, the hills on the right. The path along the northern bank used to be the military road. There are no navigation works, only occasional bridges taking minor roads across. After St Rumwold's Church, the direction alters to south-westward; the virtually straight line is stepped at intervals, the purpose being that guns could be mounted at these angles to fire along the line of the canal without hitting the defenders. Between Warehorne and Appledore, the National Trust owns the canal, which here is wide and clean, tree-lined and beautiful.

By Appledore the direction is almost southward. The path becomes a road in the village and you can drive along the bank, stopping to look at Stone Bridge where all the elements of the defence line may be examined. A mile further is Iden Lock, now unnavigable. The buildings here were the barracks and officers' quarters. Scot's Float Sluice is another mile along the road; this has double doors opening either way and can accommodate boats up to 56ft in length. The Rother is navigable up to Bodiam Bridge, 12½ miles above Scot's Float.

The junction of Rother and Brede is on the east side of Rye. The A259 Hastings road takes the line of the military road out of Rye while the Rye Harbour road crosses the Brede at Brede Sluice, a similar but smaller structure than Scot's Float. At Winchelsea, river and canal diverged by the junction of the Winchelsea Beach road with the A259. There was no lock at this point and it is unlikely that this western end of the canal was ever navigated. It is a narrow stretch of water around the north and west sides of Pett Level. At Cliff End by a stores, a cottage and a public convenience, the Royal Military Canal comes to an inglorious termination.

OS sheets 179, 189

The Thames & Medway Canal

Of the 7 miles of the Thames & Medway Canal, almost one-third is tunnel. Indeed, by far the best way of seeing this canal is by taking a train from Gravesend to Strood. For the first half of the journey the railway and canal run parallel; then, after leaving Higham Station, you plunge into the Strood Tunnel. After 1,530yd there is a brief flash of daylight, followed by another 2,329yd. On emerging, the railway turns sharply on the approach to the bridge across the Medway; the canal, however, continued in a straight line to Frindsbury Basin.

The tunnel was not part of the original plan for a canal from the Thames to the Medway. Ralph Dodd, engaged in 1799 to survey a line for a canal to connect the two rivers so that sailing barges could avoid the sometimes dangerous passage around North Foreland, proposed cutting through the chalk cliffs, but it was the recommendation of other engineers consulted that was adopted. Hence, the second longest canal tunnel in Britain was built—and by far the largest in bore. The width, including a towpath, was 26ft 6in, and the height above water-level 27ft. The canal was opened in 1824 at a cost of about £¼ million, ten times Dodd's estimate. As the number of boats using the canal at a given time depended on the tides, congestion frequently occurred and in 1830 the tunnel was opened out at the point of lowest cover for a passing place to be made: hence the flash of daylight you notice on the train.

For some years the canal was moderately busy, fruit and hops being among the cargoes carried, and the tunnel became a tourist attraction. In 1844 the canal company, noting the rapid expansion of railways in the South of England, turned itself into the Gravesend & Rochester Railway & Canal Company and constructed a single-track railway from Gravesend to Strood, passing through the tunnel with one rail laid on the towpath and the other supported from the canal bed. Trains and barges operated side by side for eighteen months; then the South Eastern Railway bought up the company, filled in the canal from Higham to Strood and laid double tracks through the tunnel. The section of canal from Gravesend to Higham traded for a further eighty-seven years, mostly carrying farm produce, until it was abandoned by its railway owners in 1934.

Part of Gravesend Basin is open and used for moorings. There are three canal cottages by the swing bridge over the river lock and on the far side of the basin is the Canal Tavern. This today is Sikh country; the turbans of the older generation are splashes of bright colour on the riverside lawns. Less colourful is the shallow and weedy canal east of the basin and only the wholly dedicated enthusiast would feel inclined to walk along it. From the train you can observe it easily enough until it diverges for about a mile before you reach Higham. The site of Frindsbury Basin and Lock is about 800yd below the bridge carrying the A2 over the Medway. The lock could take vessels of up to 300 tons. The Medway itself is still a statutory navigation up to Tonbridge, but it is not greatly used.

OS sheet 178

Bibliography

BOOKS

Barton, N. J., *Lost Rivers of London* (Dent, 1962)

Clew, K. R., *The Somersetshire Coal Canal and Railways* (David & Charles, 1970)

Dalby, L. J., *The Wiltshire & Berkshire Canal* (Oakwood Press, 1971)

Dashwood, J. B., *The Thames to the Solent* (1868, rep Shepperton Swan, 1980)

Denney, Martin, *London's Waterways* (Batsford, 1977)

Goodsall, Robert H., *The Arun and Western Rother* (Constable, 1962)

Hadfield, C., *The Canals of South and South East England* (David & Charles, 1969)

Handford, Michael, *The Stroudwater Canal* (Moonraker Press, 1976)

— — and Viner, D., *Stroudwater, Thames & Severn Towpath Guide* (1981)

Household, H., *The Thames & Severn Canal* (David & Charles, 1969)

Vine, P. A. L., *London's Lost Route to the Sea* (David & Charles, 1973)

— — *The Royal Military Canal* (David & Charles, 1972)

ARTICLES AND BOOKLETS

The Chard Canal (Chard History Group, 1972)

The Itchen Navigation (Southampton Canal Society, 1977)

Sussex Industrial History, Vols 1 and 6 (Phillimore, for Sussex Industrial Archaeology Society, 1971 and 1974)

Wey—South Path (Wey & Avon Canal Trust, nd)

SOCIETIES

Itchen Navigation Society
Kennet & Avon Canal Trust
Portsmouth & Arundel Canal Society
Southampton Canal Society
Stroudwater, Thames & Severn Canal Trust
Surrey & Hants Canal Society
Thames & Medway Canal Society
Wey & Arun Canal Trust
Wilts & Berks Canal Amenity Group

2

THE SOUTH-WEST

The Dorset & Somerset Canal

What is left of the little that was ever made of the Dorset & Somerset Canal continues to moulder away in the hilly country west of Frome. It was intended as a branch of a waterway connecting Bristol and Poole, most of which was authorised by an act of 1796 for a navigable canal between Widbrook on the Kennet & Avon and Shillingstone Okeford, about 4 miles north-west of Blandford Forum, incorporating 'a certain Navigable Branch'. Although opposition from landowners prevented the continuation of the waterway to Poole from being authorised, the proprietors felt nevertheless that enough traffic would be generated to make the undertaking viable and work on the branch began soon after the act was passed. The branch was planned to be 11 miles long from Nettlebridge to Frome; like the Somerset Coal Canal, then building to the north, it passed through mining country and its main purpose was to convey coal to the woollen mills of Frome.

Of the branch itself, only about 8 miles were ever cut and on the main line no work was done at all. Costs, as so often happened, were underestimated; what was built of the branch cost about £60,000 and no more than that was ever raised. An act of 1803 enabling the proprietors to seek further funds had no effect and no further work was carried out on the canal after that year. Although water was let in to part of the line, there is no record of any cargo being carried. As a commercial proposition, the Dorset & Somerset Canal was a total failure.

Evidence of the canal's existence, however, can still be found, and if you are exploring the Somerset Coal Canal a diversion southward is well worth while. From Radstock, take the A367 towards Shepton Mallet. About a mile after Stratton-on-the-

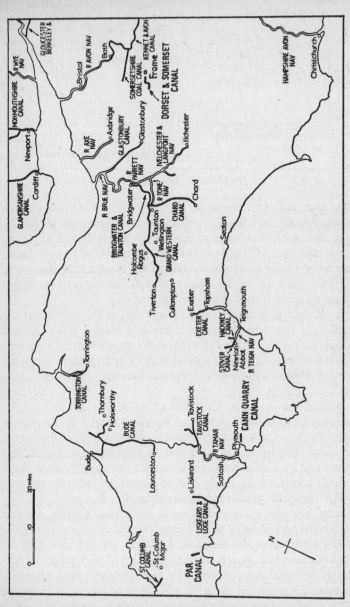

The South-West

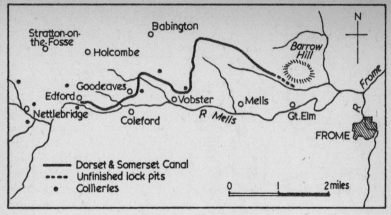

The Dorset & Somerset Canal

Fosse turn left for Holcombe. To the east of this road was the terminal basin, although its outline by now may no longer be traceable. At Edford on the south side of Holcombe the road crossed the canal. Behind the Duke of Cumberland you can find a packhorse bridge spanning the bed of the Dorset & Somerset; to the west is the site of the basin and eastward some of the line is visible with parts of it quite well preserved.

At Coleford, 2 miles from Holcombe, is the canal's largest artefact, a two-arched aqueduct across a valley. It has lost its parapet and is covered in ivy but is still a most impressive memorial. It has been said that the canal was for a short time navigable between Edford and Coleford, but documentary evidence is lacking.

Behind the chapel in Coleford a stretch of canal bed can be distinguished leading towards an intended tunnel at Goodeaves Farm. From what would have been the north portal of the tunnel the canal runs up to the road east of Highbury. A length was obliterated by a branch railway line; the next point to make for is Vobster Cross where, to the east of the cross-roads, the original bridge takes the Mells road over the canal.

Now the canal heads due north for about a mile, turning south-eastward shortly after being crossed by the Radstock-Frome railway. In the fields between the railway line and the A362 Radstock-Frome road there are sites of particular interest. So far, the canal was cut along the 425ft contour, with no locks. To meet the projected main line at Frome, however, a descent of 210ft in a little over a mile was needed. For this, the proprietors intended to use a device patented in 1798 by James Fussell, a member of the canal committee and an ironmaster of Mells. Fussell's 'balance lock' was essentially a boat lift—James Green installed similar examples on the Grand Western Canal thirty years later. It consisted of a large masonry chamber divided into two by a central buttress, the canal at the upper and lower levels being similarly divided. Each chamber contained a caisson, a watertight box open at the top, into which a boat could be floated. On the central partition was a shaft with a wheel mounted on it; similar but smaller shafts and wheels were mounted on the top of each caisson. The caissons were linked by a chain running over the central wheel, so that as one rose the other sank. Chains attached to the bottom of each caisson helped to equalise the weight. Water could be run into the descending caisson as necessary to control the descent. When a boat entered a caisson the canal was shut off by a stop gate. According to the patent, lifts up to 100ft could be achieved by this method.

An experimental lift was constructed on Barrow Hill and in the autumn of 1800 trials took place. Shortly before this, Weldon's Lift on the Somerset Coal Canal had been abandoned. The Barrow Hill trials, however, were successful; built with a descent of 20ft the balance lock operated several times with loaded boats. A public exhibition in October 1800 brought a crowd of enthusiastic onlookers and a glowing account was printed in the *Bath Chronicle*. As a result, the canal committee determined to adopt Fussell's invention and tenders were invited to construct five more lifts on the descent to Frome.

You can find the site of the trial lock about 200yd north of the railway and 500yd eastward of the Mells–Buckland Dinham road (ST 735505). Then head for a patch of woodland about ½ mile further on. Here you will see the clearly defined canal bed and the remains of the four balance locks on which work was begun, but never finished. The large pits are about 20ft deep and some fragments of stonework are visible.

Of the next mile of canal nothing remains—perhaps nothing was ever cut. If you return to the Radstock–Frome road, stop by the bridge over the railway about a mile south of Buckland Dinham. Cross a stile on the south side of the bridge and fight your way through the nettles alongside the railway. Soon you come to a clearly defined length of canal bed, lined by trees. And this leads you to the well-hidden Murtry Aqueduct, of three arches, that took the canal over the Vallis Vale stream. This cost a little over £300 to build and is similar in style to Midford Aqueduct on the Somerset Coal Canal. Note the little skew arch and the inexplicable shelter. Then return to the main road and look down on the old bridge over the stream near the railway-crossing.

It was planned that the junction of branch and main line should be on the north side of Frome, but of the Dorset & Somerset Canal there is nothing more left to see apart from a length of stone wall, intended as an embankment, on the north side of Whatcombe Farm. At the time of writing, no society or authority appears to have any concern over the relics of this canal and it is perhaps extraordinary that of a line that was never completed and never used, so much has somehow survived.

OS sheet 183

The Glastonbury Canal

Of the Glastonbury Canal there is little evidence left. Opened in 1833 from Highbridge to Glastonbury it was closed only twenty-one years later (apart from a short section at Highbridge), and drainage works and peat cutting have obliterated most of its course. It was a local project, originally conceived as a cheap method of bringing prosperity to Glastonbury. The first surveyor, a local man, Richard Hammett, proposed that it be made by utilising existing drainage cuts at a cost of £9,000. This estimate was increased as the plans were adjusted; nevertheless, over £15,000 was raised before the act was obtained, indicating both confidence and enthusiasm. Soon after work began, however, it became obvious that expert advice was needed. Sir John Rennie was called in; he recommended a waterway 8ft deep, capable of taking the Bristol channel coasters, with a sea-lock and one other, on a line rather different from that first suggested. Work was recommenced and took five years to complete at a cost of about £30,000.

For a few years things went well. The trows and barges brought building materials to Glastonbury and the town increased in size. The canal also helped to drain the Brue levels, materially assisting cultivation. It seemed as if Glastonbury might become a boom town; but it was not to be. The peat through which much of the canal was cut swelled and the bottom of the canal rose towards the top, a process accelerated in places where the canal company, seeking economy, had skimped on the clay puddling. Navigation became difficult and sometimes impossible. The canal could no longer take the flood-water which spilled into the peat moors and the upper pound began to leak into the fields alongside. In 1840 Richard and Samuel Prat, Glastonbury solicitors and heavy investors in the canal, absconded—to the dismay of their fellow townsmen—and were later adjudged bankrupt. John Bulleid, a respectable citizen and a major shareholder in the canal, committed suicide.

The Bristol & Exeter Railway opened its station at Highbridge in 1842 and within a few years was negotiating to buy the canal, despite arguments from some of its shareholders that it would prove a liability. The purchase was completed in 1848, with an obligation on the railway to keep the canal open and in good condition. It was an obligation it was quick to try to rid itself of. There were problems with the Commissioners of Sewers, who were owners of the sea-lock at Highbridge and for some time had kept the gates closed to retain a navigable depth of fresh water in the canal. In 1850 the lower levels were flooded; the commissioners opened the gates and navigation became even more difficult. The Bristol & Exeter then determined to sell the canal to its offshoot, the Somerset Central Railway, for a line from Highbridge to Glastonbury. The sale was completed in 1852. The canal was used to transport material for building the railway and was then closed in July 1854, the railway opening in the following month.

The Highbridge end of the canal, which belonged to the commissioners, was not abandoned until 1936. The sea-lock and basin were on the south-west side of the A38/B3139 junction; the site is now a car park, and there may still be mooring rings in the wall. The South Drain takes the line of the canal. Between Edington Burtle and Shapwick Lock the railway was laid alongside the canal; of the lock a few traces can be found. Towards Ashcott you can follow the canal bed and east of the site of Ashcott Station there was an aqueduct over the South Drain. At Sharpham the railway crossed the canal; ½ mile eastward the canal was carried across the Brue by a twin-arch iron aqueduct of which the abutments may still be seen. On the approach to Glastonbury, near New Close Farm, there was a sharp right-angled bend that the company lacked the funds to straighten. Glastonbury Basin is now covered by a timber yard and all associated buildings have been demolished. There were eleven swing bridges on the canal; these were fixed when the canal was closed, but some of them are likely to survive.

OS sheet 182

Somerset Rivers

The Parrett has always been a navigation and the Tone, which joins the Parrett at Burrow Bridge, formed the old water route to Taunton before the Bridgwater & Taunton Canal was made. Until 1836 the Parrett was unimproved; in that year the Parrett

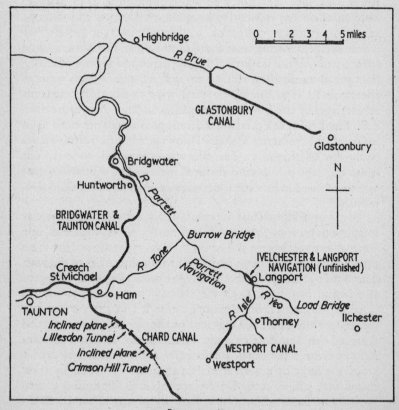

Somerset rivers

Navigation Company was formed with the intention of staving off competition from the Chard Canal then under construction. Four locks were built: at Stanmoor above Burrow Bridge, Langport, at Muchelney where the Isle joined the Parrett, at Oath, and a half-lock was built at Thorney. The navigation was extended to Westport via the 2 mile Westport Canal, and the bridge at Langport, which had obstructed vessels for centuries, was demolished and rebuilt. For some years the company traded with rather more success than the Chard Canal until railway competition and the expense of maintaining drainage proved too formidable. The navigation was abandoned in 1878, although boats continued to use it for several years. It can still be used by light craft and the Westport Canal has recently been reopened by the Wessex Water Authority, although a lowered road bridge obstructs passage. The basin at Westport has an interesting collection of buildings including a warehouse. Langport is an attractive little town whose prosperity was founded on the river; the site of the lock is a few hundred yards below the bridge. The half-lock at Thorney (ST 428227) is worth seeking out; it merited a whole page, photograph and diagram in an important article on 'Flash-locks on English Waterways' (see page 218).

So much of an obstacle was old Langport Bridge that in 1795 a navigation was planned to bypass it by improving existing drains and to join the River Yeo (or Ivel) which would be improved to Ilchester. Boats had reached Ilchester on occasions since Roman times, although probably only when the river was in flood. Otherwise, Pill Bridge or Load Bridge would have been the limits of navigation. The Ivelchester & Langport Navigation was to be 8¼ miles long with 7 locks. Some work was done on the upper section of the line and on rebuilding bridges, but there is no evidence that any of the locks were completed and the project ran out of funds in 1797. The river continued to be used as in previous years.

Improvements to the Tone are recorded in the seventeenth century, although the navigation does not seem to have reached Taunton until 1717 after improvements on the upper 3 miles including the construction of locks. On the whole, this was a prosperous navigation until the opening of the Bridgwater & Taunton Canal in 1827. By the end of the eighteenth century there were 4 conventional locks on the river, at Obridge, Bathpool, Creech St Michael and Ham, and 4 half-locks. Two more locks were built on a cut to the Grand Western Canal, known as the Parliamentary Cut as it was made in accordance with the 1832 act under which the canal company took over the river. Although the canal company was obliged to keep the river navigable, trade on the Tone declined rapidly and, with the closure of the Parrett navigation in 1878, traffic virtually ceased. The length between Burrow Bridge and Ham Mills was used until the end of the 1920s. The remains of the locks disappeared in the flood-prevention works in 1967-8.

OS sheets 182, 193

The Chard Canal

The Chard Canal was among the last of the main line canals to be made. It was opened in 1842, the same year that the Bristol & Exeter Railway arrived in Taunton, only a few miles from the canal's junction with the Bridgwater & Taunton Canal. This railway company bought both these canals in 1866-7 and closed the Chard in the latter year, although the Bridgwater & Taunton, of course, remains open today. These two canals were remnants of ambitious ideas for an English & Bristol Channels Canal which, according to one survey, would have passed through Chard itself.

The Chard Canal was a typical product of James Green, its surveyor. Like his other West-Country waterways it took tub-boats and had as few locks as possible—one and a stop-lock. The descent of 231ft from Chard was accomplished by 4 inclined planes and the hills were penetrated by 3 tunnels. All these were included in a canal only 13½ miles long. It can be explored in a day, and if you are spending a week-end in the area it is well worth taking the other day to investigate the Grand Western on the other side of Taunton.

Chard, apart from its main street not the most attractive of Somersetshire towns, lies on the A30/A358 crossing. For the whole of its length the canal lies on the east side of the A358 and never more than 2 miles from it. The site of the basin is on the north side of the town on the premises of B. G. Wyatt, Furnham Road. Two canal warehouses have been integrated into Wyatt's factory; the façade facing Furnham Road and much of the surrounding wall were built by the canal company. Immediately north of the basin the canal line ran close to the disused line of the Chard-Taunton railway, but few traces are now visible. The minor road to Chaffcombe, heading north-east off the A358, crossed the canal and leads around the northern side of Chard Reservoir. Close to the point where this road leaves the reservoir a footpath on the left leads to the Chard Common Incline (337103/339345). This was the longest of the canal's inclines, falling 86ft, but unlike the others had only a single track. It was operated by a water-wheel driven by a water-turbine at the foot, but no trace of any installations now remains.

Return to the main road, continue north and take the next turn east to Knowle St Giles. This road soon crosses both old railway and canal. If you pick up the line of the canal you may follow it to the site of the one conventional lock, just under a mile along in Bere Mills Covert. The lock was about 56ft long.

If you return to the A358, you need to turn on to the A3037 towards Ilminster to meet the canal again. The right turn to Cricket Malherbie crosses the canal in about 300yd. About ½ mile further along the main road you will see some cottages at Dowlish Ford built in the bed of the canal, which then passes under the road making for the eastern slopes of Herne Hill. A deep cutting was originally intended here, but once construction was begun this was changed to a tunnel, 300yd long. A few years ago it was possible to see evidence of the beginning of the cutting actually on top of the tunnel, but lately this area has been filled in. The north portal of the tunnel, however, has been preserved. Beyond the portal, the Ilminster incline took the canal down 82½ft; the foot of the incline was by the boundary of the school playing-field. It seems from a contemporary drawing that the incline was worked by an overshot water-wheel at the foot, operating a continuous chain to which caissons containing the boats were attached. If this was so, the water to drive the wheel must have been led off from the River Isle, several hundred yards distant.

Wharf Lane indicates the site of Ilminster Wharf. To the north of the A303 the canal crossed the Isle at a point later used by the railway. Beyond, much of the line disappeared when Merrifield Aerodrome was built. It is advisable to return to the A358 and continue as far as the minor road to Beercrocombe. Here you can see the embanked canal to the east of the church and running southward to Keysey's Dairy House. The road heading north from the centre of the village takes you close to the site of the south portal of Crimson Hill Tunnel, although there are now no signs of the portal itself.

The next place to make for is Wrantage on the A378, the Taunton–Langport road. Stop by the Canal Inn, with its misleading sign, and look for the abutments of the aqueduct which took the canal over the road. A track on the south side of the road takes you to the tunnel's north portal. Crimson Hill Tunnel is 1,800yd long, which puts it into the 'top twenty' of British canal tunnels. The shackles in the roof aided boatmen to haul the boats through—unlike narrow boats, tub-boats would not have been legged through tunnels. The lining is of stone with holes at regular intervals in the sides, possibly for drainage. Nearby, you may find the foundations of the tunnel-keeper's house. Having navigated the tunnel, boats then descended the 27½ft Wrantage incline with a sizeable pound at the foot and a length of tree-lined canal leading you almost back to the main road. The embankment continues on the north side of the road, levelling down as it meets the rising ground. By the time the minor road to Lillesdon is reached the canal is in a cutting; a stone bridge carries the road across and the towpath is visible below. The cutting continues to the south-east portal of Lillesdon Tunnel, now almost entirely filled in. The far portal of the 314yd tunnel, in comparatively good condition, is in a field on the north-west side of the road from Lillesdon quite close to the A378/A358 junction.

Thornfalcon is the next place of interest. Here the site of the fourth incline is near Canal Farm on the road leading northward from the village. This brought the canal down a further 28ft. Continue along this road, taking the left turn for Creech St Michael and turning left again at a T-junction towards Ruishton. Soon you see the abutments of the aqueduct that took the canal across the road. From here an impressive embankment with several flood arches carries the canal over the flood plains of the Tone to a handsome and elegant three-arch aqueduct, now lacking its parapet, striding across the river. The final length of canal is on a buttressed embankment with stone walls at the end of which is a private garden, the towpath serving as the garden path. The house was once an inn and is likely to have been also the Chard Canal toll house. The stop-lock and towpath bridge of the Bridgwater & Taunton have both disappeared.

Spare some time for the Bridgwater & Taunton Canal if you can. It is navigable, but only by light craft as the fixed bridges provide limited headroom. Some of the locks have recently been restored, but what is wanted is restoration throughout to proper navigable standards. The West Country needs living inland navigations; the Bridgwater & Taunton has been 'on the borderline', as it were, for far too long.

OS sheet 193

The Grand Western Canal

The Grand Western Canal, as built, was a fragment of various ambitious and imaginative schemes for an inland waterway connection between Bristol and Exmouth. One of these schemes, whose combined purpose was to eliminate the dangerous voyage around Land's End, was for a navigable canal from the Exe at Topsham to the Tone at Taunton, with three branches, the longest of them to Tiverton. The route was surveyed by John Rennie in 1794 and an act obtained two years later. The war against France, however, and the consequent economic problems put the plans into abeyance, and it was not until 1810 that in a field in the parish of Holcombe on the line of the Tiverton branch Sir George Yonge cut the first turf, at which the numerous body of spectators, with the prospect of cider to follow, testified their joy. Four years later—and a difficult and costly four years they had proved—the branch, 11 miles long from Tiverton to Lowdwells, was complete, at a cost to the canal company of nearly £¼ million, far more than had been estimated for the entire waterway under the 1796 act. Trading, almost entirely in lime and roadstone, began as soon as the branch was open; but it all moved one way, from the quarries at Holcombe Rogus and Burlescombe to Tiverton, with no back-carriage.

For several years the canal company was unable seriously to contemplate extending, let alone completing, its line. Enthusiasm revived, however, with the opening of the Bridgwater & Taunton Canal in 1827. Extension of the Grand Western to Taunton seemed to hold promise of profit and the company called in James Green, engineer of the Bude and Torrington canals, to report. With a financial limit imposed by the company, Green resurveyed the line and proposed a tub-boat canal with inclined planes, similar to his Bude Canal. In a second report he withdrew the inclined planes, except for one, and substituted seven lifts, and in 1831 construction in accordance with this report began. Five years later, with the work unfinished, Green was dismissed, chiefly because he had failed to make the inclined plane at Wellisford operate at all. The company called in an experienced engineer, W. A. Provis, to advise; he recommended installing a steam-engine at Wellisford and various improvements elsewhere to minimise wastage of water. The company raised the necessary funds, mostly from private loans including £1,000 from its own superintendent (Captain John Twisden, RN, then 80 years old), and in 1838 the line to Taunton was opened. The length from Tiverton to Taunton was 24½ miles and no more of the Grand Western Canal was ever built.

Four years later the Bristol & Exeter Railway arrived at Taunton, reaching Exeter in 1844. In 1848 the railway branch line to Tiverton was finished—and so, after a mere ten years, were the prospects of the canal. It was not long before the canal company leased the Grand Western to the railway, which in 1864 purchased it outright for £30,000, under one-tenth of what it had cost to construct. Green's tub-boat section from Taunton to Lowdwells was closed in 1867. Some stone traffic continued on the Tiverton Branch until 1924; thereafter this length fell into gradual decline, used by anglers and towpath-walkers, but unnavigable. The navigation rights were extinguished in 1962, the same year in which the Tiverton Canal Preservation Society was formed. The society defeated a move to infill part of the canal in 1966 and then took part in negotiations with the British Waterways Board to ensure the canal's future. These negotiations led in 1971 to the transfer of the canal to Devon County Council, together with the sum of £38,750 to cover future liabilities. Following restoration work, navigation—in unpowered craft—is again possible, and you can enjoy a trip in a horse-drawn passenger barge.

The restored section of the Grand Western is clearly marked on the Ordnance Survey map and Devon County Council has published two leaflet guides. Tiverton Basin is on the south-east side of the town; if you enter the town on the A373, turn left at the roundabout and in a few hundred yards you will find the basin on your left in what is now a mainly residential area. It is signposted almost everywhere. In a yard adjacent to the basin are the remnants of lime-kilns. On the south side of the basin were several wharves.

From Tiverton you can either walk the towpath or take the A373 through Halberton to Sampford Peverell; the canal is never more than a mile from the road. There are several good stone bridges and it is worth diverting from the main road to see them. Near East Manley a twin-arched aqueduct with an iron trough took the canal over the Tiverton Branch of the Bristol & Exeter Railway. Hereabouts the canal, following the contours, swings north, is crossed by the main road and loops around the north side of Halberton; this was a notoriously leaky section of waterway. Greenway Bridge, made of local sandstone, is the nearest to Halberton. Halberton Wharf was nearly a mile east of the village, by Rock Bridge where the A373 moves to the north side of the canal again. Rock House nearby was built for Captain John Twisden, and Charles Hadfield, most scholarly of canal historians whose account of the Grand Western is contained in his *Canals of South West England*, lived in Rock Cottage during 1928. In about a mile the canal and main road cross again in the middle of Sampford Peverell where the site of the wharf is conveniently indicated by the Wharf Guest House. Several cottages in this village were demolished for the construction of the canal, and it was here during the cattle fair in 1811 that 300 navvies, angry at delays in their wages, rioted; one of them was shot dead when attacking the house of a local resident.

From Sampford Peverell to Lowdwells you can continue along the towpath or take to the minor roads. There are 9 road bridges in the distance of 5 miles. On the north side of the canal by the bridge—the second from the village—that takes the lane to Boehill Farm are the remains of the pit which supplied the clay for puddling the canal. Ebear Bridge carries the minor road to Westleigh; north of the village were the quarries which provided the canal's main cargo. About 600yd further along, the canal swings due north. This was the point where the Tiverton Branch left the proposed main line, which would have continued southward roughly along the line of the present main line railway. The next bridge leads to Canonsleigh and the site of more quarries, and by the one after that, Fenacre, a road runs alongside the canal. At Whipcott there were lime-kilns and quarries, one of which was the last to send stone by the canal in the 1920s. Then comes the short Waytown Tunnel taking the canal beneath the road to Holcombe Rogus. There was no towpath through the tunnel, the boats being pulled through by the boatman hauling on a chain; you can see a short length of chain near the southern portal. By the north portal was a small wharf and the wharf house still survives. The canal was fed by springs in the bed at either end of the tunnel. Another 600yd brings you to Lowdwells and the end of the watered section. Here is Lock's Cottage, once a mill cottage, and the remains of the 45ft long lock which had a fall of 3½ft. The lock was built by James Green and dates from about 1832; it was intended to take four tub-boats up to the summit level. Recent attempts to excavate it were halted as its condition below water-level was too unstable, although Provis in his report had remarked on its excellent workmanship.

From Lowdwells to Taunton the canal closely follows the course of the River Tone. Following the footpath from Lock's Cottage you come to a minor road where you can detect the abutments of an aqueduct that once carried the canal across it. An embankment in the field on the far side of the road holds the dry bed of the canal which leads you in about ⅓ mile to the site of Greenham Lift. The restored lift-keeper's cottage is privately inhabited. Of the lift itself, which with a fall of 42ft was by far the largest—and most troublesome—of the 7 lifts Green constructed on the Grand Western, there are no substantial remains; indeed, all that you can see is a riot of greenery, reputedly concealing a double-decker bus, at the edge of the cottage garden. If you walk down the slope to the lower level, you can see bits of stonework at the foot of the old retaining wall.

Green's lifts were similar to James Fussell's trial lift which was built for the Somerset & Dorset Canal on Barrow Hill. He described and illustrated them in the *Transactions of the Institution of Civil Engineers*, Vol 2, 1838 (since reprinted separately). To solve problems that arose in use, locks had to be added to the first three lifts to be completed—those nearest Taunton. Thereafter they worked reasonably well, apart from occasional breakages and failures.

A fine accommodation bridge crosses the canal near the foot of Greenham Lift. You can follow the line across a muddy field until it is crossed by a road on the south-east side of Greenham Church. It holds the same direction for over a mile, passing Elworthy Farm and coming up alongside a minor road near the site of Cothay Manor. It swings eastward to be crossed by the road from Thorne St Margaret to Higher Wellisford. Some 2 miles along the canal from Greenham Lift is the top of Wellisford incline; it is $\frac{1}{2}$ mile north of Thorne St Margaret and is accessible from Bughole Lane, which takes you to Incline Farm. Among the farm buildings are two cottages for the incline-keeper and his assistant, and the engine-house, now used for storage.

The Wellisford incline, 440ft long, lowered the canal 81ft. Green planned it to operate on the bucket-in-well system, like the much longer incline at Hobbacott Down on the Bude Canal. Both inclines were double track, but at Wellisford the boats were moved up and down the incline on wheeled cradles whereas the Bude Canal boats were fitted with wheels themselves. Green, however, was unable to make the Wellisford incline work. After his dismissal, Provis considered that Green had seriously under-estimated the weight of water necessary to operate the system, especially when a loaded boat had to be raised when there was nothing going down in return. To solve the problem the canal committee installed a steam-engine and it was this that powered the incline during its working life.

The well at the top of the incline has been filled in, but you should be able to identify the slope and the basin at the foot. A road between Holywell Lake and Langford Budville crosses the Tone; south of the bridge another road turns off west and between this road and the river is the site of the basin with the mouth of the adit, intended to take off the water from the well, close by.

It is best now to make for Wellington and take the B3187 road towards Milverton. At Tonedale, just over a mile along, the road crosses the canal; if you find yourself crossing the river you have gone too far. There was a wharf at Tonedale. A footpath leading westward is on the line of the canal; it crosses a mill leat and in about 500yd brings you to the site of the 18ft Winsbeer Lift. There are no masonry remains but only bumps in the ground; the ruins of the lift cottage may still be visible. You can continue walking through fields to the foot of the incline, with the river below on your right and old sandstone quarries on your left.

Returning to the B3187, you can either walk along the line of the canal eastward—not impossible, although the bed is not always discernible—or go into Wellington, take the A38 Taunton road and turn northward to Nynehead about a mile on. The Nynehead road crosses the canal about 300yd north of the railway bridge. Here there was a wharf and the wharf cottage is by the roadside. A few minutes' walk westward through a small wood brings you to the remains of Nynehead Lift. Around the site the trees have been cleared and you can examine the considerable remains of the masonry chamber. The lift cottage has been demolished, but its foundations have been traced. Now embanked, the canal continues and soon crosses the drive to Nynehead Court by a stately single-arch aqueduct.

A larger aqueduct survives to the east of the Nynehead road. You can either try to force your way along the overgrown canal bed or divert around the edge of the field. In a few hundred yards you come to the aqueduct over the Tone, a handsome 30ft span of stone and brick. Note the iron trough that held the water.

The Grand Western stays close to the river but now on its northern bank. For the site of the next lift continue into Nynehead, turn right and in ¾ mile right again on to the road to Bradford-on-Tone. Just past East Nynehead on the south side of the road is Lift Cottage, privately owned. In the garden, underneath the railway embankment, are the remains of the second largest lift, Trefusis, with a rise of 38½ft. If you continue towards Bradford and take the next turn, sharp left, you cross the canal twice. There was a wharf by the second bridge on the north side of Tone Green.

Now the canal lies between railway and river. For Allerford Lift make for the Victory Inn at Allerford, a mile south-west of Norton Fitzwarren. There was a wharf near the inn and the wide ditch of the canal is clearly defined, leading to the site of the 19ft lift. No masonry is left, but the difference in height is obvious. The lift cottage nearby has been renovated. Similarly, the masonry of the Norton Lift, with a 12½ft rise, has disappeared. Its site is a mile north-east of Allerford; turn south in Norton Fitzwarren, cross the railway by a footbridge and across a field you come to the bed of the canal. Again, notice the change in level at the site of the lift.

Some traces of the Grand Western can be found on the approach to Taunton, notably at Silk Mills Bridge on the road from Staplegrove to Bishop's Hull. In Taunton itself the railway bridge over Station Road occupies the site of an aqueduct and the relief railway line takes the line of the canal. Canal Road leads you to the final few yards of the Bridgwater & Taunton Canal; the junction with the Grand Western was on the north side of the bridge, near Firepool Lock. The boundary of the railway goods yard is on the line of the canal; the railway has obliterated the regulating lock and the Taunton Lift. Part of the retaining wall of the lift, which had a rise of 23½ft, can be seen at the end of the garden of one of a row of cottages backing on to the railway property. In the 13 miles from Lowdwells to the terminus at Taunton, the Grand Western descended 262ft.

OS sheets 181, 193

The Stover and Hackney Canals

The short Stover Canal in South Devon has an interesting link with one of the longest and busiest of the narrow Midland canals, the Trent & Mersey. The connection is clay. The Stover was built in the early 1790s by James Templer, a local landowner whose estate was rich in deposits of clay. Via the canal, clay was shipped to the Teign estuary and thence to the Mersey. Then it was off-loaded into narrow boats heading for Stoke and in particular for the Etruria Works of Josiah Wedgwood. After the opening of the Haytor Granite Tramway in 1820, granite was also exported by the Stover and shipped to London for major building works.

The Stover enjoyed many decades of prosperity. The Templer family sold it to the Duke of Somerset in 1829, together with the tramroad. He rented out the navigation; then in 1862 he sold it to the South Devon Railway for £8,000. The railway continued the same policy and the canal continued in trade until 1939 with the lessees, Watts, Blake & Co, shipping the clay in their own steam-tug towed barges from their clay cellars at Teigngrace.

Originally, the canal began at Teigngrace, but James Templer's son John had it extended to Ventiford to connect with the Haytor Granite Tramway. If you take the A382 Okehampton road out of Newton Abbot you will find a right fork for Teigngrace about a mile out of the town. Continue through Teigngrace for Ventiford, about ¾ mile. Under the railway bridge and to the right is the canal basin, its outline still traceable. The tramway came in from the north-west and much evidence of it can be found if you have time to explore.

At Teigngrace you find the canal by first seeking out the railway line and the old station. About 50yd south a farm track crosses the line and also the canal. Here is Teigngrace Lock, its chamber made of granite. The Stover locks were designed to take two boats, 54ft by 14ft, end-on. They were bow-hauled or sailed until the introduction of steam towing. The canal runs parallel to the railway and you can follow it (advisedly with wellington boots and a machete) to the next lock, Graving Dock, with much difficulty.

Driving southward from Teigngrace you come to a T-junction. Turn left and shortly the road crosses the canal at Teignbridge. To the left are the remains of Teignbridge Lock; to the right, by the old railway station, the overgrown site of the wharf. Here used to be extensive clay cellars belonging to Watts, Blake & Co. See if the interesting old paddle-gearing still survives on the lock.

For the junction with the estuary you take the A380 Exeter road from the centre of Newton Abbot and make for the traffic lights. Look for a track across Jetty Marsh and follow it towards the railway. The canal locked into the Whitelake Channel about ¼ mile beyond the A380 railway bridge. There is a double lock, once walled with wood. You may find a couple of decaying boats in the vicinity. Jetty Marsh was just about the head of navigation in the Teign, which was busy with the clay trade until well into the present century, with 100,000 tons being moved in 1905, most of it by water. Granite from the tramway continued into the 1850s; the National Gallery and the British Museum are built of Haytor granite.

The clay trade led to the building of the Hackney Canal by Lord Clifford in 1843. This 5 furlong waterway was cut from a point on the Newton Abbot-Kingsteignton road (A380) about midway between the two. Clay cellars were built by the road to store clay from the Kingsteignton area. They are still there but now used as workshops. With permission, you can follow the canal outside the south-west perimeter of the race-course as far as the entrance lock to the Hackney Channel. Beside the channel there are remains of clay cellars which antedate the canal. You can accompany the channel to the sad-looking estuary and cheer yourself up at the nearby pub. Traffic on the Hackney Canal ended in 1928. It was quite a busy little canal in its time, used by eight barges, and producing a comfortable return for the Clifford Estates.

OS sheet 176

The Tavistock Canal

The Tavistock Canal was built for more purposes than navigation. It was designed by John Taylor, at that time manager of the
Wheal Friendship Mine, to link Tavistock with the ancient port
of Morwellham, to provide a water supply from the Tavy to
drive the mills and mining machinery on its route, and by the
construction of its tunnel to help in the prospecting for further
lodes of ore in this copper-rich district. It was opened in 1817 and
enjoyed a moderate success for some years with tolls averaging
rather under £1,000 a year until the opening of the South Devon
& Tavistock Railway in 1859. By the 1870s traffic had virtually
ended and a visitor to the area in 1896 wrote: 'The canal, once a
new and successful enterprise, was unused, partly because the
mines whose ores used to be carried in its barges closed, partly
because the railway had superseded it.' However, the canal was
not filled in and the water remained flowing. In the early 1930s it
was cleaned out and the water was led off from the south end of
the tunnel through a culvert and two short tunnels to a reservoir
above Morwellham whence it was piped to power a generating
station, as it still does today.

Tavistock Wharf is now a car park at the end of Canal Street.
The canal's water supply is led off the Tavy at a weir by Abbey
Bridge; the feeder enters the car park running through it and
under a building which belonged to the old canal company.
Emerging from this building is the Tavistock Canal. You can
follow the towpath out of the town past meadows, cottages built
by the Duke of Bedford (who owned most of the land hereabout), under the A386 near Drake's statue and around the school
and Crowndale Farm, where Drake was born. Soon trees line the
canal as you approach the valley of the Lumburn. Near a cottage
the waterway narrows and it has been suggested that this was the
site of a lock. Locks were mentioned in the Canal Act and in a
notice dated 1854 inviting tenders for work on the canal there is a
reference to 'locks, hatches and wooden bridges between the
Tavistock Wharf and the Tunnel's mouth'. The canal took tub-
boats approximately 31ft by 5ft; the length of this presumed lock
is 50ft, which is a multiple of 12ft 6in, as the act required the
length of a lock should be. A semi-circular cut in the side of the
canal might have been made to permit the opening of a lock gate.
It has additionally been suggested that the lock's chief purpose

was to control the flow of water along the canal.

The canal now turns sharply to the north, running parallel to and above the Lumburn on an embankment. It crosses the river by a single-arch aqueduct. By the next bend is the junction with the Mill Hill Branch, 2 miles long, leading to a slate quarry. You can follow the dry bed of this cut to the A390 Tavistock-Liskeard road. It was replaced by a tramroad in 1846 and from the A390 it follows the tramroad embankment as far as Mill Hill cross-roads. To the west you will find evidence of a bridge that once took the branch over the road. On the far side of the road is the likely site of an inclined plane that lifted the branch 19½ft. The top length of the branch is conjectural; examine the lie of the land and come to your own conclusions.

From the junction a short stretch of canal leads to the portal of the tunnel through Morwelldown. This tunnel, only 8ft high and 6ft wide, is the smallest bore navigable tunnel on the British waterways. It is 2,540yd long and took 13 years to complete. The date of commencement, 1803, is inscribed over both portals. The tunnel was very difficult to excavate; conditions inside it were foul and Taylor designed two pumps operated by water-wheels, one to clear the air and the other to remove the water flowing through the workings. During the excavation copper lodes were found, but they did not prove especially remunerative. The tunnel had no towpath; boats going from Tavistock to Morwellham floated through with the current, but those returning had to be legged, a slow procedure against the the flow of water. Various schemes were tried, including drawing the boats through by a wire rope powered by a water-wheel at each end. None of them was wholly satisfactory and the problem remained for the lifetime of the canal. On the open canal the boats were horse-drawn, an extra horse being attached for the journey to Tavistock.

The south portal of the tunnel, the rest of the canal and the inclined plane are now in the care of the Morwellham Open Air Museum, which has done much investigative and restoration work in the past few years. They form part of the Canal and Woodland Trail, which begins at one of the museum buildings in the port—it used to be a malt-house—and continues through Morwellham Farm, where you can see old farming machinery and implements, across the long incline of the Devon Great Consols Railway to the inclined plane of the canal. This was double-track with a rise of 237ft and was operated by a water-wheel. The boats, according to the best evidence, did not use the incline, but the cargo was off-loaded into iron wagons with larger wheels at the front to keep them level. You can see the sleepers and a stretch of iron rail on the slope. The railway ran to the quayside at Morwellham, with a branch to a storehouse above the river.

From the incline the trail takes you to an old tin/copper mine and through a wood to the canal towpath. The channel here is shallow and good for frogs. You walk alongside it to the south portal of the tunnel, which marks the end of the museum trail. Returning to the museum, you can gain a good idea of the rest of the Morwellham story by taking the Port and Mine Trail. This takes you from the Ship Inn, once a haven for ships' captains and traders but now no longer licensed, past lime-kilns, chutes from the branch of the canal inclined-plane railway through which ore was tipped into the sheds, a section of this railway, cottages built by the Duke of Bedford in 1856 for the increasing population of the port during the copper boom, a manganese-grinding mill, and other industrial relics, until you return to the docks and quays—having enjoyed a trip on the mine tramway half-way round.

As a result of the discovery of rich veins of copper at Blanchdown, 5 miles away, trade at the port increased enormously after 1844. The new mines—five of them—were brought together in the Devonshire Great Consolidated Mining Company which built new quays at Morwellham and a dock to take the 300-ton schooners. The other docks included one for manganese; furthest downstream is the medieval dock, built where a tributary once joined the Tamar. The Devon Great Consols did not use the canal, the trade on which was dwindling away as the port's prosperity grew. Between 1850 and 1860 was the busiest period; then the productivity of the mines began to decline, and so did the port. For a few years arsenic became more important than copper as an export, but all trade ended with the century until in 1901 the Great Consols Mine stopped altogether.

The revival of Morwellham began in 1970, thanks to the trustees of Dartington Hall and the Dartington Amenity Research Trust. There is still an enormous amount to be done but remarkable progress has been made to dispel the melancholy decay which characterised Morwellham.

OS sheet 201

The River Tamar and the Tamar Manure Navigation

For vessels of any size, Morwellham marked the head of navigation on the Tamar. It was possible, however, for barges to be bow-hauled a further 2 miles upstream to a fish-weir near Gunnislake. Towards the end of the eighteenth century various schemes were proposed for extending the navigation inland by canal. The most promising followed a survey by John Rennie in 1795; this envisaged cutting a canal 1½ miles long across a bend in the river, bypassing the weir, and constructing a tub-boat canal to link up with the projected Bude Canal near Tamerton Bridge. The Tamar was to be dredged and improved below and above the canalisation, and the whole navigation would be about 20 miles long.

An act was obtained in 1796 and work was begun. It stopped a few years later, all that was completed being the dredging of the lower stretch of river from Morwellham, a lock 70ft by 20ft and a 500yd length of canal. A quay was built above the lock, with a granary, stabling and kilns. The Tamar Manure Navigation Company, the owners of the navigation, continued in business for nearly 120 years carrying coal, bricks, lime, manure and granite. Gunnislake Gasworks were built by the quay and supplied with coal well into the 1920s. All trading ceased in about 1929 when the navigation silted up; the company went into liquidation in 1942.

Today, the lock and canal have been designated an ancient monument. The A390 Tavistock–Liskeard road crosses the Tamar at Gunnislake and you can reach the site by taking a minor road leading south-east and downhill from the centre of the village. The lock is a few hundred yards from the gasworks. The granite chamber is in good condition; the top gates have been replaced by a concrete block wall and the lower gates are derelict. The upper part of the length of canal is filled in and vehicles and cattle can cross it to the lock island.

With the revival of interest in Morwellham, attention has also turned to the Tamar Manure Navigation. A committee has been formed and its members have organised clearing of the river banks and channel to encourage boaters to use this stretch. It is claimed that the 1796 act is still operable and the committee members hope that the conflict between fish-breeding—for which part of the river bed in the area is used—and navigation will be resolved. A boat-launching ramp at Calstock is also being planned to enable trailable boats to be used on the Upper Tamar.

Below Morwellham the Tamar is navigable at high water by craft drawing up to 5ft; it is a very beautiful waterway. In 'Crossing the Brook', exhibited at the Royal Academy in 1815 and now in the Tate Gallery, J. M. W. Turner gives a somewhat Italianate view of the Tamar Valley, with a water-wheel and indications of industrial activity in the distance. Those with keen eyesight or imagination may convince themselves that there are also the lock gates of the Tamar Manure Navigation.

OS sheet 201

The Liskeard & Looe Union Canal

In some ways the Liskeard & Looe Union is reminiscent of the canals of South Wales. It is squeezed into a valley, along with a river, a railway and—for part of the distance—a road; it is heavily locked and emerges into an estuary and for several years was busy and profitable.

A canal link between Liskeard and Looe was first proposed in 1777 when Edmund Leach produced a plan for a contour canal about 15 miles long which would distribute lime to the hillside farms and descend by means of inclined planes. The proposal lapsed, however, and was not revived until 1823 when a committee was established to recommend the best way to improve communication between Liskeard and Looe. James Green, at that time Surveyor of Bridges in Devon, was consulted and reported in favour of a tub-boat canal, $6\frac{1}{4}$ miles long, with 2 inclined planes falling 180ft. Although there was plenty of enthusiasm, funds were not immediately forthcoming and no action was taken. Then in December 1824 a meeting in Liskeard decided to promote a canal with locks and a towing path wide enough for gentlemen's carriages from Moorswater near Liskeard to Terras Pill above Looe, about 6 miles, with road connections to Liskeard and Banka Mill. The plans were by Robert Coad and Richard Retallick, who became the company's engineer and superintendent respectively.

The canal, with 25 locks taking vessels 50ft by 10ft, was opened in 1828. It was thought that coal, agricultural produce and lime— burnt in kilns alongside the canal and used as fertiliser—would be the main traffic, but with the discovery of copper on Caradon Hill, copper ore soon became the principal cargo. The canal became so busy in the mid-nineteenth century that water shortages began to occur and congestion became a problem. The canal company, with both money and land at its disposal, built first a horse railway connecting the mines with the basin at Moorswater and then a steam railway alongside the canal, opened in December 1860 and later extended to East Looe, where the harbour had been greatly improved. Within a short time the canal above Sandplace ceased to be used and the quays at Sandplace were either destroyed or cut off from the waterside by the railway. Between Sandplace and Terras Pill some navigation continued, but with difficulty as the bridges taking the railway over the canal provided insufficient headroom. Conditions on this short stretch continued to deteriorate and after the GWR took over the railway in 1909, all boat traffic stopped.

No longer is the canal marked on the OS map, but some traces of it still exist. At Moorswater the construction of the Liskeard bypass caused much destruction and the area around the quays has been developed into the Liskeard Industrial Estate. The canal reservoir, fed by the Crylla leat, has been obliterated, but the site of the quays themselves has not yet been built on. Alongside the railway clay-works siding you can find the side walls of one of the two quays; close by is a bank of lime-kilns, a reminder of the reason for which the canal was originally constructed. The Moorswater Viaduct strides across the valley.

Part of the canal near Coombe Junction was destroyed when the extension railway to Liskeard was made between 1898 and 1901. Southward from here you can follow the canal bed by keeping close to the railway, although in places it is much overgrown. Between St Keyne and Landlooe Bridge the railway was laid in the canal bed. Several of the lock chambers survive and can be found by the present-day overbridges—three-arched to take railway, canal and river. These bridges were rebuilt by the GWR in 1910 from the original Liskeard & Looe Railway bridges. At the tails of some of the locks you may find sections of the road bridges built when the canal itself was constructed. By now the basin at Sandplace is likely to have been filled in; it was just above the hamlet and close to the former Bullers Arms. It was John Buller's quay that was destroyed by the building of the railway in 1859. Terras Lock, now a sluice, is a short distance southward, on the north side of the Terras level-crossing.

The scenery of the Looe Valley is spectacular; the hills rise sharply on either side and, except in high summer, there is comparatively little traffic. The canal bed is dry—or at best damp— but the river bubbles along close by. The railway history and relics in this area are especially interesting and, if you are exploring hereabouts, it is worth obtaining a copy of Michael Messenger's book, *Caradon and Looe*, which will help you make sense of what you see.

OS sheet 201

The Cann Quarry and the Par Canals

These two short—and short-lived—West-Country canals should not be overlooked. Each had a particular point of interest, although there is very little left of either of them today.

The Cann Quarry Canal was an attempted solution to the problem of transporting slate from Lord Morley's quarry to Plymouth. The quarry was in Plym Forest on the east bank of the river and about $\frac{1}{2}$ mile north of Plym Bridge. Alternative solutions proposed by the engineer J. M. Rendel were the construction of a horse railway with inclined plane or the canalisation of the River Plym, but Lord Morley favoured the idea of widening an existing mill leat to take trains of wheeled tub-boats, such as Rendel had seen in Shropshire, which could be run off on to a private branch tramroad and thence to the Plymouth and Dartmoor railroad, which already existed. The leat itself came off the Plym by a weir on the north side of the quarry and ran close to the river for about 2 miles to Marsh Mills. Then it was led off to join the River Tory, a tributary of the Plym.

Rendel improved the leat by widening and embanking it and straightening out some awkward curves. A 4ft wide towpath was built on the western side. There were no locks, but there was a gradual slope down to the mills, where a small basin was built.

The canal was opened in 1829 and operated for about seven years. Then, possibly because of the amount of transhipment involved, it ceased to be used and Lord Morley's tramroad was extended northward along the towpath to the quarry. With the ending of boat traffic the canal became once more a leat and in 1855 the quarry itself was closed. Building of the Tavistock

Branch Railway later obliterated many traces of the tramroad.

You may still find the course of the leat to the north of the site of Marsh Mills Station close to where the A374 crosses the Plym. And close to Plym Bridge the Tavistock Railway used to cross the leat; here the towpath was widened to carry Lord Morley's tramroad and the evidence of this should still be visible. It is as a converted mill leat, however, that the Cann Quarry Canal claims its place in waterway history.

The Par Canal was west of Plymouth, midway between Fowey and St Austell. Its interest lies in its date; it was constructed well into the railway age, being opened in 1847. It was the remnant of an earlier idea for a coast-to-coast canal, from Padstow to Fowey. This never materialised, but what was later made was a tramroad with a short canal—the Par Canal—at its southern end.

The canal was just under 2 miles long. It connected at Pontsmill with the Treffry tramway, named after J. T. Treffry, a wealthy Cornish mine-owner. Here at the foot of the Carmears incline a basin was built. Most of the traffic came off the tramway: clay, and tin and lead ores. This was off-loaded from trucks into the canal boats and taken down to Par Harbour. It is likely that the canal also served the works at Pontsmill.

Such was the productivity of the mines that within a few years it was decided to extend the tramway to the harbour to avoid the delays of transhipment. This was done in 1855, although the canal was not closed until 1873 when the Cornish Mineral Railway, now the owner of the Treffry tramway, built its line from Par to Fowey. The canal water was piped under the railway-crossing as it was used by a lead-smelting works and for sluicing the harbour.

The size of boats used on the Par Canal is not known, but one lock was built on it about half-way down. If you seek evidence of its existence, follow the line of the old railway due north from Par Harbour to Pontsmill—but do not be too optimistic.

OS sheet 201

The St Columb Canal

This canal is something of a mystery. It was planned by John Edyvean of St Austell, who put up the money himself for a horseshoe-shaped canal from Mawgan Porth to St Columb Porth, 13 miles long, with an inclined plane from the cliff top to the shore at each end. The purpose was to distribute sea-sand around the local farms, for use as fertiliser, and general merchandise. Stones were to be collected in the boats and shot down the inclines, whence they were taken away in ships—though what stones and for what purpose is part of the mystery. An act was obtained in 1773 and in the following years two sections of canal were cut. One was at a height of about 200ft from Trenance Point, above Mawgan Porth, for some 4½ miles to a point about ½ mile below Whitewater, where it took in water from a river. The other ran from Lusty Glaze, just south of St Columb Porth, past St Columb Minor to a road junction leading to Rialton Barton. This section was about 2 miles long but was only 100ft above sea-level. Locks or an inclined plane would have been needed to connect the two sections, but no connection was ever made. Evidence that the canal was building comes from contemporary advertisements, but there is no reliable evidence of its use. It seems to have been disused by 1781, in any event. The writer of an article in *The Monthly Review* in 1791 related how he went to see the canal in 1779 and met Edyvean, who by then was blind, 'groping his way by the side of his canal, and leading a miserable little horse ... He conducted us to all the parts of this ingenious work ...', but sadly no further informative details are given.

The ground today yields little evidence. The depression of the canal bed can be found behind St Columb Minor Church; a path from the churchyard crosses the line by a packhorse bridge, most of which has been filled in. You can follow the canal for several hundred yards in both directions. At the Trenance Point terminus parts of the canal bed were traceable on the cliff top, but by now these may all have disappeared beneath bungalow gardens and other developments. I do not believe that firm identification of the inclined plane sites is possible, nor is it certain that both of them were built. A description printed in Rees's *Cyclopaedia*, 1805, may refer to one of them; this states that the plane was covered with planks, and the boats, hauled out of the canal by a wheel and drum, shot their load of stones down the slope. Boxes of coal or sand were raised by the same wheel and drum and loaded into the boats at the top.

Apart from the act I do not know of any records of the St Columb. What does exist, however, is a prospectus of 'an intended Canal from St Columb Bridge to Mawgan Porth', dated 1829, in which Robert Retallick, surveyor of the Liskeard & Looe Union Canal, estimates an expenditure on the works of £6,150. This would include 22 locks, to cope with a rise of 147ft, and 'machinery for bringing sand from the Beach to the Canal'. The length of this canal was to be just under 5 miles. There is no evidence that any action was taken on this proposal, but it seems strange that in the prospectus and the few accompanying letters that survive there is no mention at all of any previous canal undertaking in the area.

What evidence is there, then, of the existence and trading history of the St Columb Canal? That is the question which any interested reader is invited to answer.

OS sheet 200

The Bude Canal

Recently the Bude Canal, most of which was abandoned in 1891, has received a good deal of attention. At least two books have been devoted exclusively to it, as well as a number of chapters and articles in other publications, and those dwelling along its line must be quite used to investigators prodding among the hedges and discovering large stones and pieces of iron. It is not surprising; the canal's history is fascinating and a journey along its course takes you through beautiful and remote countryside. Also, there always seems something new to find. Such is the terrain through which the canal passes that it is unlikely for most of it to be disturbed by major building or engineering operations in the foreseeable future; so the attraction of the Bude Canal for explorers should continue.

The original intention of the canal's promoters was a 95 mile waterway climbing from Bude Harbour and winding around the district with tub-boats carrying sea-sand, a valuable fertiliser. This plan proved too costly and was shelved for over forty years. In 1817 the idea was revived and, following a survey by James Green and Thomas Shearm, an act was obtained for a short barge canal and over 40 miles of tub-boat canal in 3 branches. In the event, a total of 35½ miles of canal was constructed, opened throughout in 1825. It comprised 2 miles of barge canal, with 2 locks and a sea-lock; then the main line of tub-boat canal

ascended by 3 inclined planes to a terminus at Blagdonmoor
Wharf, near Holsworthy. A branch from Red Post headed
southward, keeping close to the Tamar, falling through 3 inclines
and ending at Druxton Wharf; another branch, a navigable
feeder from Tamar Lake, joined the main line near the top of the
Venn (or Veala) incline. Although the canal, by bringing down
the price of sea-sand, brought a measure of prosperity to the local
farmers, it did not do its own shareholders much good. The first
dividend was not paid until 1876, when the canal was carrying
about 55,000 tons a year. Now the railways were edging into the
South-West and both traffic and revenue declined. After several
years of struggling and uncertainty the canal company gave up,
abandoning all except the barge canal and the navigable feeder.
These lengths were sold to the Stratton & Bude Urban District
Council in 1901 to be used for water supply.

The lower length of the barge canal, including the lock gates
and the pound of the sea-lock at Bude, is in good condition. The
canal entrance is protected by a substantial breakwater and the
lock permitted vessels up to 300 tons to enter. Beside the lock are
the remains of a narrow-gauge edge-railway; trucks could run
down to the sand and load up there, being drawn back by horses
to be off-loaded into the boats. Barges took the sand to tub-boats
at Helebridge Wharf, or the tub-boats might be brought down to
be loaded at Bude. You can walk the length of the barge canal
along the towpath, past the two derelict locks, Rodds Bridge and
Whalesborough, noting the deterioration in the condition of the
waterway as the distance from Bude increases.

The A39 crosses the canal at Helebridge, about 2 miles south of
Bude. The wharf is filled in, but you should be able to discern its
outline. The house overlooking the site was the engineer's house,
lived in by George Casebourne, James Green's successor, for over
forty years. To the east of the wharf is the foot of Marhamchurch
incline; a footpath runs up beside the slope and on the other side
is the minor road to the village. This incline took the canal up
120ft on a slope 836ft long. It was operated by a water-wheel, like
all the inclines on this canal except Hobbacott Down. There were
two tracks and the boats were fitted with wheels to engage with
rails on the plane. You can see the remains of a tub-boat with a
wheel still attached at the Exeter Maritime Museum. These boats
were operated in horse-drawn trains of four or six. The leading
boat had a pointed bow and the train was steered from the second

boat by a boatman using a handspike. The boats, it seems from the company records, banged about all over the canal and frequently fell down the inclines.

There is a road bridge over the line of the canal in Marhamchurch village. The line then winds away northward for about $1\frac{1}{2}$ miles until it reaches the foot of Hobbacott Down incline, the greatest on this canal and the second highest in the country. This worked on the perilously simple bucket-in-well system. From the top, two wells descended to the lower level of the canal, a distance of 225ft. In each well a bucket was suspended by a chain winding over a large drum. As the full bucket, holding 15 tons of water, descended, so a boat was drawn up the incline by the other end of the chain. When the bucket reached the bottom (and the boat the top) the water escaped through a valve and flowed along a horizontal channel—the adit—to the lower pound. The theory worked; in practice, however, the chain often broke, sending either boat or bucket, and sometimes both, crashing down. In the first six months of 1826 chains broke nine times. Repair bills were major items in the canal company's budget and the passage of boats could be halted for several days. Other machinery gave trouble, too. John Honey, the resident engineer, wrote on 12 August 1831:

> The Beam of the Chain Wheel at Hobbicott Down being so much decayed as to render it almost immediately necessary to put in a new one ... The Wood work of the Drums and Brakes at Hobbicott Down are very much decayed, there is no wood in hand to repair it; something must be done soon otherwise the whole will fall a wreck together.

A steam-engine was installed at Hobbacott Down to operate the incline when the buckets were out of action. It consumed so much coal, however, that Mr Honey was reluctant to use it and in any event the breaking chains often damaged other parts of the machinery as they whipped about. When the Secretary to the Exchequer Loan Commissioners reported on the canal in 1834, he found that:

> the complex method of movement by perpendicular Water Buckets with multyplying Wheels etc invented by Fulton the late famous American Engineer [had been] subjected to repeated accidents of a serious nature, leading to great expense in repairs, causing impedi-

ment in the Traffic, want of confidence in the Traders, and consequent loss of Revenue, so that the Canal and Works have got into a
state of dilapidation without remedy unless the course of management is very materially altered.

The course of management remained much the same and the
inclined plane continued to operate spasmodically until the
closure of the canal, following which the wells were filled with
concrete. And this was despite the secretary's comment that
'there is a prospect of an increasing and remunerative traffic if the
chief difficulty can be removed'.

Today you can climb up the slope of the incline to the engine-
house and the incline-keeper's cottage at the top. You may find
traces of the coping of the wells; you will certainly find a superb
view towards the coast. If you are approaching the incline from
the top, make for Thurlibeer Farm on the south side of the A3072
midway between Stratton and Red Post. Ask at the farm for
permission to see the Hobbacott Down inclined plane.

From Thurlibeer Farm the canal runs eastward and parallel to
the road as far as the cross-roads at Red Post. A few hundred yards
south of the cross-roads the Druxton Branch leads away to keep
the Tamar company for several miles. The main line then swings
north; the main road bridge over it has been flattened, but there is
a good bridge surviving at Anderton. There is another bridge at
Burmsdon, $\frac{3}{4}$ mile further north, and a sturdy single-arch aqueduct over the Tamar. The canal turns east to the foot of the 500ft
Venn incline which takes it up 58ft to the summit level. At the
top are the filter beds of the waterworks. Water is still fed from
Tamar Lake along the feeder to these beds, whence it is piped
beneath the incline and underground to Stratton. Soon the feeder
leaves the main line, winding its way north through Puckland
for 4 miles to Tamar Lake, with the remains of a wharf at
Virworthy.

The main line follows a sinuous course to the east, crawling
along the contours. All the minor roads on the north side of the
A3072 between Red Post and Holsworthy cross the canal, and
here and there you will see traces of it. On the north side of
Holsworthy, which still describes itself as a port town, were two
wharves. Stanbury Wharf was beside the A388 Bideford road,
about a mile from the town. There are still a warehouse and a
wharfinger's cottage. Vivian & Sons, the last firm to trade on the

canal, had their depot here. Blagdonmoor Wharf is reached from a minor road forking right off the A388, ½ mile from the centre of Holsworthy. The canal houses have been incorporated into the farm and the warehouses and stables are now farm outbuildings. The wharf itself is grassed over. From the eastern end of the wharf the canal line continues, to end in a cutting which was intended to lead to a tunnel on the way to Thornbury, the original proposed terminus of the canal. Some digging was begun at Vagglefield Farm, by the far end of the projected tunnel.

For the Druxton Branch of the canal you follow the B3254 south from Red Post. The branch keeps close to the 250ft contour line on the west side of the Tamar, descending by between 50ft and 60ft at each of 3 inclined planes. The first of these is Merrifield. The road crosses the track of the old Holsworthy-Bude Railway 3 miles south of Red Post. A lane to the east leads to the site of Whitstone & Bridgerule Station from which you can make out the incline a few hundred yards to the east. The entrance to the wheel-pit, which forms an impressive cavern below ground, is visible at the top. The energetic may follow the line of the towpath southward, with occasional diversions: there are mileposts to be found and indications of bridges; or return to the B3254 and continue south to the North Tamerton road. About 400yd past the church is the site of Tamerton Wharf. A low aqueduct used to take the canal over the road; you should be able to find the abutments. The bungalows on either side of the road were converted from wharf buildings: the one on the north stored coal and that on the south stored sand.

To reach the Tamerton incline you can try to follow the canal line south, past a lay-by, but you will have to divert around ploughed fields; or you can take the road opposite the church for ½ mile and fork left on to a track just past Tamerton town. Follow the line of the hedges and you will come to the foot of the incline. Recently, part of the slope has been ploughed, but the top is hidden among trees and shrubbery. Penetrating this you will find the entrance to the wheel-pit, although the pit itself has collapsed. The sill and two channels with masonry sides leading to the head of the incline can be found in the undergrowth. This is a beautiful but lonely place; look on the map to see how little habitation there is hereabout. Legend says that one of the early incline-keepers used to be summoned from his part-time farm work by his wife ringing a large bell when a line of boats came into view. So efficient was this keeper—Thomas Smale—that he was promoted to Werrington incline, less isolated, with a better house and more money—but not enough, it seems, as he died in the workhouse in 1849. Bushes from the incline-keeper's cottage garden still grow near the top of the Tamerton slope.

The canal continues south through Eastcott Wood and Bradridge Copse. The road crosses it at Boytonbridge, but no trace of the bridge itself remains. Here you can detect the outline of a basin and wharf, but there are no buildings. Take the road south from Boyton and fork left for Bridgetown. Turn left for Tamartown and look out for a 'low bridge' warning sign. The low bridge is the Werrington incline, now incorporated in a farm. Ask permission to see the water-wheel pit. There is a wharfinger's house here also. You may continue along this road to the site of an aqueduct at Tamartown, demolished early this century. If time permits, try to find the little accommodation bridge known as Hunch Bridge and note the narrowness of the canal.

Between Bridgetown and Crossgate the canal crosses Tala Water by an aqueduct built to replace the original one which was destroyed by floods in 1835. The line then edges nearer to the road which crossed it by a bridge, now disappeared, near the north side of a copse. A few hundred yards brings you to the site of Druxton Wharf—Druxton is a minute village ½ mile away and the place to look for on the map is Crossgate. The outline of the basin is clear and there are several canal-associated buildings around it including a warehouse, wharfinger's cottage and stables. As on the main line, the branch never reached the terminus intended for it; Green had planned to take the canal 3 miles nearer to Launceston, but the company could not afford this.

Everyone who comes across the Bude Canal wants to know more about it. Here I can give only a brief guide and commend the two books referred to at the beginning of this section: *The Bude Canal* by Helen Harris and Monica Ellis, a thorough study of its history with a mass of supporting information, an itinerary and a discussion on inclined planes, and *Along the Bude Canal* by Joan Rendell, an informal survey with interesting illustrations and personal stories of the canal workers.

OS sheet 190

The Torrington Canal

The Torrington Canal disappeared from the Ordnance Survey map years ago, but there is still plenty of evidence of its existence to be discovered. It was a private undertaking, the only completed element of an ambitious scheme for a network of Devonshire tub-boat canals, thought up by a Torrington landowner, Denys Rolle. Inspired by the Bude Canal proposals, Rolle's idea was to supply farms with sea-sand (for manure), lime and coal by several narrow canals with the gradients being overcome by inclined planes. It was Denys's son John, Baron Rolle, who revived part of the idea in 1823, twenty-six years after his father's death. Limestone, to be burnt in his kilns and then sold to local farmers, was to be the principal cargo, while farm produce would be taken down to Bideford in return. With James Green as engineer, the Torrington (or Rolle) Canal was opened in 1827 from Torrington to the River Torridge near Bideford, a distance of 6 miles. The works included a tide-lock, an inclined plane and a splendid aqueduct. The canal lasted until 1871 when Lord Rolle's son Mark forsook it to the South Western Railway, which wanted to use part of its bed for the construction of a branch line to Torrington.

You can make out the line of the canal from Castle Hill, Torrington, high above the Torridge. The track of an old road curls round the foot of the hill; this was made on the bed of the canal. The terminal basin was by Town Mill, the lordly-looking castellated building to your left. This was built by Baron Rolle. Note the extra arch for the canal in the bridge that takes the A386 over the Torridge in front of the mill. To the right, the old road ends by a toll house by the next bridge at Taddiport. The Torridge Inn at the bottom of Mill Street used to be the Canal Tavern. Westward, there is a factory on the line of the canal, but at the railway station you will see another canal arch beneath the road bridge.

The canal followed the east bank of the river through the grounds of Beam House. To the west of the house it crossed the river by a five-arched stone aqueduct, impressively substantial. A print after Thomas Allom shows navigation in progress at this point. A besmocked yokel leads a white horse drawing a train of two boats, the first with a pointed bow, the second a squarish tub. The first boat is empty apart from a gesticulating boatman; in the second there is a little indistinguishable cargo. A similar train follows closely behind. The artist has abbreviated the height of the aqueduct, possibly to diminish the contrast between its massive structure and the apparently toy-town operation it was built to support. Today, the canal and aqueduct form part of the drive to Beam House. An almost illegible inscription records Baron Rolle's laying of the foundation stone, an event marked by the firing of a cannon which burst and injured John Hopgood, compensated by Lord Rolle with a year's salary!

From the aqueduct the canal course is squeezed in between the river and the A386, much of it destroyed beneath the railway. The Weare Gifford inclined plane lowered the canal 6oft; it was powered by a water-wheel and had two tracks. It is probable that the tub-boats had wheels, like those on the Bude Canal. Don't look for the incline at Weare Gifford but continue north on the A386 until you reach a lane heading eastward signposted to Ridd's Cottage. The incline crossed this lane and continued into the field on the south side. The upper part of the incline was cut across by the railway embankment, by which you may find traces of the water-wheel pit. The foot of the incline is marked by a small stone shed.

The canal remained close to the river until joining it at Pillmouth; follow the line of the railway from Landcross to find the site of the tide-lock. Here there was a shipyard, building schooners as well as smaller vessels. The premises were owned by the Rolle Canal Company and its first vessel was named—as if one needed telling—*Lord Rolle*. A pity it was a schooner and not a tub-boat; how splendid to have had the *Lord Rolle* cross the Rolle Aqueduct on the Rolle (or Torrington) Canal!

OS sheet 180

Bibliography

BOOKS

Booker, Frank, *Industrial Archaeology in the Tamar Valley* (David & Charles, 1969)

Clew, K. R., *The Dorset & Somerset Canal* (David & Charles, 1971)

Ewans, M. E., *The Haytor Granite Tramway and Stover Canal* (David & Charles, 1966)

Hadfield, C., *Canals of South West England* (David & Charles, 1967)

Harris, Helen, *The Grand Western Canal* (David & Charles, 1973)
— — and Ellis, Monica, *The Bude Canal* (David & Charles, 1972)
Messenger, M. J., *Caradon and Looe* (Twelveheads Press, 1978)
Rendell, Joan, *Along the Bude Canal* (Bossiney Books, 1979)

ARTICLES AND BOOKLETS

'Cann Quarry Canal and Railway', Edwin Welch, *Transactions*, Devon-shire Association, Vol 100
Let's Explore Old Waterways in Devon, Arthur S. Clamp (Westway, nd)
Morwellham in the Tamar Valley, Frank Booker (DART pub no 24, 1976)
The Tavistock Canal, Carolyn Hedges (DART pub no 16, 1975)

SOCIETIES

Tiverton Canal Preservation Society

3

THE WELSH BORDER AND SOUTH WALES

The Herefordshire & Gloucestershire Canal

At first sight, the Border counties seem about the least likely area of Britain for canal transportation. The contours are irregular and apparently random; there are no signs of industry and no obvious sources of water supply. In the eighteenth century Herefordshire was regarded as the most idyllic of counties, breeding sheep and contentment. Beautiful though the countryside was, and is, however, the economic pressures were as real in Herefordshire as elsewhere, although its reputation as a haven of peace and plenty, fostered particularly by the eighteenth-century poets John Philips and John Dyer, tended to obscure this.

Like the other cities of the Three Choirs Festival, Gloucester and Worcester, Hereford has suffered from the planners, developers and despoilers of the post-war years. Of course, all has not been lost: the cathedral, though much restored, is mostly splendid and there are some pleasant old narrow streets nearby. The city is still worth a visit; but be warned—it is not easy to find anywhere to eat, especially if you are teetotal, so come prepared. On the north side of the city is the railway station, and a few yards from the station buildings is the site of the terminal basin of the Herefordshire & Gloucestershire Canal.

The object of the local promoters of the canal was to transport coal from pits near Newent which had been worked to little profit for many years. Hereford in particular was to benefit from cheaper coal. The idea of giving Hereford a better water connection than the Wye provided was mooted by Robert Whitworth in 1777, but it was not until 1790 that action began and the line was surveyed by a former assistant of Whitworth, Josiah Clowes. Three years later, with the act obtained and money raised, Hugh

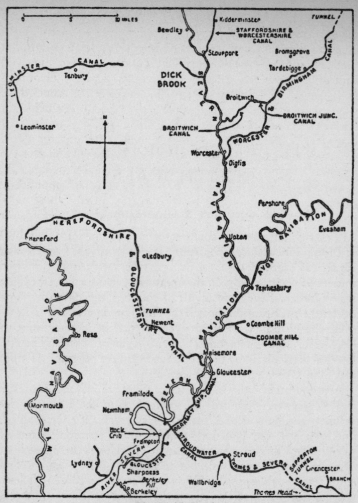

The Welsh Border

Henshall was called in to re-examine the line; he proposed moving it nearer to Newent, across particularly difficult country, to avoid constructing a 3 mile branch. This plan was adopted—to no one's advantage as it transpired.

The story of the H & G has been recently researched and told by David Bick. From the economic angle it is a miserable tale. By 1798 the canal was open from Gloucester to Ledbury—'a sixteen mile ribbon of water serving a few villages and a couple of small market towns practically devoid of industry in any form', as its historian puts it. There were 13 deep locks up to the summit at Ledbury and the narrow Oxenhall Tunnel, 2,192yd long and enormously expensive and troublesome to cut—'Henshall's Folly' might be a fitting name for it. South of the tunnel there was a short branch intended to serve the Newent coalfield, but both branch and coalfield fell into disuse a few years later. A manager, William Maysey, was appointed at Ledbury for £30 a year and under his surveillance a little trade trickled on into the nineteenth century, turning over a few hundred pounds annually.

On Maysey's retirement in 1827, the committee appointed as his successor a young local man, Stephen Ballard, whose energetic and ambitious drive has left its mark on the Herefordshire countryside. He quickly became convinced that it was both possible and desirable to complete the route to Hereford, carrying the committee along with him on the wings of his enthusiasm. With hindsight, it now seems extraordinary that at the beginning of the railway age anyone with any sense would put up money for such an undertaking, estimated to cost £76,000, but in 1837 work began. From Ledbury the line edged its way in the general direction of Hereford. The Ashperton Tunnel, with its spectacular deep cutting, was completed and so was the vital feeder from the River Frome, essential for the canal's water supply. In January 1843 the wharf at Canon Frome was in use, the date marking, so the *Hereford Journal* said, 'the desertion of the River Wye as a navigation for the conveyance of foreign produce'. A year later, at a celebration dinner at the City Arms, Hereford, in honour of Ballard, marking the opening of the canal to Withington, 4 miles outside the city, at least seventeen gentlemen spoke, their observations going to show, according to the *Journal*'s report:

that the line of the Canal had been completed in the most satisfactory manner, the work being done in a superior style, and there having been no offensive conduct to others on the part of the navigators, and fewer on their part than usual among labourers of that description ... that a plan would shortly be submitted for completing the Canal to Hereford; that many shares had been sold at a premium, and that although there had been considerable apathy on the part of the inhabitants of Hereford, yet that it was now fast wearing away.

This last observation was notably ill-founded; when the canal did reach Hereford in the following year there were no celebrations, no one appeared to watch the basin being filled and Ballard, in some distress, departed to a new appointment. As soon as the canal was completed the West Midland Railway offered to buy it. The offer came to nothing, however, and when it became clear that Hereford would have to wait some years for the railway the canal company was forced to try to make its line pay.

This to some extent it succeeded in doing, through efficient management, rate cutting and the carriage of materials for railway companies. Eventually, under the astute chairmanship of William Price, who was also chairman of railway and other canal companies, the H & G leased itself to the Great Western Railway for £5,000 a year. Through the 1860s and 70s, a few thousand tons a year continued to be carried, including coal, stone, bricks, grain, cider and groceries. At last the GWR decided to replace the Ledbury-Gloucester section with a railway, using the canal to bring materials up from the Severn. The last cargo passed in 1883, although the company itself remained in being until nationalisation in 1948, continuing to pay dividends on its £5,000 income. The railway, built for the most part along the line of the canal, carried passengers until 1959 and freight until 1964; the rails have since been lifted and most of its structures demolished.

Although not so improbable as the Leominster Canal—to which it was at one time suggested that it should be connected— the Hereford & Gloucester was an unrealistic, if optimistic, undertaking. Much of the eighteenth-century construction was obliterated by the railway, but a good deal of Ballard's work remains. It is to explain the presence of these tunnels, bridges, aqueducts and embankments in unexpected places in rural Herefordshire that I have recounted some part of its history. Between Hereford and Ledbury many wharf buildings survive, notably at Withington Marsh, by the A465, Kymin, a mile south of Ocle Pychard, Crews Pitch Wharf, on the Hereford-Worcester road a mile south-west of Newtown, and by the A417 a mile west of Canon Frome. The canal buildings are red brick and the cottages, seen end-on, remind you of conventional signal-boxes in profile. On the wharfinger's house at Withington Marsh it may still be just possible to discern the words 'William Bird, Wharfinger' and a warehouse at Canon Frome carries the legend 'Salt'. At Ledbury an engineering works occupies the warehouse at what for thirty years was the canal's terminal basin; the wharf house, much enlarged, stands close by.

All the places mentioned are shown on the OS map and are easy to find. In Hereford itself there is very little to see. By the railway station imagination will have to work hard to reconstruct the wharves and buildings of the old terminal. At the north end of Widemarsh Street there is a bridge that used to cross the canal, widened since it was originally built. The other reminder in Hereford is the ¼ mile Aylestone Tunnel, immersed in the Holmer Trading Estate but with a portal visible near the Bridge Inn.

From Hereford you can either follow the course via the wharf buildings already mentioned or take the A4103 Worcester road. About 8 miles along there is a minor road to Monkhide, a scattered hamlet where the one road crosses the canal twice within a few hundred yards. The first crossing is by a splendid skew bridge, described rightly by David Bick as a 'little gem of civil engineering'. He suggests that Ballard may have designed it for his own pleasure and satisfaction; certainly it was built in a place where few would come to admire it. To the east of the second, more ordinary, bridge is a surprising sight: a wide stretch of the Hereford & Gloucester, fully watered and apparently fit for navigation. It is only a short stretch, however, and soon the water ends where the bed and banks have been filled in and planted with trees.

Return to the main road, continue to the Newtown crossroads and turn south-east. At Stretton Grandison a minor road leads westward to Yarkhill; ¼ mile along, a bridge crosses the canal course which can be clearly seen crossing the fields. There are more traces on the other side of the main road, towards Canon Frome by the gates of the school. From here you can follow the canal southward to Ashperton Tunnel, or you can return to the main road and take the next turning east, which soon swings to run alongside the canal. The tunnel, 400yd long, is in a deep cutting; it was difficult to excavate and is still impressive as well as precipitous. Here in 1842 Ballard planted a yew tree, which can still be found. The canal bed holds water hereabouts and is crossed by two bridges. There was also a tunnel house near the south-east portal.

Follow the road to the A4154, and turn south towards Ledbury. There is a wharf house at Staplow. Behind Prior's Court on a minor road east there is a length of embankment across the Leadon Valley, with an aqueduct over the river and another across a farm track. The embankment is much overgrown, but among the trees and bushes you may find the remains of a stop-gate. From Prior's Court it is now due south for Ledbury. The canal entered the town parallel to the A417; there used to be six locks and a wharf at Bye Street. This was a favourite haunt of John Masefield when a boy, and in a poem he recalls the building of the railway in Ledbury along the line of the canal.

From Ledbury to Gloucester most of the old canal of the 1790s has been obscured by the railway, although the persistent searcher walking the railway track—most of which can be followed quite easily—will frequently detect variations between the relatively straight line of the railway and the alternating curves of the canal. Between the wharf by the Ledbury-Ross road and Dymock there is little of interest to note. Just south of Dymock, however, the railway swung away westward where the gradients were easier, leaving untouched Oxenhall Tunnel and the length of canal to its south.

The north portal of the long and narrow tunnel, with such a small bore that it 'looked more like a sewer than anything else', according to Henry Williams who navigated it in 1875, is in the grounds of Boyce Court where John Moggridge, a partner in the mines which the canal was intended to exploit, lived when the tunnel was dug. The canal is clearly defined through the grounds of the Court and the drive crosses it by a brick bridge. The stonework of the portal has gone, however, and rough brick-work is exposed. The M50 crosses the tunnel near this portal, about 300yd west of the bridge taking the B4215 across the motorway; tunnel-spoil heaps can be seen on the south side. The south portal is behind Holder's Farm; access can best be found from the B4221, a mile west of Newent. Make for Oxenhall; there's not much there apart from the church. Near here were the mines which were the reason for the canal's existence, and also some of the most interesting relics of its past.

The canal can be found where the road crosses it about 200yd east of Oxenhall Church. The branch to the Newent coalfield locked into the main line on the north side of the bridge, although the site of the lock cannot now be discerned. The branch itself swung south of the church (you can trace its line around the foot of an embankment), continuing for about 2 miles keeping close to the Oxenhall-Gorsley road and the Ell Brook. A mile northward along the main line is the portal of the tunnel. Walking along the canal bed is difficult and it is better to take the road running parallel, from the church to Hilter's Farm, and approach the canal from the bridge 400yd east of the farm. First, though, note the furnace pond for the old Newent Ironworks, alongside the canal at Oxenhall.

The stone-faced portal, still in reasonable condition, is in a comparatively shallow cutting. Henry Williams claimed that it took him and his friends only 35 minutes to leg through; he also said the tunnel was by no means straight. There was a horse-path across the top, of which remains can be seen at the north portal, while near the south end there is an excavation in the cutting which may have been a shelter or stable.

Back at Oxenhall you can follow the towpath south past the privately owned lock house and House Lock, the chamber of which is virtually complete. Then there is the site of another lock, with no masonry traces, and an aqueduct across the Ell Brook, pierced now so that any water collecting in the canal channel falls neatly into the brook beneath. The railway also crossed the brook close by and, within a few yards, again obliterated the canal. The B4215 crosses the canal at Newent and the basin was just behind the fire station. The remaining locks, apart from the one into the Severn at Over, have all disappeared. It is worth remembering the double locks 3 miles south-east of Newent, if only for Henry Williams's experience there. He described the structure as 'an immense thing with about 30 feet fall and a pair of gates in the middle'. He and his companions had no idea how to operate it. They were coming from Gloucester and were confronted with it early in the morning when it was pouring with rain:

We took the boat in, shut the rear gates and let down the sluices, then opened the middle gates and let in the water at the top sluices, but by some extraordinary means the water, as soon as it came in, rushed out again through some invisible exit and as there was a ledge across the middle of the lock we could not get sufficient in to float over.

It took them half an hour to manhandle the boat through.

Apart from a few curves of canal bed there is little to see on this last stretch and the final traces at Gloucester, apart from the site of Over Lock, have vanished beneath new roads and buildings. The canal left the Severn just south of the entry of the River Leadon; you can see the lock house but little more. Do not stop to trace that part of the canal that used to run across Alney Island to a point near Gloucester Quay and was abandoned in early days. Until a few years ago some of it was visible, but it is now obliterated—and the road traffic is particularly ferocious hereabouts.

For many people, the Hereford & Gloucester is the archetype of the abandoned canal. It has all the features that a canal needs, set in beautiful and comparatively unfrequented countryside. Its history is interesting, and nobody is going to reopen it. The formation of a trust or society to preserve discreetly such artefacts as the tunnels and aqueducts and the canal bed at Oxenhall and Monkhide would be welcome; unprotected as the H & G has been, it is fortunate that so much of it survives.

OS sheets 149, 150, 162

The Leominster Canal

On the A49, 12 miles north of Hereford, is Leominster, a good starting-place for exploration of the impressively named Kington, Leominster & Stourport Canal. This was intended to provide a route for agricultural produce to reach the Severn and thence the industrial Midlands and to open up Herefordshire to the industrial products of the Birmingham area in return; there was also the prospect of moving coal from mines in the hilly country near Newnham and Mamble into the market town of Leominster. The project, however, was an extreme example of so-called 'canal mania', and the proposed line makes the Hereford & Gloucester seem rational by comparison. Thomas Dadford, Jr, the engineer who surveyed the route, planned 4 tunnels—the longest over 2 miles in length—3 major aqueducts and a large number of locks of which 16—about a quarter of the intended number—were built. The undertaking was locally sponsored and was estimated (or underestimated) to cost £150,000. In the event, 18½ miles from Leominster to Southnet Wharf were opened, costing £93,000. The shareholders' optimism went unrewarded; no dividend was ever paid.

Between Kington and Leominster very little work was done; there may have been some preparatory digging north of Kingland near the proposed aqueduct over the Lugg, but nothing more. On the Ludlow road heading north from Leominster is the Wharf House, about 400yd past the level-crossing. The site of the

wharf is beside the house; an inconvenient distance from Leominster, it seems, but the canal had to keep on the north side of
the town to avoid a second crossing of the Lugg. From the wharf,
the canal heads northward for about 6 miles; the railway line, to
the west of the A49, follows generally the same direction.

The first substantial remains of the canal, apart from an isolated
lock house ¾ mile from the wharf, are found by taking a minor
road heading north-west off the A49, 4 miles out of Leominster—
the second turning left after the entrance to the National Trust
property, Berrington Hall. In 1¼ miles this road crosses the railway and a few yards further on it takes you over the top of Putnal
Field Tunnel. Construction of the tunnel had been difficult and
expensive, although it is only 330yd long. Both portals with their
shallow approach cuttings, sometimes holding water, can be
reached through the fields on either side of the road. The stonework, untended for well over a century, is in surprisingly good
condition and the narrow high entrances are sound, although the
tunnel has collapsed in the middle.

From the tunnel the canal continues north-eastward very close
to the railway, which eventually crosses it by the site of Woofferton Wharf and Locks just over a mile further on. To reach this
point by road, continue along the A49 through Brimfield to the
junction by the Salway Arms. Turn on to the B4362 and find the
canal south of the road opposite the old Woofferton Station. To
the west of where the railway crosses the canal are the remains of
Woofferton Locks; the north wall of the top lock is substantially
intact and a piece of timber on the wall has rooted and puts forth
leaves. The house nearby was the lock house.

To follow the canal take the A456 Kidderminster road. Much
of the next few miles has been obliterated by the Tenbury Railway, which bought it up in 1860. A major canal relic is the Teme
Aqueduct, the centre arch of which was blown up, with some
difficulty and by our side, in World War II. This is about a mile
east of Woofferton; you can pick up the track of the old railway
on the north side of the A456 and follow the diverging canal
embankment to the riverside to inspect the aqueduct remains.
The canal keeps very close to the A456 until Newnham but, apart
from Easton Court Bridge at Little Hereford and a few traces of
the canal line itself, there is nothing to see.

At Newnham, just before the A456/A443 junction, it is best to
turn left along a minor road, leave your car and find the bridge

over the Tenbury Railway track. You may be able to pick up the
line of the canal just to the north of the bridge and follow it along
a farm track, past the site of the 94yd Newnham Tunnel (of
which the portals were destroyed a few years ago) and through a
field where a canal cottage stands isolated. If you don't want to
face the farm and caravan site, follow the railway track, from
which you will soon be able to see the canal cottage. A few
minutes' walk brings you to a cutting where you can detect the
course of the canal on either side. Leave the track and follow the
old towpath eastward; within a few minutes you will find yourself on top of another of the canal's major structures, the single-
arch brick aqueduct over the River Rea. From the top you gain
little idea of the aqueduct's massiveness; the narrow trough that
held the water is disconcertingly insignificant. So descend to the
river bank to admire the crumbling splendour; it is easy to believe
the local story that it contains a million bricks. Several thousand
of them are now missing and it is worth examining some that are
strewn around; they are exceptionally heavy. Nothing is being
done to preserve the Rea Aqueduct, and in any event it is probably too late for anything but the most expensive and visually
obtrusive measures.

From the top of the aqueduct there is a fascinating and mostly
beautiful walk to the Wharf House at Marlbrook. You pass the
easily detectable sites of six locks and a lock cottage. Some years
ago there was an attempt to create fisheries here, which explains
why the canal bed is comparatively well preserved. The wharf
house itself is a handsome building, much grander than its
counterpart at Leominster. The openings on either side of the
central bay were docks into which boats could be drawn for
repair. Here coal was brought down from Sir Walter Blount's
collieries by the Mamble tramroad; on the day the navigation
was opened from here to Leominster, in December 1796, fourteen boat-loads of coal were carried along its length to be sold in
Leominster at 15s a ton. The canal continued a short distance
further east to Southnet Wharf and a lane carries on to the A456.
The 18 miles 5 furlongs between Southnet Wharf and Leominster
Wharf is the total length of continuous waterway that was made.

On the opposite side of the main road is the site of the northern
portal of Southnet Tunnel. This, one of the most intriguing of all
canal tunnels, was 1,250yd long. It was completed in 1795 but
collapsed in the same year, never to be repaired. Rumour says

that two men and a boat lie entombed therein. The south portal, of similar exaggerated section to Putnal Field, could be found by taking the A443 Worcester road and turning north by the Nag's Head. Where the minor road turns sharply east a farm road branches off; a short stretch of canal cutting, with the tunnel entrance, is in a field nearby. About 2 miles further east a short stretch of cutting was begun near Dumbleton, but apart from that no traces of construction have been discovered between Southnet and the Severn: no long Pensax Tunnel and no splendid flight of locks down to the river. In June 1797 one spadeful of earth was dug opposite Stourport to mark the intended junction of canal and Severn, but by this time it was becoming obvious that the project would not be completed. There was not enough trade and no more money. A proposal to complete the line to Stourport by tramroad came to nothing—or to very little, it being possible that some construction was begun. Other proposals for extension or continuation likewise failed. The canal company limped on through the first half of the nineteenth century, with very little trade and very little water to carry it, eventually managing to negotiate a sale to the Shrewsbury & Hereford Railway for £12,000. In 1859 the canal was closed.

OS sheets 138, 149

Border Rivers: the Wye and the Lugg

Both the Wye and its tributary the Lugg are old navigations, although evidence of the works has been swept away. There is a reference to navigation on the Wye in 1296, but the first major attempt at improvement was that of Sir William Sandys, appointed in 1662 to make the rivers navigable for goods and passengers. He built, it seems, a few flash-locks on the Wye, but it is unlikely that he achieved anything on the Lugg at all. There were further attempts to improve both rivers in the eighteenth century and it was possible in favourable conditions for barges to reach Hay, bow-hauled by gangs of men as on the Upper Severn. On the Lugg at least three half-locks were built early in the eighteenth century, at Lugg Bridge, Longworth and Mordiford, and it was possible to reach Leominster by barge. These locks still existed in 1906 and traces of their remains were recorded a few years ago. The Lugg probably ceased to be used after about 1860.

An important improvement to the Wye Navigation was the opening of a towpath between Lydbrook and Hereford in 1811. Coal from the Forest of Dean upward and timber downward were the main cargoes. The river trade to Hereford stopped when the city was connected to the railway and the towpath company was wound up in 1855. Silting brought the head of navigation lower down the river which, apart from an occasional adventurous voyager, is now used only for rowing and canoeing. It is possible to conjecture the sites of at least some of the flash-locks, but no visual evidence is left.

OS sheets 149, 162

The South Wales Canals

With the exception of the Brecon & Abergavenny, none of the South Wales canals is now a navigable waterway. Each of the heavily locked valley canals—the Monmouthshire, Glamorganshire, Neath and Swansea—contributed enormously to the pros-

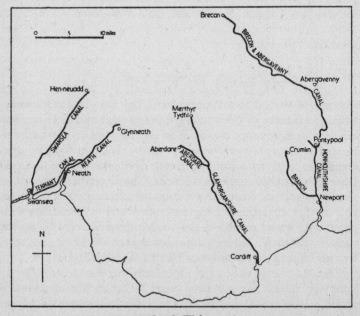

South Wales

perity of the town it principally served and each gave way to the railway and main road squeezed beside it in the little room there was. Fortunately, they have all left good evidence of their existence and they are for the most part easily accessible.

The Monmouthshire Canal

Opened in 1799, the Monmouthshire Canal was constructed with two arms stretching up from Newport into the valleys of the Usk and the Ebbw. The eastern arm, the main line, makes an end-on junction with the Brecon & Abergavenny at Pontymoile Basin by Pontypool. In its 11 miles there were 42 locks and in the 1840s, when Newport exported more coal than Cardiff, it was carrying over 800,000 tons a year, some of it off the Brecon & Abergavenny, but much fed to it by a network of tramroads. While trade was still profitable the canal company determined to become a railway company also and hence forestall competition; this it succeeded in doing and in 1852 the Newport–Pontypool line was opened. The Monmouthshire Railway & Canal Company then bought the Brecon & Abergavenny, bringing more traffic on to its railway line. In 1880 the Great Western Railway bought the Monmouthshire company. Canal receipts continued to decline, but a little trade was carried on until 1938. Part of the main line was abandoned in 1954, when bridges in the area of Cwmbran New Town were levelled and the locks converted to weirs, and the remainder was closed in 1962.

From Pontymoile Basin to Newport the canal still carries water, which is sold for industrial use. The towpath is also walkable throughout. Before walking southward, however, you may wish to explore a short stretch of the canal from the basin to Pontnewynydd, closed by 1853. Pontnewynydd was the original terminus of the canal, just over a mile north-west of the centre of Pontypool up a flight of 11 locks. The maintenance yard at Pontymoile Basin lies on this section of the canal. Seek for traces of it in Pontypool, including part of a lock on a traffic roundabout on the east side of the town. Much of the section, which was usually short of water, was used by the subsequent railway; this gives you an indication of the line of the canal.

The Monmouthshire's junction with the Brecon & Abergavenny at Pontymoile was made when the latter canal was opened in 1812. This is a fascinating place, with the Brecon & Abergavenny aqueduct over the Afon Lwyd to the north, a toll house and gauging stop, old railway bridges and an accommodation bridge. The Monmouthshire Canal is navigable here for almost 1½ miles to the culverted Crown Bridge at Sebastopol. South of the bridge there is a pleasant ¾ mile, with the 87yd Cwmbran Tunnel, navigable for very light craft; then a road has been slammed down across a lock and navigation must cease. This is Five Locks Road, the lock being the top of a flight of five, now ornamental cascades in a public park. If you continue towards Newport you pass several more locks and many other canal features, including mileposts. It is possible to canoe on some stretches and Gwastad Lock, the lowest on the main line, has been re-gated. The local authorities have put this part of the canal back into good order.

The junction with the western arm, the Crumlin Branch, comes just after the M4 has crossed the canal—with, be it noted, ample navigational headroom. The towpath on the main line carries on for another mile, past Bridge 1 to the short tunnel under Barrack Hill. On the far side of the tunnel the water is taken off by culvert to the Usk. Most of the remains of the canal in Newport have been obliterated by road works in the past ten years. The canal line is under Mill Street Bridge and Kingsway, along Llanarth Street to Canal Parade. There was a further extension to Potter Street, with a lock, opened in 1818 and closed in 1879, but I do not think there are any traces of this or of the short private branch below it.

Return to Malpas Junction by the M4 to follow the Crumlin Branch. The towpath still extends for 9 of the original 11 miles of its length. To start with, the branch runs parallel to the motorway beneath the hill called Allt-yr-yn, the declivity of the ash trees. This is Newport's 'Little Switzerland', although it has its own distinctive attraction and does not need this sobriquet. Allt-yr-yn Lock with its stone bridge and cottages has all the essence of the canal scene—except for boats. There are four more locks in this flight. The canal then swings to dive beneath the motorway in a culvert. Now you are at the foot of the Rogerstone or Cefn flight of fourteen locks, the best-known site on the Monmouth-shire and one of the greatest achievements of canal engineering in South Wales, lifting the branch 168ft. The Gwent and Newport Councils have laid out a trail around the locks; there is an interpretation centre and picnic area and the locks themselves have been cleaned out and tidied up. Some of the side ponds have also

been cleared. Access by car is from the A467 Risca road, ½ mile
from Exit 27 on the M4. A turning signposted Henllys takes you
into Cefn Walk, which leads you to the site. The locks themselves
are arranged mostly in pairs, with a very short pound separating
each pair. There is a complicated system of bypass weirs and
culverts to prevent flooding. Note the extra-wide 'sea-lock' and
try to work out for yourself why it was built like that. Commercial vessels last used the locks in 1930 and the Crumlin Branch
was finally abandoned in 1962.

From the top of the flight you can follow the towpath to Risca
or take the A467 which runs between the canal and the Ebbw.
The canal is culverted in places, but generally it is in fair condition. A sad recent loss was Gile Aqueduct at Pontymister, demolished in 1974 for road widening; this originally took the canal
over a road to Risca House. As you go on there are quarries in the
hillside to the north-east. Continue through Risca and Cross
Keys, where the Sirhowy Valley branches off to the west, to
Pontywaun. Here the A467 crosses to the east side of the canal. A
few hundred yards further, on the approach to Cwmcarn, the
canal ends near the point where the Nant Carn stream feeds water
into it. For the next 2 miles the main road has been built on the
canal. You may find part of a lock wall at Abercarn and a short
stretch serving as a watercourse a little further north. Another
road covers the canal between Newbridge and Crumlin, its
gradient denoting the whereabouts of the Newbridge locks. The
Navigation Inn at Crumlin indicates the canal's terminus; originally the branch ended further north but was cut short when the
Crumlin Viaduct was built. As the Navigation Inn reminds you
of the canal, so the Viaduct Inn commemorates that remarkable
structure that dominated the valley for a hundred years—the
railway engineer's answer to Pontcysyllte.

So much of the Monmouthshire Canal has survived because
the local authorities have taken an interest in it and given it a
measure of priority in their planning. Details of the treatment
may not please everyone—but how much more pleasant and
useful it now is than a rat-infested linear rubbish dump, the fate
of many canals in fringe urban areas before they are finally
eradicated.

The Glamorganshire Canal

Arguably the greatest of the South Wales waterways, the Glamorganshire Canal has fared less well since abandonment than its neighbour, the Monmouthshire. It was opened in 1794, 24½ miles in length from Merthyr Tydfil to Cardiff Docks, with 49 deep locks taking it down the valley of the Taff. Since its closure in 1942 much of it has disappeared beneath new roads and it is sad that today so little can be found of the canal on which the prosperity of Cardiff and the Taff Vale was founded.

The Merthyr ironmasters, led by Richard Crawshay, promoted the Glamorganshire; they both owned the canal and traded on it, garnering the dividends and the receipts from tolls. They also quarrelled with each other—one result of this was the Penydarren tramroad on which Trevethick's first locomotive ran to Abercynon in 1804, built by the ironmasters of Dowlais who had failed to get the better of Crawshay and were consequently ejected from the canal committee. What united the ironmasters was their common enmity to the Marquess of Bute, who frustrated their efforts to improve the Cardiff terminal basins as he had plans of his own for Cardiff Docks.

The canal basin in Merthyr is near the Georgetown roundabout and the bus depot. The Merthyr-Abercynon section was abandoned in 1898, but recently some part of the basin has been excavated and the keels of two boats have been exposed. Plans to flood the top basin have proved impractical and the canal bed is to be paved with the keels left in position. Alongside the canal are three rows of early nineteenth-century cottages. That on the east is Chapel Row which has recently been restored and includes the birthplace of the composer Joseph Parry, who as a child worked in both the mines and the ironworks before his family emigrated to Pennsylvania in 1854. This cottage is now the office and exhibition centre of the Merthyr Heritage Trust. At the north end of the terrace and integral with it are the substantial ruins of Crawshay's Anglican chapel for Georgetown, latterly used as a canal warehouse.

To anyone interested in industrial archaeology, Merthyr has much to offer. Nearby there are two splendid viaducts on the old Merthyr-Brecon Railway, the Ynysfach ironworks and the Penydarren tramroad tunnels. Above Merthyr to the north-west is Cyfarthfa Castle, built by William Crawshay II. It is now a museum, with a few relics of the canal and tramroad among the large collection drawn from the industrial past. You can enjoy an ice-cream on the terrace from which the Crawshays used to survey their empire. Despite their fearsome reputation, the Crawshays were not particularly worse than most other business-men of their time—and in some ways they were more en-lightened. And at least one of their workmen followed their example as masters to good effect. This was John Hughes, born in Merthyr, who learnt his trade at the Cyfarthfa Works and emi-grated to found in 1869 the Russian iron town of Yuzovka (Hughesovka) which, with his skilled Welsh workmen, he ruled autocratically in conditions that sound reminiscent of Merthyr at its harshest.

In the early days of construction a short extension of the canal was made from Merthyr to Cyfarthfa; this was the first length to be abandoned in 1868. Cyfarthfa was also the terminus of another canal—the Cyfarthfa Canal for tub-boats, 2 miles long from the Canaid Brook, opened in about 1776 and disused by 1835. On your walk along the Glamorganshire to Abercanaid you may be able to discern traces of this cut on the right. At Abercanaid there used to be two docks, but they have been filled in. Further south you pass the fan house and Cornish beam engine-house of the Gethin mine. The canal continues on the west side of the Taff through Aberfan where one of the locks at 14ft 6in had the greatest fall of any on the British canals.

At Abercynon, 8½ miles from Merthyr, the Glamorganshire was joined at the top of the town by the Aberdare Canal. From Incline Top the waterway descended through several double locks. At the foot of the flight is Navigation House, built beside the terminus of the Penydarren tramroad—note the memorial plaque. Abercynon was not only an important junction but also a boat-building centre for the canal. It was here that the Taff was crossed by both the canal and the turnpike road and the substan-tial rendered arch that carries the A4059 over the river today is, in fact, the original stone aqueduct/viaduct with a steel girder wid-ening on its north elevation. From this point on, however, much of the Glamorganshire has been obliterated by improvements to the A470 Merthyr–Cardiff road.

In Pontypridd a length of canal is now kept as a nature reserve and is looked after by the Glamorgan Naturalists' Trust. You find it on the east side of the town behind the Bunch of Grapes. This section is known as Nightingale's Bush and includes derelict locks, an attractive bridge and some canalside cottages. A short branch led into the Brown Lenox Works, spanned by a cast-iron swing bridge which still survives; this firm and the Mid-Glamorgan County Council are responsible for reclaiming this pleasant length of canal.

South of Pontypridd the A470 again encroaches. Among the sites that have disappeared beyond recall is the great treble locks at Nantgarw. Each of the locks was about 14ft deep; they formed a staircase of three, with footbridges, and were lit by gaslight in the busiest days of the canal in the mid-nineteenth century. That no preservation order was obtained is an indication of the casual manner in which the industrial relics of the Welsh past were regarded a few years ago.

A section of canal, however, has been preserved further south. This can be reached by a minor road forking right at Tongwynlais, or from Velindre Road at Whitchurch off the A4054. This is also a nature reserve cared for by the trust; the towpath makes easy walking, the canal is stocked with fish and there are two more lock chambers. At the Whitchurch end is the old Melingriffith Works; the Harfords of Melingriffith were among the original promoters of the canal and shortage of water for the works had caused many quarrels on the canal committee. On Rennie's recommendation a water-wheel and pump were erected in about 1809 to return to the canal the water that had been led off through a feeder into the works; somehow this structure has survived and in 1980 was restored to good order.

From Whitchurch south there is not much left to see. The car park on the east side of Cardiff Castle takes in a section of canal and the pedestrian subway beneath Kingsway incorporates a canal bridge and a few yards of towpath. Look for the bases of gas lamps originally installed to light the canal. Under Queen Street there used to be a 115ft tunnel through which boats were hauled by chains affixed to the walls; presumably some of it is still there in the basements of department stores and shops. South of Queen Street there are reminiscences of the canal in East and West Canal Wharf, the Custom House and the New Sea Lock Inn; a series of car parks has been built on the canal line, leading to a grassed stretch and an old warehouse. Features of interest include bollards that were originally made as cannon barrels but were rejected because of flaws, and the barge-weighing machine—although you will not find this in Cardiff but outside the Waterways

Museum in Stoke Bruerne. You may find part of the sea-lock near the outfall of the Taff.

Until the late 1860s the Glamorganshire Canal was highly profitable and extremely busy, so busy in fact that there was considerable congestion especially at Nantgarw, Melingriffith and at the approaches to the Queen Street Tunnel. Traffic came not only down the canal from the ironworks and mines of the Merthyr area, and from the Aberdare Canal, but also upwards, iron ore and cinders being major items. Boats moving up the canal had to be loaded less heavily as there was a constant downward current caused by the working of the locks. There was congestion also at the canal dock in Cardiff as the hostility of Lord Bute prevented the canal company from improving their facilities as they wished.

For some thirty years the canal successfully withstood competition from the Taff Vale Railway. Authorised in 1836, this was promoted by ironmasters and mine-owners who had quarrelled with the reigning Crawshay and left the canal committee. It took over the Penydarren tramroad and shortly became the most prosperous railway company in Britain, yet such was the volume of trade engendered in the valley that both railway and canal were able to co-exist. In time, however, collieries and industrial works became connected to the railway rather than to the canal and the expansion of the Bute Docks, with their railway connections, began to draw trade away. In 1885 Lord Bute bought the canal, and with it the Aberdare Canal. By then it was in poor condition; some improvements were made, but little trade was attracted. A move to use much of the canal bed for a railway line came to nothing, but for many years there was little boat movement except on the lower reaches. The Merthyr–Abercynon section was bought by Cardiff Corporation in 1920 and water pipes were laid under it. Traffic elsewhere ended in 1942 when the canal burst its banks at Nantgarw.

The Aberdare Canal

Of the Aberdare Canal there is very little left. It was opened in 1812, $6\frac{3}{4}$ miles long from Aberdare to a junction with the Glamorganshire at Abercynon. During the 1820s it fell under the Crawshays' sphere of influence, but its greatest days came later in the century with the steam-coal trade. As with the Glamorganshire, it maintained its trade for many years despite railway competition in the Aberdare Valley. The year 1864 marked the beginning of a decline in its fortunes although trade continued until almost the end of the century. It was closed in 1900 and sold to the local authorities in 1923.

The canal was cut on the north side of the Afon Cynon and much of its bed has been used for widening of the Aberdare-Abercynon road. Recently, the basin at Aberdare has been restored; it can be found by the Ynys Sports Centre off the A4059. At Mountain Ash, cottages that used to be canalside now back on to the road and you should be able to trace the line of the canal as it approaches the junction at the top of Abercynon. The remains of the stop-lock may still be concealed in undergrowth.

The Neath Canal

Westward, the Neath Canal is the next of the South Wales valley canals to be explored. It was opened in 1795, 13 miles long with 19 locks, with coal and iron ore as the chief cargoes. The iron ore was intended for works at Neath Abbey. For a time sea-going ships used the port of Neath, but with the opening of the Tennant Canal most of the coal-carrying craft continued to Swansea, a more convenient and better developed port.

Unlike its neighbours to the east, the Neath Canal has escaped even partial obliteration by the main road with which it shares its valley. Consequently, its restoration—by the Neath & Tennant Canals Preservation Society—is not an impossibility, although the task is formidable. On your tour of these canals you should see plenty of evidence of the work that has been achieved since the society was founded in 1974 with the ambitious aim of the restoration of navigation throughout.

From its terminal basin at Glyn-neath to the junction with the Tennant Canal at Aberdulais the Neath Canal is so close to the A465 valley road that a detailed itinerary is unnecessary. For Glyn-neath Basin you need to find Oddfellows Street on the south-east side of the A465. The preservation society has cleared much of the towpath and repaired some of the bridges; work has also been carried out on many of the lock chambers, although to date funds to replace lock gates are not available. At Maesgwyn, 2 miles from Glyn-neath, you will find a lime-kiln beside the lock, and there are boat-houses for pleasure craft that belonged to Maesgwyn House nearby. At Resolven it is planned to create an industrial history park of which the canal will be a central feature.

Between Rheola and Resolven there are two cast-iron aqueducts made at the Neath Abbey Works in 1838, a canalside cottage and a number of bridges and locks. South of the canal bridge at Resolven near Farmer's Lock you can find the ruins of a chapel of rest for canal-borne funerals. Southward the canal is in water, which it feeds to local industries. The Ynysbwllog Aqueduct across the River Neath was destroyed in the floods of 1979; it was in poor repair before then, lacking one parapet and with the canal water piped across. One reason for the canal's endurance is that up to this point the river separated it from the Vale of Neath Railway; hence the canal continued to serve the pits on the north-west of the river even when the railway was in full operation. Towards the end of the nineteenth century the newer collieries linked themselves to the railway direct, and the older ones, not to be outdone, built bridges over canal and river. Little trade continued into the twentieth century and the navigation was abandoned in 1934.

Aberdulais Basin can be reached from a lane behind the Railway Inn on the road to Tonna off the A465. The basin has been cleaned out and the walls rebuilt; light craft are permitted to use it, although they are not allowed to navigate the canal. The Neath towpath can be walked for about 2 miles in either direction. A remarkable skew bridge takes the Neath towpath over the Tennant. You can also see a toll house, lock and lock-keeper's cottage. The Dulais Falls are nearby, close to the meeting of the Neath and Dulais rivers. The Tennant Canal crosses the River Neath just above this junction by a formidable 11-arch aqueduct, 340ft long.

In Neath itself, the river, now widening into its estuary, separates the two canals. South of the town access to the canal is difficult as it runs through railway territory. If you follow the A474 to Briton Ferry and turn right at traffic lights along Brynhyfryd Road to Zoar Chapel, you will find the Giant's Grave Bridges, built in 1930 by Neath Council, crossing the canal a few inches above water-level. Here the Giant's Grave extension to the Neath Canal begins; this was a private undertaking opened in about 1815, further extended a few years later by the Briton Ferry, or Jersey, Canal. The total extension is about ½ mile long and runs alongside a rolling-mill until it terminates close to the massive viaduct carrying the A48 across the estuary. Once the canal reached the riverside, but the last section has been filled in.

The Tennant Canal

The Tennant Canal, first known as the Neath & Swansea Junction, is still privately owned and used as a water-supply channel. George Tennant, a local landowner, developed it from the 3½ mile long Glan-y-wern Canal, opened in 1790 from the Glan-y-wern Colliery to the north of Crymlyn Bog to a point beside the River Neath nearly opposite Giant's Grave. Tennant leased this canal from the Earl of Jersey in 1817, enlarged it and made a connection with the river through a lock at Red Jacket. He also took it across to the Tawe at Swansea. This river-to-river navigation had its limitations and it soon became apparent that a further development was necessary. In 1821, therefore, Tennant, without obtaining a parliamentary act, began an extension to join the Neath Canal at Aberdulais. As it was a private undertaking, negotiations for land purchase proved difficult; nevertheless, Tennant persisted and his canal was opened throughout in May 1824.

> To his noble genius, great merit is due,
> The increase of traffic, he'll daily pursue;
> Employ to poor labourers, it is known full well,
> He gave them by making Neath Junction Canal

wrote Elizabeth Davies who composed verse and sold lollipops in Neath. When completed, the Tennant Canal was the most important private venture of its kind in Britain.

At the Swansea termination of the canal Tennant wanted to develop a wet dock but lacked the resources to do so. The growth of Port Tennant, as the area around the terminal was known, was thereby restricted and in the 1850s the larger Swansea Docks were opened higher up the estuary. Later, a wet dock was built at Port Tennant—the East Dock, opened in 1881, on the northern arm of the canal. More recently, the King's and Queen's Docks were constructed on Port Tennant, with a surviving length of canal alongside the King's Dock North Wharf. It is worth noting that the development of the port of Swansea had been foreseen by Tennant, whom we can remember as one of the greatest developers (but not exploiters) of the wealth of South Wales.

As it is privately owned, access to the Tennant Canal is restricted and you cannot stroll along the towpath freely as you can along the Neath Canal. From Aberdulais it swings to the west of Neath, passing Neath Abbey in a deep cutting. It runs close to the railway along the east side of Skewen; you can approach it from the B4290 which crosses it by Jersey Marine. Thence the canal cuts across the southern edge of Crymlyn Bog, terminating by industrial works and railway sidings on the south side of the housing estates of Port Tennant on the approach to Swansea.

The Swansea Canal

Cut along the Tawe Valley for 15 miles from a basin between Abercrave and Ystradgynlais to Swansea, the Swansea Canal was opened in 1798. Many of the Neath Canal promoters were involved and it was a successful undertaking from its earliest years. It incorporated the Duke of Beaufort's short Trewyddfa Canal to the south of Morriston and had a number of private branches and associated tramroads. In the peak years of the mid-nineteenth century the Swansea carried twice the tonnage annually of the Neath Canal, although its figures never approached those returned by the Monmouthshire or Glamorgan. Nevertheless, it remained a profitable concern for a longer period than any other South Wales waterway. When it was sold to the GWR in 1873 it fetched over twice its construction costs and, although the upper section ceased to trade a few years later, the lower reaches showed a profit until 1895. Some short-haul traffic continued on the lower 6 miles until 1931.

Much of the canal is still in use as a water channel and there is easy access from the A4067 Sennybridge-Swansea road. The terminal basin remains as a marshy bog behind the Rheolau Arms, a petrol station and bus garage to the north-west of the valley road on the south of Abercrave. The keel and lower skeleton of a canal boat still awaits loading alongside the hillside quay. The best access for a view of the basin is reached through a farm gate one field north of the Rheolau Arms. A walk from here to the upper basin, beside the top feeder of the canal, runs alongside the interesting remains of the Abercrave Ironworks. The Royal Commission on Ancient and Historical Monuments in Wales has recently excavated the pit for the water-wheel that drove the blast for the furnace, the remains of which lie immediately to the south-west of the pit. The wheel itself is gone, but its dimensions—35ft in diameter and 8ft wide—have been worked out from its striking outline worn into the south-west side of the pit. The wheel's existence was due to the Swansea Canal Company's late decision to replace their original engineer, Charles

Sheasby, Snr, with Charles Roberts and to require a resurvey of the canal. Sheasby had constructed the fine feeder-weir to the north of Abercrave (you can see this from the valley road and the recreation ground in the village) and the large feeder to the point where the Abercrave village road leaves the main valley road. Here an underground canal arm on the model of Clyn-du (see below) was to span the river on an aqueduct—the existing Yard Bridge—and enter Ty-mawr Level to the east. This did not happen, however; Roberts decided to terminate the canal further south, dispensing with two locks, with a short tramroad connection northward to Abercrave 'Yard' on the flat ground below the village. From here tramroads led to Ty-mawr Level over the proposed aqueduct to limestone quarries above Abercrave and to more collieries further north. The feeder ran steeply down from the Yard to the canal basin as built, with a substantial head of water available for the taking.

South of the basin, the canal, its bridges and aqueducts at Ystradgynlais and Ystalyfera have been destroyed. The next evidence is traces of the Godre'r-graig Locks staircase at Cwm-taw-isaf Farm at the foot of the new valley road slope. Then at Ynysmeudwy you will find the canal in water and you can follow the towpath to Pontardawe, noting lock chambers, bridges and a single-arch aqueduct. South of Pontardawe the canal is in water as far as Clydach where, at Coed-Gwilym Park, Lliw District Council now hires out canoes. There is a renaissance of interest in the Swansea Canal in this area; a job-creation scheme has enabled the towpath to be cleared and bridges and aqueducts to be repointed, and local amenity groups will be making varied use of the waterway.

To the north of Clydach by an overflow are the remains of a wheel-pit of the Graigola Basin Fireclay Mill, powered by the canal's surplus water. According to its act the canal had to return all its surplus water above Lock 7 to the River Tawe and various industrial undertakings were established to take advantage of this power supply. Evidence of more than forty-six of these undertakings has been found although at only two sites are there visible remains. The nearby dock on the east side of the canal has disappeared beneath a golf course.

In the centre of Clydach by the bridge you will find a pair of lock gates with cut-off balance beams; there is also an aqueduct over the River Clydach, found by following the 'Gentlemen' sign by the Public Hall. The convenience itself used to be splendidly equipped by Ducketts of Burnley; perhaps it still is. At the south end of the watered section of canal in Clydach is the small tinplate-works of John Player & Son Ltd, on the east side of the A4067. This originally had a water-wheel powered cupola furnace driven by surplus water coming off the bypass at Lock 5. In later years the wheel was replaced successively by two turbines. The wheel/turbine house was demolished in 1980 to provide a new access for small industries located in what used to be Clydach Foundry and now is part of the tinplate-works. The rest of the foundry buildings, including wooden cranes, a steam locomotive and a travelling gantry-crane of the 1880s, have survived.

Between Clydach and Swansea nothing now remains of the canal except for a roving bridge recently re-excavated as a feature in the Morriston conservation area. South of this, at the point where the road from Neath crosses the canal line shortly before joining the Swansea Valley road, is the presumed site of the first underground canal in Britain—the Clyn-du Navigation Level. Its portal is marked by a man-hole cover to the east of the Neath/Swansea Valley road junction on the west side of a disused railway cutting. This underground canal was constructed in 1747 and later connected with Morris's Canal, cut in about 1790 from Landore to copper works below Morriston. Morris's Canal was absorbed into the Trewyddfa Canal, $1\frac{3}{8}$ miles in length from Landore to Trewyddfa opened in about 1796, which in turn became a constituent of the Swansea Canal two years later. The Clyn-du Level was the first of three underground mining canals in South Wales which pre-dated the famous Worsley Levels of 1760; the other two were at Gwauncaegurwen, near the head of the Swansea Valley, and at Rhandir-mwyn, Carmarthenshire.

In Swansea the docks that the canal was built to serve have been reconstructed. Part of the filled-in canal bed can be found by the remains of the Brunel bridge that carried the South Wales Railway over the Tawe. There are also some traces of the Llansamlet or Smith Canal, a 3 mile waterway made in about 1784 by John Smith, a colliery owner, to serve his and other mines. The basin of this canal, which closed in about 1852, is west of Port Tennant near the site of the old Midland Railway bridge. In this vicinity there used to be several copper mines supplied with coal by canal.

In the Swansea Industrial and Maritime Museum a large permanent exhibit on the subject of the Swansea Canal has been prepared by the Royal Commission on Ancient and Historical Monuments in Wales; you will find this and the accompanying guidance map of great value if you intend examining the canal's remains. The commission has been much involved in the last few years in recording the structures and examining the documents of the Glamorgan canals and I am most grateful for being permitted to make use of some of its findings.

OS sheets 159, 160, 161, 170, 171

The Kidwelly & Llanelly Canal

There is a sizeable collection of old canals in south-west Wales, most of them unpronounceable by the Englishman and all but invisible to the naked eye. Investigating their remains demands time and dedication; it is easier to discern their traces after heavy rain—when, of course, it is more difficult to approach them because of the morass thereby created. The most considerable of these canals was the Kidwelly & Llanelly—inappropriately named, as it turned out, as it merely skirted Kidwelly and got nowhere near Llanelly at all.

Included in the K & L was an earlier canal, Kymer's, the first Welsh canal to obtain a parliamentary act, which opened in 1769. This was made by Thomas Kymer to connect his mines and quarries with the quay at Kidwelly and avoid the uncertainties of navigation on the Gwendraeth Fawr. Although only 3 miles long, it proved to be useful, and when in the early nineteenth century proposals were made to develop Kidwelly Harbour and improve communications generally, Kymer's Canal was seen as an integral part. Llanelly and Kidwelly were to be linked by a canal which would incorporate Kymer's, and a branch was to be built up the Gwendraeth Valley for several miles. Other branches or tramroads were also suggested, the whole to form a transport network. Not all the necessary funds were forthcoming, however, and work proceeded in fits and starts. What was to be built of the K & L was finished in about 1838. This comprised a line from Kymer's Canal up the valley as far as Cwm-mawr, and another from a junction near Spudder's Bridge, $1\frac{1}{2}$ miles southeast of Kidwelly, to Burry Port. The best way to comprehend what was built is to look at the single-track railway line on the

OS sheet, as this was built generally on the bed of the canal.

The first plan was to use locks for the descent down the valley to Kidwelly, but when, after some interval, work restarted in the 1830s, the plan was altered. That interesting engineer, James Green, was called in, a man who, as his work on the West-Country canals shows, would never use a lock if he could think of an alternative. He proposed three inclined planes with a total fall of about 200ft. To be fair, however, it cannot be proved that the substitution of inclines shortened the canal's life. For it was a short life; in 1865, aware of the threat of loss of traffic to competing railways and troubled by problems of maintenance and the difficulties of keeping a channel in Kidwelly Harbour, the K & L turned itself into a railway company, joined with the company running Burry Port, and within a few years built railway lines over its canals.

Evidence on the ground of the existence of the K & L is fragmentary. Opposite Kidwelly Church a road leads to the railway station. On the far side of the level-crossing the northernmost of two tracks leads to a sewage farm and also to a bit of the Kymer's section of the K & L—the last few yards with a small stone-walled basin. There was no connection with the estuary, a silted expanse with something of a hopeless air about it. Back a short distance along the canal there is indication of a branch that was intended to go to Kidwelly Bridge, but may not have done so.

There are a few things to see in the vicinity of Spudder's Bridge, on the B4308, one of which is the old bridge itself, now bypassed. About ½ mile downstream, the branch line to Burry Port crosses the river using the aqueduct constructed for the canal in 1815, according to its inscription. A short walk south-westward is the end of the Moat Farm Branch of the canal, which was connected by tramroad to collieries at Trimsaran. Further up the valley there are signs of the canal bed by the bridge over the railway at Pontnewydd. At Ponthenry was the first of the inclines; again, the railway indicates the site on the south side of the village. Little is known about the K & L inclines, except that they seem to have been worked by water power and took small tubboats. Goods were presumably transhipped into larger boats somewhere on the canal's lower reaches. The head of the Ponthenry incline is conveniently marked by the Incline Hotel in the village. Another incline was at Clos-isaf, 1½ miles up the valley from Pontyberem (the incline used to be called Hirwaun-isaf); the stone structure marking the head of the incline is beside an ungated level-crossing a few yards along a minor road on the north side of the B4317. This was the top incline; Charles Hadfield believes that it was never used and that the canal after Pontyberem was no more than a water channel. Between the two inclines mentioned was another one, which has disappeared under coal workings.

The canal ended at Cwm-mawr, near the derelict railway station. It has been suggested that it crossed the river to a basin on the north side, but this does not look likely and evidence on the ground is lacking.

Of the southern arm of the canal there are some traces south of Burry Port, at the east side of the golf links. There are also a few traces of the Pembrey Canal, which lost most of its purpose when the K & L was made. These include a bridge over Pembrey Halt and a terminal building, Glo-Caled, north of the A484 between Pembrey and Burry Port. The bridge over the railway just before the B4317 joins the A484 was adapted from a K & L canal bridge.

One feels that there should be a lot more to add, but it would need research of a microscopic kind. The results of an aerial survey of the region would be invaluable to the earthbound scrutiniser.

OS sheet 159

Bibliography

BOOKS

Bick, David, *The Hereford & Gloucester Canal* (The Pound House, 1979)
Gladwin, D. D., *Canals of the Welsh Valleys* (Oakwood Press, 1975)
Hadfield, C., *Canals of South Wales and the Border* (David & Charles, 1967)
Kissack, Keith, *The River Wye* (Terence Dalton, 1978)
Stevens, R. A., *A Towpath Guide to the Brecknock & Abergavenny and Monmouthshire Canals* (Goose & Son, 1974)

ARTICLES AND BOOKLETS

A Glimpse of the Past (Wales Tourist Board, nd)
'Herefordshire & Gloucestershire Canal' and 'The Leominster-Stourport Canal', I. Cohen, *Transactions*, Woolhope Field Club, Vols 35 and 36

Navigation on the Wye, B. J. Stevens (Monmouth Borough Council, 1955)

SOCIETIES

Neath & Tennant Canals Preservation Society
Newport Canal Preservation Society
Torfaen Canal Society

NOTES

All information on the water-power uses of the Swansea Canal comes from: S. R. Hughes, 'The Swansea Canal: Navigation and Power Supplier', *Industrial Archaeology Review*, Vol 4, No 1, Winter 1979–80, pp51–69.

Information on underground mining canals comes from: S. R. Hughes, 'The Development of British Navigation Levels', *Journal* of the RCHS, Vol xxvii, No 1, March 1981.

All descriptive information on Swansea Canal remains that does not fit into the above two categories is taken from the Royal Commission on Ancient and Historical Monuments in Wales's forthcoming inventory on *The Industrial Archaeology of the Swansea Canal and its Associated Water and Transport Systems* (Cardiff, HMSO, 1981). Some information on the Glamorganshire Canal is from a similar forthcoming publication on the industrial archaeology of that waterway.

4

MID-WALES AND THE WEST MIDLANDS

The Montgomeryshire Canal

In 1944 the Montgomeryshire Canal, along with much more of the Shropshire Union network, was abandoned by its owners the London, Midland & Scottish Railway. Eight years earlier the bank had burst near Frankton and the railway had found itself unable, or unwilling, to commit the necessary funds for repairs. Had the Llangollen Canal not been needed as a water channel, that would have gone as well. Those many thousands who enjoy cruising the Llangollen today might spare a thought for the Montgomeryshire, and perhaps a few pounds towards the costs of those fighting so hard for restoration of this very beautiful waterway.

Recently, 5 miles of the canal north of Welshpool have been reopened and a boat for handicapped children is now based at Buttington Wharf. Work is also in progress at Frankton Locks by the junction with the Llangollen, and elsewhere along the line. There is little problem in finding the canal as the whole length, including the dewatered sections south of Frankton and between Maesbury Marsh and Crickheath, is shown clearly on the OS sheets, access from the road is generally easy and there is plenty of towpath left.

The least-known length of the Montgomeryshire is the top section between Newtown and Welshpool of which restoration in the nearer future at least is not likely. Newtown Basin has been filled in; to find the site look for Lower Canal Road, a turning off the B4568 road to Llanllwchaiarn less than ½ mile from Newtown centre. There is a terrace of wharf cottages and other canal-related buildings all of early nineteenth-century brick. South-east of the basin were twenty-two lime-kilns. Some of the canal's

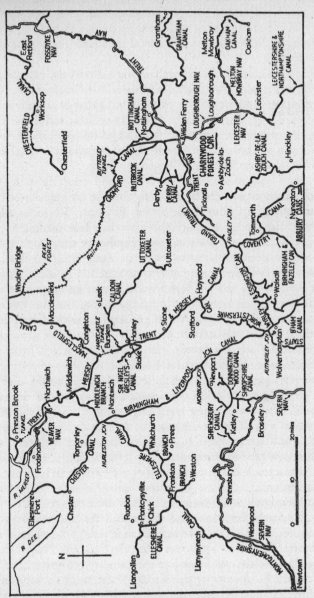

The Midlands

water supply was raised from the Severn; the pump-house has been converted into a garage and its chimney recently demolished. There are traces of two bridges in this area. The Wool Producers of Wales factory is a useful landmark for exploration in Newtown.

Behind the church at Llanllwchaiarn is a clearly defined section of canal bed crossed by a bridge with an iron-railing parapet. The road now takes the north side of a hill while the canal line keeps close to the Severn on the south. You may be able to follow it on foot to Penarth Weir, designed by Josias Jessop and built by John Williams in or about 1818. North-east of the weir the canal is in water, below the chamber of Freestone Lock.

By road continue along the B4568 and turn right on the B4389, which crosses the canal at Aberbechan by a girder bridge of four cast-iron beams made at the Brymbo Works in 1862. North of the bridge and accessible from a lane leading to an automobile scrapyard is a small and handsome three-arch aqueduct of sandstone ashlar that takes the canal over the Bechan Brook. Canal and Severn are very close together here and remain so for a further $3\frac{1}{2}$ miles. There are locks south of Abermule and at Dolforwyn, just north of the bridge taking the A483 across both waterways. Here is the site of a coal wharf with a Shropshire Union galvanised-iron warehouse and two wharfinger's cottages, one of which was the recent victim of a fire attack by those Welshmen who oppose holiday homes.

The main road accompanies the canal closely, crossing it three times in the next 3 miles, the canal being culverted on each occasion. The third crossing is at Garthmyl, the junction between the Eastern and Western Branches of the canal. The Garthmyl-Newtown Western Branch, $7\frac{3}{4}$ miles long with 6 locks, was completed in 1821 and engineered by John Williams. It was constructed as a result of the prosperity of the Eastern Branch but by a separate company, the intention being that the companies would merge when the Western Branch dividends reached 5 per cent. This never happened, however, and the undertakings remained separate until the Western Branch joined the other in the Shropshire Union in 1850. At Garthmyl by the Nag's Head realignment of the road has left the canal overbridge standing parallel to it by the site of the wharf. There were six lime-kilns here, lime and limestone being for many years the principal traffic on the canal.

The Eastern Branch, 16¼ miles long from Garthmyl to Carreghofa, had the Dadfords, father and son, as engineers. Their aqueduct over the Rhiw at Berriew was rebuilt in 1889. The canal is now piped across it. Scouring of the river bed has revealed that the central pier was seated on baulks of timber, presumably to protect the foundations. There are two road arches on either side of the central spans. Just over a mile north is a contrasting aqueduct across the Luggy Brook. This has a cast-iron trough with ornamental railings and was installed in 1820 to replace an earlier one, probably of masonry. The Luggy Aqueduct is accessible from a minor road ½ mile north of the B4390 junction. It lies to the south of the bridge carrying this road over the canal. Below the locks, close to the Horseshoe Inn, is a bank of lime-kilns. This was Brithdir Wharf. The blue brick of the lock house is not what it was first built of; look at the chimney to see what it was like originally.

There is another interesting site at Belan Locks, 2 miles further on just before the A490 joins the A483 from the south-east. Here there is a lock each side of the bridge, another bank of lime-kilns, a beautifully constructed overflow weir, a lengthsman's or lock-keeper's house and, on the north side of the bridge, the remains of two boats trapped when the canal burst in 1936. At both locks the impressive ground paddle-gear survives. This was probably designed by G. W. Buck, engineer to the canal in the 1820s and early 1830s. It operates paddles placed horizontally in the canal bed and seems to be unique to the Montgomeryshire. It was Buck who also installed iron lock gates, the pair from Welshpool Lock now an outside exhibit at the Waterways Museum at Stoke Bruerne.

On the approach to Welshpool the canal draws close to the road to be culverted beneath it and continues on its eastern side to the town. Just before the crossing at Whitehouse Bridge is a saw-mill built over a small stream. This belongs to the Earl of Powis, whose ancestor was a principal promoter of the canal. It seems probable that the presence of a saw-mill on this site determined the line of the canal hereabouts. Certainly the canal served the mill, timber being the main cargo from this area. Nearby there used to be a bone-mill and the inevitable lime-kilns.

Welshpool Wharf is accessible from Severn Street (B4381) in the centre of Welshpool. The lock has been recently restored; a warehouse and other canal-associated buildings stand close by and the whole site is as attractive—and potentially useful—a town canal site as you can find anywhere. There is another warehouse north of the bridge and an iron-trough aqueduct over the Lledan Brook, erected in 1836 and similar to that at Brithdir.

On the reopened length of canal, places to see include Buttington Wharf, Pool Quay (the old head of navigation on the Severn), and Burgedin Locks, beside the B4392, with the junction with the short Guilsfield Branch, now a nature reserve. Tyddyn Basin, 2 miles south-west along the B4392, still has derelict wharf buildings; timber for Liverpool used to be loaded on to boats here. Between Burgedin and Carreghofa the canal has been dredged and the towpath cleared, but to restore navigation the A483 bridge at Maerdy will have to be raised. The heavy and leaky Vyrnwy Aqueduct is on this stretch. Between the aqueduct and Carreghofa is Bridge 96—Williams Bridge—which, despite a massive press campaign and whatever pressure canal enthusiasts could exert, was culverted by Powys County Council in 1980, adding another obstacle to through restoration. Although the council says that this is only a temporary measure forced on it by shortage of funds, reconstruction of the bridge will inevitably be expensive and cannot be envisaged in the near future. Meanwhile, the Shropshire Union Canal Society volunteers will doubtless continue restoring Carreghofa Locks for which the British Waterways Board will provide the gates.

The Eastern Branch of the Montgomeryshire ends north of Carreghofa Locks. From here to Frankton, strictly speaking, it is the Carreghofa Branch of the Ellesmere Canal. Points of access include Crickheath Wharf, Redwith on the B4396, Maesbury Marsh, with a crane and a Navigation Inn, and the Queen's Head on the A5, from which a minor road to Rednal is the most useful to follow. Note the canalside building just before canal and road part company by the railway bridge. After Rednal, turn westward at the T-junction for Lower Frankton, the locks and the crowded waters of the Llangollen.

OS sheets 126, 136

The Shropshire Union Branches

The Weston Branch

The Ellesmere Canal as planned was to have four terminal points: Ellesmere Port, Chester, Ruabon and Shrewsbury. The Weston Branch was part of the intended Ruabon-Shrewsbury line, which extended to Pontcysyllte, a distance of 17¾ miles. The Pontcysyllte section became part of the Llangollen Canal, but nearly all of the Weston Branch, from Lockgate Bridge to Westonwharf, was disused by 1917 when its banks burst at Dandyford.

Lockgate Bridge is on the minor road between Welsh Frankton and Hordley. Exploration of the remains of the branch does not take long as much of the line has been ploughed in; an hour of daylight after touring the Montgomery will be enough. There was a basin north of Hordley on the west side of the road about ¼ mile from the village. There is evidence of the cut at Lower Hordley and you may be able to follow it north to Dandyford and look for the site of the burst. South of Lower Hordley the line wriggles south-eastward; the road to follow goes through Bagley and Nillgreen. Due west of Wycherley Hall a bridge stands isolated in the fields (SJ 414272). South of Nillgreen is Westoncommon, where a very minor road leads westward to Westonwharf (420257). The wharf itself is clearly defined, with a warehouse and lime-kilns nearby. The cut extended a short distance south of the wharf itself.

The Prees and Whitchurch Branches

A short and lockless branch to Prees was opened from the Ellesmere Canal on the south side of Whixall Moss to Quina Brook— as far as it ever reached—in 1804. Quina Brook is on the B5476 between Tilstock and Wem; there were lime-kilns here, later absorbed into a farmyard. At Edstaston there was a wharf and a Shropshire Union warehouse which may still survive. Further north the canal is watered and the towpath makes a pleasant walk. It passes through the hamlet of Waterloo with accommodation bridges north and south of the road-crossing. There are two lift bridges on the final length and there may still be some Shropshire Union notices to be found. Part of this branch has been restored for use by a boatyard.

The Prees Branch was abandoned with the rest of the LMSR

waterways in 1944, having ceased trading before World War II. The short Whitchurch Branch shared these dates. Much of this branch has been obliterated. The wharf in Whitchurch was near the Victoria Jubilee Park; there was—and perhaps still is—a Wharf Gun Shop which indicated the site. The canal ran along the boundary of the park and out of the town to Chemistry village on the north of the A525. There is a cruiser base on the Llangollen Canal by the junction with the branch.

OS sheet 126

The Upper Severn

In the mid-eighteenth century the Severn, according to Richard Whitworth, was navigable by a vessel of 50 tons as far up as Welshpool except in times of excessive drought, 'and not a lock the whole way'. The vessels were barges, carrying a single square sail, or trows, rather larger with more sail area. When the wind failed they were bow-hauled by gangs of men, a task which attracted, it was said, persons of bad character—the only ones who would follow such a degrading occupation. Horse-towing became possible only when towing paths were made. The first long stretch of 24 miles between Bewdley and Coalbrookdale was opened in 1800 and within a few years the path was extended to Gloucester. The locks between Stourport and Gloucester were not built until the 1840s.

With railway competition and deterioration of the condition of the river, the upper reaches gradually fell into disuse. Traffic above Shrewsbury ceased in 1862 and above Bridgnorth in 1895. Stourport is now the limit of navigation, but with the closing of the oil wharves there and at Worcester commercial traffic above Gloucester has virtually ended.

In the great days of the Severn as a trading river, Pool Quay was the head of navigation. This is 3 miles north of Welshpool on the A483; the Montgomeryshire Canal is on the west side of the road and the river on the east. According to Thomas Harral (*Picturesque Views of the Severn*, 1824) the number of vessels trading between here and Gloucester amounted to 400, 'mostly navigated by three or four men each, robust and resolute fellows'. I do not think there is any evidence of works connected with navigation on these upper reaches, however; whatever there was

Chamber of the first lock on the Baybridge Canal
(Adur Navigation)

Lock chamber,
Liskeard & Looe
Union Canal

Lower Belan Lock,
Montgomeryshire Canal

Paper Mill Lock,
Ipswich & Stowmarket
Navigation

Shipmeadow,
or Geldeston, Lock,
River Waveney

Staircase pair on the Rogerstone, or Cefn, flight of fourteen locks, Monmouthshire Canal (Gwent County Council)

The River Nar at Narborough

Prestolee Aqueduct, Manchester,
Bolton & Bury Canal

has been destroyed by floods. It is not likely that the works were substantial; there was no controlling navigation authority and hence no major engineering works.

At Uffington, where the Shrewsbury Canal came within a few hundred yards of the river, there are remains of ferry installations, and at Preston, a mile south, is a good example of one of the several islands created in the construction of bypass channels around fish weirs. If you take the B4380 road from Shrewsbury you come in 9 miles to Leighton; south of the village there is a stone towpath-bridge where the Leighton Brook joins the river.

As the river enters Ironbridge Gorge evidence of its trading past accumulates. Most notable is the Gothic-styled Severn Warehouse, built by the Coalbrookdale company in the 1840s and recently renovated and transformed into a display centre for the Ironbridge Gorge Museum. Castings from the ironworks, and other goods, were brought down to the riverside by a tramroad, of which part of the track has been reinstated. The Upper Severn Navigation Trust plans to construct a replica trow and moor it by the warehouse.

There are more warehouses on the north bank of the river before you arrive at the Severn's major industrial monument, the Iron Bridge itself. Opened in 1779 and now restored and conserved with the greatest of care it dominates the river scene and its daring complexity draws wonder and admiration. To the west are the wharf walls close to the Bedlam furnaces, which are also part of the museum. And at Coalport you can examine the remains of the canal/river interchange close to Coalport Bridge, built early in the nineteenth century on the site of Preens Eddy Bridge which seems to have been another iron bridge built soon after its great neighbour. There are remains of a wall at Swinney Wharf, a few hundred yards further down, and at Sutton Wharf, accessible from a turning off the A442 south of Sutton Hill, there are traces of works on the site of the terminus of the tramroad from Oakengates which operated from about 1800 to 1814. The first iron boat was launched at Willey Wharf, on the west bank of the river near Swinney Farm; traces of the wharf may still be found.

Bridgnorth has treated its riverside with some respect and a walk along the west bank is rewarding, with several pieces of evidence of the trading past of the river. From Bridgnorth, take the minor road through Eardington and onwards until the road turns to cross the Mor Brook. Where the brook joins the river there is an iron towpath-bridge dating from 1824; on this stretch are traces of the towpath which was surfaced with debris from ironworks and potteries. There is another towpath-bridge 4½ miles further south; continue through Highley, take the B4555 and then follow a track a few yards before the road turns sharply west. The track leads to the confluence of the Borle Brook and the river; this bridge dates from 1828. At Highley and Arley sandstone was loaded on to boats; south-east of Highley village you may find millstones both in the river and on the bank.

At Bewdley, according to Thomas Harral:

> the navigation of the Severn presents a very busy appearance; and it is the boast of the inhabitants that their trows and their sailors are the best upon the river. On each side of the stream are extensive and commodious wharfs.

There is no navigation at Bewdley now, owing to shallows further down, but it remains a dignified and mostly beautiful town. As at Bridgnorth, you can find evidence of the trading past if you walk along the riverside. From Bewdley it is less than 4 miles to Stourport, the entrance to the Staffordshire & Worcestershire Canal, and the pleasure boats.

The Shropshire Tub-boat Canals

The new town of Telford sits not only on its namesake's London-Holyhead A5 road but also on the network of tub-boat canals which helped greatly in the development of the coalfields and ironworks of the area during the Industrial Revolution of the late eighteenth century. This network consisted of the following canals, in order of their opening dates: the Donnington Wood (also known as the Marquess of Stafford's and the Duke of Sutherland's), 1768; Ketley, 1788; Wombridge, 1788; Shropshire, 1792, and Shrewsbury, 1796. The Newport Branch of the Birmingham & Liverpool Junction, which became the Shropshire Union, was opened in 1835, connecting with the Shrewsbury Canal at Wappenshall. This was a narrow-boat canal, however, and its boats were unable to penetrate the network. They could not even use the Shrewsbury locks which, although long enough to accommodate them, were too narrow.

The Donnington Wood Canal was built by Lord Gower and it is from his and his son's further ennoblement that the canal acquired its alternative names. He owned mines at Donnington Wood and the 5½ mile canal was used to convey coal in trains of tub-boats to a wharf on the main road near Newport. A branch with three short arms was built a few years later to connect limestone quarries and limeworks at Lilleshall and Pitchcroft with the main line. The branch, 2 miles long, was on a lower level than the main line and originally the connection was made by a twin-shafted vertical tunnel at Hugh's Bridge, with goods being raised or lowered through the tunnel by crane. This was replaced by an inclined plane. There were also seven locks on the branch, which continued in use until about 1880. Traffic on the main line of the Donnington Wood ceased in 1904.

The Wombridge Canal, 1¾ miles long, was cut by William Reynolds, ironmaster of Ketley, to carry coal and ironstone from Wombridge to the Donnington Wood Canal and thence to furnaces in Donnington Wood. The Wombridge was made on the higher level and when the Shrewsbury Canal was opened a few years later they met at the top of the Trench inclined plane. The Shrewsbury took over most of the line of the Wombridge, which continued to operate until about 1904.

Reynolds opened the Ketley Canal about the same time as the Wombridge. This began as a short, isolated waterway designed to carry coal and iron from Oakengates to his Ketley Works. It was the first British canal to use an inclined plane, an idea which Reynolds may have obtained from the Continent or from tramroad inclines nearer home. The Ketley incline was double track; the boats floated into cradles and the descending load drew up the other. As the ironworks were on the lower level, nearly all the loads went downwards. When the Shropshire Canal was opened the Ketley became a branch of it, but it closed when the ironworks shut in 1816.

Many of the ironmasters joined with Reynolds to construct the Shropshire Canal, which formed the major element in the tub-boat system. Telford described its route 'carried over high and rugged ground, along banks of slipping loam, over old coal mines and over where coal mines and iron stone are now actually worked under it ...', concluding that its construction proved 'there is scarcely any ground so difficult but where ... a water conveyance may always be obtained'. At its northern end the Shropshire connected with the Donnington Wood via Wrockwardine Wood inclined plane, while southward it divided into two arms, one to Brierly Hill, above Coalbrookdale, the other descending by two inclined planes to the bank of the Severn at Coalport. From the foot of the Hay incline the short Coalport Canal was constructed parallel to the river with extensive wharves. There was no water connection with the Severn, but platforms were built over the riverside from which coal and other goods could be shot into the barges below. Much of the Shropshire Canal was closed in 1858 by the London & North Western Railway, which had bought it and wished to build its own line to Coalport. Short sections in the southern half survived longer, the stretch below Windmill Hill incline, used for carrying coal to Blist Hill furnaces, not closing until 1944.

The Shrewsbury Canal at 17 miles was the longest of the East Shropshire navigations. It supplied Shrewsbury with coal and was another tub-boat canal, the locks being long enough to take a train of four. Like the Shropshire Canal it became part of the Shropshire Union Railway & Canal Company in 1846 and continued trading throughout its length until 1921. In that year the Trench inclined plane, the last to be operated in Britain, was closed and Shrewsbury Basin was abandoned in 1922. Commercial traffic finished in 1931 and the canal was abandoned, along with another 160 miles of waterways, by its then owners, the London, Midland & Scottish Railway, in 1944.

Newport makes a convenient starting point for an examination of the remains of the tub-boat canals. The terminus of the main line of the Donnington Wood was at Pave Lane, 2 miles from Newport on the A41 Wolverhampton road. Part of the drive to Lilleshall Hall, now the National Sports Centre, was constructed on the canal which swung westward, passing beneath the drive to Little Hales Manor Farm, and across the fields to Hugh's Bridge, the junction with the Lilleshall arm. Lilleshall village is off the A518, about 2½ miles from Newport, and you may still be able to find traces of the canal in the fields east of the village. The arm ended at Pitchcroft, about ½ mile north of Lilleshall; the wharf has been mostly obliterated, but there may be traces of a bridge near some cottages. This length had seven locks, but you are unlikely to find evidence of them on the ground.

For Hugh's Bridge follow the minor road from Lilleshall to Lilleshall Hall. You cross the bridge in less than a mile. Take the track northward to Incline Cottages; this runs parallel to the main line of the canal. From a farm gate you can discern the slope of the incline, 123yd long. The upper basin has been filled in and the engine-house has gone, but the entrance to the tunnel that preceded the incline is in the garden of the cottage on the east side of the slope. From Hugh's Bridge you can follow the canal south to the ruins of Lilleshall Abbey. It continues through Abbey Farm and across fields to Muxton Bridge Farm. Muxton Bridge itself is on a minor road from the A518 through the village of Muxton. From Muxton Bridge to the foot of the Wrockwardine Wood incline the canal is no longer traceable.

The Wrockwardine Wood incline site is 1¼ miles north of Oakengates centre. Look for the Bellevue Inn and close by is the junction of Furnace Lane, Plough Road and Moss Road. This is close to the foot of the slope which runs up past the Methodist church; from here the Donnington Wood headed north-east-ward and the Shrewsbury Canal, incorporating the Wombridge line, of which you may find a fragment down Furnace Lane, headed west. The inclined plane itself belonged to the Shropshire Canal; it was double-track and operated by a steam-engine, with a rise of 120ft.

Little is left of the northern length of the Shropshire Canal. There were two tunnels, at Snedshill and Stirchley, which have disappeared. The junction with the Ketley Canal was at Oaken-gates; the top of the Ketley incline was near Ketley Hall and the foot, 73ft lower, close to a pub called the Wren's Nest, which you can find on a housing estate to the south of the A5 by turning off this road at the Seven Stars. Owing to building development over the last few years you will find no evidence of the incline or canal hereabouts today. The docks have been sealed beneath new buildings. If you continue to the south side of the M54 you may find traces of a disused railway on the east of Dawley. This was the Coalport Branch line and took the course of the Shropshire Canal.

The junction of the Coalbrookdale and Coalport branches has been obliterated by the A442. Join this road in Dawley and head south. Look for a sign reading 'Aqueduct'; this points to a hand-ful of houses on a dead-end road on the west side of the A442. Here is an aqueduct that carried the branch to Brierly Hill and here you are close to the site of the junction. You may be able to follow this branch or to approach it by climbing the hill on the west side of the A4169 above the museum at Coalbrookdale. There are two Telford-designed cottages by the canal, which ended 2¾ miles from the junction at the head of an inclined plane. Originally, there were two vertical shafts leading down to a tunnel; coal and iron were lowered and limestone raised by cranes, the loads being in iron crates. After a year or so this system was replaced by an inclined plane, which did not count as part of the canal as the loads travelled up and down it in wagons, not boats. The foot of the incline was by Styches Weir, on the Coalbrookdale Stream, and there was a rail connection with the Severn.

Shortly after the junction, the main (Coalport) line of the canal descended the Windmill Hill inclined plane, a fall of 126ft. Road construction has obliterated this site, which lies to the south of the Brookside Estate. The final stretch of the canal, however, has been preserved by the Ironbridge Gorge Museum Trust. It runs around the western side of Blists Hill and now forms one of the exhibits in this fascinating open-air museum of the industrial past. Floating in the canal are a couple of tub-boats, one of them once belonging to the Lilleshall Company and rescued from use as a farm drinking-trough. You can walk along the towpath to the top of the Hay inclined plane where you can examine the remains of the docks and the engine-house. Rails have been laid down the slope. On the walk down you pass over the bridge carrying the incline over the disused Coalport Railway. The docks at the foot are being cleared. Close by is the entrance to the Tar Tunnel, also part of the museum. This was another enterprise of William Reynolds, driven in 1787 for about 1,000yd with the probable intention of serving the collieries as both a drain and a navigable level. A spring of tar was struck and tar was extracted, in diminishing quantities, until the 1840s.

With the opening of the canal, Reynolds encouraged the development of a housing and industrial area on the north bank of the Severn, backing on to the riverside wharves and warehouses which had followed the opening of the Preens Eddy Bridge in 1780. In the mid-1790s John Rose and Edward Blakeway moved their porcelain factory to this site. This became the famous Coalport China Company which continued in operation here until 1926. Now the site has become the Coalport China Works

Museum, part of the Ironbridge Gorge complex, and the Coal-port Canal which used to serve the factory has been restored for part of its length. The rest of this short canal to Coalport Basin will also eventually be dug out and rewatered.

For the Shrewsbury Canal we have to return to the north of Telford. Trench is on the A518 Newport-Wellington road and the site of Trench inclined plane is on the east of the roundabout junction with the B4373. You will find the Trench Reservoir and a track leading uphill past the Shropshire Arms. The incline rose 75ft and, like the others, was double track and operated by a steam-engine. It remained in use until 1921. The Wombridge Canal came in at the top of the incline and a few fragments of brickwork mark the entrance to the upper basin.

On the north side of the A518 the canal passes through a factory site and heads north-west across Hadley Park. In the park are two locks—there is another in the factory area—with enough left of their chambers and mechanism to give you a good idea of their dimensions and method of working. At 6ft 4in they were among the narrowest locks on the system, able to take tub-boats but not narrow boats. Some very narrow boats were built, in fact, to be used on the Shrewsbury Canal after the junction was made with the Newport Branch. At the lower end they had guillotine gates, originally operated by a counterweight that hung down over the canal. This was later altered so that the weight was led down the side of the framework into a pit beside the lock.

There are good remains at Wappenshall Junction including warehouses, a toll-collector's house and the towpath bridge of the Newport Branch, now preserved as an ancient monument. You can walk alongside the Shrewsbury Canal southward from here to the next road. The canal continues westward across Eyton Moor with a lock on the north side of Eyton-upon-the-Weald Moors which you reach from a turning off the A442. This main road crosses the canal at Long Lane; there is a caravan site beside the canal to the west of the crossing.

From Long Lane make for Longdon-on-Tern and continue through the village to the bridge over the river. A few yards north the Tern was crossed by the canal, carried on an iron aqueduct, an unhandsome but workmanlike structure fitted on to the stone abutments of a conventional aqueduct destroyed by floods in its early days. The Longdon Aqueduct was the precursor of the famous monument at Pontcysyllte and only the second iron aqueduct to be built. It is—or is on the way to become—an exhibit at the Ironbridge Gorge Museum. Further along the road is the site of Longdon Wharf with a Shropshire Union Canal Company warehouse.

Between Withington and Rodington the canal crossed the River Roden by a three-arched aqueduct, but there are no traces in this area. You can, however, pick up the course again as it encircles Withington on the south side of the church. From here it runs parallel to the Tern roughly a mile distant from its northern side. It is adjacent to the Withington-Atcham road between Frogmore and the fork for Uffington. In the angle of the fork is the site of Berwick Wharf where the canal turns 90° to head north-west again. There is a watered—or damp—stretch about 500yd along the Uffington road and you can battle alongside it to the portal of Berwick Tunnel, now bricked up. It is finely proportioned and faced with stone, although the tunnel itself is brick-lined, with the date 1797 inscribed on the keystone. It was the first major tunnel to be built with a towpath and is 970yd long. You may spot a ventilation shaft about half-way along. The northern portal is in fields on the south side of the Preston-Upton Magna road; you should be able to see the canal midway between Preston and the railway bridge. At Uffington there are good traces of the canal bed to the north and east of the village. Then take the B5062 into Shrewsbury. Most of this stretch of canal has been obliterated, but you can seek for evidence near the gasworks. There was no connection with the Severn, but you may find some relevant buildings near Spring Gardens.

OS sheets 126, 127

The Newport Branch of the Shropshire Union

Abandoned in 1944, the Newport Branch of the Shropshire Union Canal was a sad loss. A move to restore it was begun in the mid-1960s but met with insufficient support. Since then, more of the canal has been infilled and the prospects for restoration now are by no means hopeful.

The branch was opened in 1835 to connect the Shrewsbury Canal with the main line of the Birmingham & Liverpool Junction. It was a little over 10 miles long with 23 locks, most of them concentrated above Norbury Junction. The junction itself, with boatyard and pub, is a popular halt on the Shropshire Union, and the first short section of the branch is used for moorings, with a dry dock in what used to be the bottom lock. Immediately above this dock, the locks and canal have been eliminated.

To find the canal by road make for Norbury, which lies to the south of the A519, 4 miles north-east of Newport. The right fork south of Norbury crosses the branch at Parton's Bridge, where you can see Lock 5. Following the canal towards Newport you will see that some of the locks of the Norbury flight still survive. Return to the A519 and head for Forton, turning south at the cross-roads in the village. This minor road joins the canal to cross the River Meese by the three-arch Forton Aqueduct. There is a good skew bridge close by. Here the canal is dry, but a few hundred yards further along, past Meretown Lock, it becomes a waterway by courtesy of the local authority. Part of the canal on the north side of Newport can be followed; there is a lock cottage by Haycock's Lock and a wharf building and another good bridge at the site of Newport Wharf. You can continue to walk past two more locks, Tickethouse and Polly's, before the infilling recommences.

From Newport to the junction with the Shrewsbury Canal at Wappenshall there is not much to be seen. Much of the canal has disappeared, including Kynnersley, or Duke's Drive, Aqueduct, an elaborate iron trough that took the canal over a drive between Kynnersley and Hincks Plantation and used to bear the arms of the Duke of Sutherland on either side. To the south of the aqueduct was the short Humber arm; if you fight your way along you may come to the remains of a boat in the overgrown bed. At the end of the arm, which can be reached from the minor road between Preston-upon-the-Weald Moors and Lilleshall, there is a rail-canal interchange building by Lubstree Wharf, once busy with traffic from the Duke of Sutherland's mines and works at Lilleshall.

At Preston there is a bridge and a pool that once was a winding hole. From Preston take the road to Wappenshall, the junction with the Shrewsbury Canal. The branch between Wappenshall and Newport was not used after 1939.

OS sheet 127

The Droitwich Canals

The salt town of Droitwich was connected with the Severn in 1771 by the 6¾ mile Droitwich Canal. In 1853 it was linked with the main waterway network of the Midlands by the short Droitwich Junction Canal. Both these canals were abandoned in 1939, after many years of decay. Chunks of the Droitwich were filled in, including a stretch in the centre of the town. Then, with some of the infilling still looking rather raw, voices advocating restoration began to be heard. The town council looked favourably on the idea, but it was not until the formation of the Droitwich Canals Trust in 1973 that action began. In October of that year a large-scale and nationally publicised 'dig' took place organised by the trust which, unlike most restoration bodies, had obtained a lease of their canal and had full control over its length. In six years nearly half the Droitwich Canal was disinterred and restored—in fact, the summit pound. This was watered and opened to small craft by the end of 1979. However, what remains to be done will be more difficult and costly—the section to the Severn, with eight locks, and the shorter section to the terminus in Droitwich. After that, the trust intends to reopen the Droitwich Junction; but that is a project for the longer term.

The Droitwich Canal runs roughly parallel to the River Salwarpe. Over the centuries there were several attempts to make the river navigable, although there is no firm evidence that any of them succeeded. It was claimed that five locks were built under an act of 1662, but these particular works were unfinished. Further attempts also failed and it was as a consequence of these repeated failures that the Droitwich Canal was proposed. In its early years the canal was moderately successful, with salt a principal traffic. The nineteenth century saw it pass into the hands of the Worcester & Birmingham Company; then in 1874 the two navigations with the Droitwich Junction were taken over by the Sharpness New Docks Company, which improved the canals and fought a strong rearguard action against the forces of rail and road. Only the Worcester & Birmingham survived, however.

In the centre of Droitwich the last ½ mile of canal has disappeared under Vine Park. At one time it was lined with salt warehouses, but the area is now cleared and grassed over. The trust intends to dig this out again, nearly along the original line, and construct a marina at the terminus. Then the canal will once again draw its water from the Salwarpe. You can follow the line westward; the canal left the town by the Railway Inn. It swings south, to be crossed by the A4133, and then south-west to the village of Salwarpe. This is the restored section. At Salwarpe the canal lies in a deep cutting. You can gain access to it through the churchyard. Two things to note in this village are the bridge-plate of the Sharpness New Docks and Gloucester & Birmingham Navigation Company, to give it its full title, and the splendid Elizabethan Salwarpe Court. From Salwarpe, walk along the towpath to Ladywood Lock, where the trust has its operational headquarters. You can continue to walk the towpath past five more locks, noting a restored circular overflow weir by Lock 3 and an attractive lock cottage by Lock 5. There are some good red-brick bridges and the brick lock-chambers are in generally sound condition. The trust intends to make the replacement lock gates in its workshops by Ladywood Lock.

From Lock 5 onward, canal and river are close together. About ¾ mile after Lock 6, however, the A449 dual carriageway has flattened the canal, culverted beneath it. Here is a major restoration problem, with the alternatives of inserting a navigable tunnel beneath the road or diverting the canal into the river via two new locks. There are further problems to the west of the road where the remains of Hawford Lock into the Severn are in the garden of a private house. Lock Lane, to the west of the A449, takes you in the right direction.

For the Droitwich Junction, go to the east end of Vine Park. The canal locked out of the Salwarpe; there were two sets of gates facing each way here, to overcome any problem of relative levels. You may find traces of it near the A38 crossing and behind the Barley Mow on the B4090—this road was the old Salt Way, and a Roman road. Part of the canal line has been built on, but you may find the remains of seven locks on the north side of the B-road. The Junction Canal met the Worcester & Birmingham at Hanbury Wharf, where there is a bridge. It may be difficult to discern the actual junction, but it is quite easy to find the Eagle at the end of your journey.

OS sheet 150

The Dick Brook

In dimensions, the Dick Brook is one of the less significant of the Severn's tributaries. It joins the main river about 3 miles south of Stourport, on the northern edge of Shrawley Wood. Road access is at Glasshampton Bridge on the B4196, where there are footpaths along the brook in both directions. Here—and it is hard to realise it—you are in the midst of an important mid-seventeenth-century industrial site and the little brook, overhung by trees, is one of the earlier man-made navigations.

This is the county of Andrew Yarranton, born in Astley, a village a mile upstream of the bridge, who recorded his undertakings and aspirations in two volumes entitled *England's Improvements by Sea and Land* published in 1677 and 1681. Yarranton was a strong believer in water transport and put forward several schemes for siting granaries and various industrial enterprises by river navigations. In the second part of his book he referred to iron workings in Astley, of which no signs were evident until 1924, when the dam of an ornamental lake burst and disclosed remains which provided the essential clue. The remains were those of a round furnace that had once stood 12–15ft high on a square base. Subsequent investigation has established the ground plan of the site in some detail and has also shown that the life of the furnace was comparatively short as the lining was burnt out

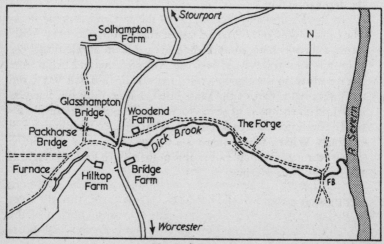

The Dick Brook

and there was no trace of any relining material.

From Glasshampton Bridge follow the track to Glasshampton Monastery, continue between two lodge cottages (pausing to admire the aviary of beautiful rare birds on your left) and turn into the wood where you will come to the Nutmells Stream which leads you to the furnace site. Don't expect to see anything impressive; it seems at first just a rough clearing in the wood with a few mounds and bits of stonework here and there. A large notice board will tell you that you are in the right place, however, and you will also see that this is an historic monument. Its connection with Yarranton cannot be conclusively proved, but it can rest as a reasonable assumption until more evidence appears.

The Nutmells Stream connected with the Dick Brook, which is crossed by a packhorse bridge a few hundred yards away—the bridge can be approached by a path from the road along the north side of the brook. This path can also be followed downstream towards the Severn. In $\frac{1}{2}$ mile you will see ahead of you a three-storey cottage and on your right a semi-cleared rough-and-tumble area bordering the brook. This is the site of a forge. Excavations have shown that it functioned also as a flint-grinding mill and a paper-mill; a heap of tin-plated buckles was also discovered. The works were powered by water from a leat taken off the brook near the bridge operating an overshot wheel on the north side. The forge and furnace were connected by a track—substantially the present footpath—which probably incorporated the packhorse bridge.

There is evidence at the forge site of wharves, so now we come to the navigational interest of the brook. To serve both forge and furnace the Dick Brook was made navigable, 2 locks being built in the bottom 300yd. If Yarranton's account can be relied on, the locks originally date from about 1653. The bottom lock is close to the junction with the Severn; to inspect it the best plan is to follow the path past Forge Cottage and carry on until you can cross the brook by a footbridge. This enables you to see the northern wall of the lock, the better preserved of the two. It is about 70ft long. Decide for yourself whether it was a pound or flash-lock; both suggestions have been made. Whichever it was, at this point cargoes would have been transhipped from the river barges or trows into tub-boats; unless the configuration of the brook has changed beyond the powers of nature, only tub-boats could have been hauled around its bends.

The site of the second lock is about 100yd above the footbridge and less easy to discover. Its dimensions have been adjudged similar to the other, but it does seem impossible that it was anything other than a flash-lock of some sort. It has been suggested that there might have been further flash-locks between the forge and the bridge, but there is no evidence and no apparent reason for their existence.

The Dick Brook and its associated sites provide an unexpected link with seventeenth-century industrial history. To get the full flavour of the area, and of the other enterprises with which he was associated, it is sensible to read Yarranton's own account, which brings you into contact with a man of remarkable energy and vision even if, at times, his imagination may have outrun his performance. In the 1660s he was a member of a group which extended the navigation of the Warwickshire Avon by building locks above Evesham and he also negotiated to improve the Salwarpe, although in this instance it seems that nothing was actually done. His largest undertaking was the Worcestershire Stour, on which he built several locks between Kidderminster and Stourbridge in 1665-7. He claimed that the river was then successfully used for coal traffic but that shortage of money prevented his plans from being completed. Floods, it is thought, destroyed the works in or about 1670 and they were not resumed. So the Dick Brook locks and the associated industrial sites remain his only tangible memorial.

OS sheet 150

The Arbury Canals

If you are cruising along the Coventry Canal between Nuneaton and Hawkesbury Junction you will notice the entrances to two short branches leading off to the west. The first of these is the Griff Hollows Canal, opened in 1787 to serve the colliery at Griff and carrying commercial traffic until the closure of the colliery in 1961. The canal itself remained navigable until the building of the Nuneaton Ring Road in 1973, and still supplies water to the Coventry Canal. A mile further south is the entrance to the Arbury canal system, a network of short private canals constructed in the Arbury Estate between 1769 and 1796. The water supply came from Seeswood Pool (you can see this from the

B4102, 2 miles north-east of Astley) and was used to power a corn-mill and a worsted-mill as well as provide for the lockage. It was Sir Roger Newdigate, mine-owner and MP, who developed this canal system out of the various streams, pools and leats on his estate. The total length of the system was 11,066yd; it included 13 locks, each 40ft by 6ft, the rise from the Coventry Canal to Seeswood Pool being 93ft 6in.

The canals were used for moving coal and carrying produce around the estate. After Sir Roger's death in 1806 their use declined and by 1819 the upper levels were no longer navigable. Weirs were constructed at the locks and the lock mechanisms and parts of the chambers were removed for use elsewhere on the estate. Only the communication canal that joined the network to the Coventry main line was usable after that date, apart from the Griff Hollows Canal which was not connected to the main system.

Arbury Hall, rebuilt by the energetic Sir Roger as a splendid example of the Gothic revival style, is open to the public at advertised times and you can examine the remains of some of the canal network on your visit. Here you are on the upper level. West of the hall is the Holly Kidd Double Lock and above it the Triple Lock, Y-shaped with two separate entrances from above. One led to the Seeswood Canal, constructed on the line of a feeder from Seeswood Pool, and the other to the short branch to Hall Pool, one of the pools on the estate where water was stored. At Hall Pool there was a boat-house and water was led down cascades to Garden Pool on the south-west side of the hall. This area has recently been cleared and restored and the Coventry Canal Society has cleaned out the double and triple locks and the connecting channel. This water near the hall was known as Swanland and was ornamental as well as useful. If you wish to inspect the rest of the upper level you will have to obtain permission from Mr F. H. M. Fitzroy Newdegate, Temple House, Arbury. This includes Seeswood Canal and Coton Lawn Canal. Garden Lock, south of the hall, has its chamber virtually intact, but it has been roofed over.

Of the lower level not much survives because of new roads and housing developments. Coventry Wood Upper Lock has been covered over in the garden of a house near Lane's Mill, but you may find a few remains of the lower lock. The Bedworth bypass destroyed a length of canal and much of Kenilworth Pool. There used to be a four-rise lock at Collycroft with an aqueduct across carrying water to the worsted-mill. The lock chambers survived until 1953 and were then obliterated by garages; the mill was demolished in 1966—Catherine Ward Hall, a residence for old people, has been built on its site. Griff Wharf was on the minor road to Arbury from the Nuneaton–Coventry road and was reached by a cut from the basin above Collycroft locks.

In 1819 Mary Ann Evans was born at The South Farm, daughter of the agent of the Arbury Estate at the time. She later became famous as George Eliot and her novels portray vividly the Warwickshire countryside in the years following the closure of the Arbury canals.

OS sheet 140

Some Birmingham Canals

With more than 50 miles of lost canals in the Birmingham area and with much of modern central Birmingham built on the site of old canal basins, it is not possible to do more than give a few indications of what might be found. Exploration by boat is, if possible, advisable as it is often only from a boat that the entrances to abandoned loops of the Birmingham Canal Navigations can be seen. A good cruising guide and a street map are essentials. If you are on foot, you might care to know that Baskerville House and the Hall of Memory stand on the site of Baskerville and Gibson's Basins and James Brindley Walk lies on the line of the Newhall Branch. Much of the canal redevelopment of the late 1960s by Farmer's Bridge was constructed on the wharves of this branch.

Motorway construction has done surprisingly little damage to the Birmingham canals, although it has made access more difficult. New roads are carried in tunnels across the main line near Galton Bridge. Close by are the three surviving Smethwick locks on the old upper level of the line, engineered by Smeaton. Above these locks near the Old Navigation Inn are traces of Brindley's original main line laid out in 1769. You can reach this area by walking along the main line from Farmer's Bridge or by approaching from the other direction via Engine Street, Oldbury.

Charles Hadfield in *Canals of the West Midlands* listed sixty branches of the BCN, of which almost half had been abandoned by 1961. He also gave a plan showing the terminal basins of the BCN in 1884 which gives a good idea of what lies beneath the segment bounded by the Birmingham & Fazeley and the Birmingham level of the main line. Another useful book is S. R. Broadbridge's *The Birmingham Canal Navigations, 1768-1846*, but the later volumes must be awaited for a full account.

An abandoned canal in this area that is practicable to follow is the Wyrley & Essington, closed from Birchills Junction to Huddlesford on the Coventry Canal in 1954. It is simpler to begin at Huddlesford, 2 miles west of Lichfield, by The Plough. The canal makes to the south of Lichfield, running alongside the A51 for a short stretch. It passes through Sandfields and is crossed by the A461 to the south of Pipehill. There are several locks on this canal and you should still find traces of some of them, although the bed is being—or has been—obliterated in many places. On the north-east side of Brownhills the Anglesey Branch came in from Chasewater Reservoir. From Brownhills to Horsley Fields in Birmingham the canal is still open. There was a proposal in 1975 to restore the Lichfield section, but too much had vanished by then.

OS sheets 128, 139

The Canals of Newcastle-under-Lyme

Of the three Newcastle-under-Lyme canals there are few traces left. Into the town from the Apedale collieries 3 miles north came Sir Nigel Gresley's Canal, which from 1776 to 1856 supplied Newcastle with coal. In 1798 this was extended a mile further south by the Newcastle-under-Lyme Junction Canal, whose promoters intended to connect their waterway with the 4 mile Newcastle-under-Lyme Canal, cut from the Trent & Mersey at Stoke and entering Newcastle from the south. The proposed connection was to be made by an inclined plane, as the Newcastle Canal was constructed on a lower level. The money was not forthcoming, however, and the incline was never built.

On the three short canals there were neither locks nor major engineering works. It is not surprising that so much of them has been obliterated, and in view of the road improvements in the area any account of the remains is likely to be soon out of date. Working from north to south, you look in the first instance for the site of the terminal basin of Gresley's Canal. Apedale Road leads off westward from the A52 at Chesterton and traces of the weed-choked basin are near Binley Farm. A football pitch has been created on the canal bed and the parapet of a bridge and the tops of two bridge arches may be discerned on Apedale Hall Road. Nearby, the lower basin still holds water and from here the canal can be seen heading south towards the ironworks. It crosses the valley on an embankment approaching the speedway stadium and then disappears in an area of spoil heaps.

Evidence of the Junction Canal lies behind houses on the south side of St Michael's Road and on the west side of Hempstall Lane. Brampton Bridge and the bricked-up arch of the bridge on Brunswick Street can also be found. Stubbs Walks on the south side of Brunswick Street lie on the final few yards of canal, and Occupation Street marks the position of the proposed inclined plane.

The basin of the Newcastle-under-Lyme Canal has been filled in. The section nearest the basin was closed in 1921, but a double row of trees by London Road Hospital denotes the line from the basin at Brook Lane. A length of canal bank lies behind Riverside Crescent, Trent Vale. The rest of the canal, from Trent Vale to the Trent & Mersey, was abandoned in 1935. A fine bridge at Racecourse Road survives with a length of canal bed at Oak Hill. In Boothen the Coronation Gardens lie on the canal and the Timothy Trew Memorial commemorates a tram conductor who was drowned in 1894 while rescuing a child who had fallen into the water. Corporation Street and Campbell Place both crossed the canal and indications can be found. A length of rather less than 100yd remains as moorings off the Trent & Mersey; this can be seen from the back of Stoke Town Hall. The junction with the Trent & Mersey is apparent from Glebe Street Bridge. Much of the Newcastle Canal was used for road widening as it was given to the Corporation of Stoke-on-Trent when the canal closed.

OS sheet 118

The Uttoxeter Branch of the Caldon Canal

In 1974 the restored Caldon Canal was reopened from Etruria to Froghall, a delightful waterway 17½ miles long. The length in the Churnet Valley from Cheddleton to Froghall past Consallforge and the Black Lion Inn is one of the most scenically remarkable in the country. There were many lime-kilns at Froghall, lime being brought by tramroad and inclined plane from Caldon Low for burning and carriage to Stoke by canal. The canal was initially successful and after a few years an extension to Uttoxeter was proposed. This was opened in 1811, but when in 1846 the North Staffordshire Railway bought the Trent & Mersey, including the Caldon, it required the Uttoxeter extension for the line of its Churnet Valley Branch and closed this length of canal in 1847.

Froghall lies on the north side of the A52 about 10 miles east of Stoke-on-Trent. To find traces of the branch follow the course of the old railway. After a bridge you may be able to make out the site of a coal wharf and, further along, the chamber of California Lock. There were more locks at Oakamoor, but they were obliterated when railway sidings were built. Between Oakamoor and Alton a road runs alongside the Churnet; it is advisable to follow this, cross the river at Alton by the entrance to Alton Towers, admire the Gothic railway station and follow the railway track. At Alton by the road-crossing there used to be a short tunnel. At Lord's Bridge the canal should be evident. It runs along the foot of Abbey Wood, diverging from the railway as it leaves the wood. The towpath should be discernible and along it an accommodation bridge, Seventy Bridge, may still survive. A few hundred yards on, the canal crossed the river on the level above Crumpwood Weir. The lock on the south bank of the river was called Flood Lock.

In Denstone the canal has been built over and it is doubtful whether there are any traces in Rocester either. On the west side of the B5030 Rocester-Uttoxeter road it was widened to form an ornamental lake in the grounds of Woodseat. Then it merged again with the railway, but you may be able to pick it up again on the east side of Stramshall by a white cottage. From here it swung westward to cross the River Tern by an iron trough aqueduct of which the abutments and traces of the central pier can be found. It entered Uttoxeter on the southern side of the A50; the basin at the north end of High Street has been filled in and a warehouse beside it has been converted into a factory.

There will be, I am sure, more to find of the Uttoxeter extension than has been mentioned here and its exploration takes you through a fascinating stretch of countryside.

OS sheet 128

Bibliography

BOOKS

Broadbridge, S. R., *The Birmingham Canal Navigations*, Vol 1 (David & Charles, 1974)

Cossons, N. and Trinder, B., *The Iron Bridge* (Humanities, 1979)

Hadfield, C., *Canals of the West Midlands* (David & Charles, 1969)

Trinder, Barrie, *The Industrial Revolution in Shropshire* (Phillimore, 1973)

ARTICLES AND BOOKLETS

'The Arbury Canals', Philip Weaver, Railway and Canal Historical Society *Journal*, Vol XVI, Nos 1 and 2 (January and April 1970)

'The Archaeology of the Montgomeryshire Canal', S. R. Hughes, *The Montgomeryshire Collection*, Vol 69 (1981)

The BCN, A Cruising Guide, K. D. Dunham and R. B. Manion (1969)

The Caldon Canal (The Caldon Canal Society)

'The Canal Inclined Planes of E. Shropshire', W. H. Williams, *Industrial Archaeology*, Vol 2, No 3

'The Froghall-Uttoxeter Canal', A. E. and E. M. Dodd, *North Staffs Journal of Field Studies* (1963)

(Several useful pamphlets are published by the Ironbridge Gorge Museum Trust)

SOCIETIES

BCN Society

Caldon Canal Society

Droitwich Canal Trust

Shropshire Union Canal Society

Upper Severn Navigation Trust

5

THE EAST MIDLANDS

Oxford Canal: The Old Loops

As originally constructed, the northern section of the Oxford Canal from Hawkesbury to Napton Junction followed the contours as if it was stuck to them. From Hawkesbury to Hillmorton it took the line of the 300ft contour; then, having ascended through three locks, it followed the 325ft contour to Napton. A 16 mile flight for a crow became a 44 mile voyage for a boat. To combat a proposal made in 1827 for a London & Birmingham Junction Canal—a wide waterway designed by Telford, which would have bypassed the Oxford completely—the Oxford company decided to modernise its own line. Within a few months plans were produced to shorten the line by nearly 14 miles, with embanked cuts and large aqueducts replacing the meandering loops. Although the London & Birmingham proposal eventually came to nothing, the Oxford went ahead with its scheme which, in view of the profits the company was making, it could well afford. In May 1834 the new line was opened. Not all the planned alterations were effected and the line was shortened by just over 11 miles.

Many traces can still be found of the Oxford Canal's disused loops. Handsome iron bridges carry the towpath of the present canal over the entrances of the loops. You will find one of them at Braunston, spanning the entrance to what is now the Ladyline Boatyard. The watered section of the loop now ends by the A45. It used to pass, however, under the road; then it swung westward past some cottages and turned south, to be crossed by the embankment of the railway from Weedon to Leamington which was built after this part of the canal was abandoned, as the railway has been for many years. You can find evidence of the canal bed on both sides of the embankment. It continues southward for

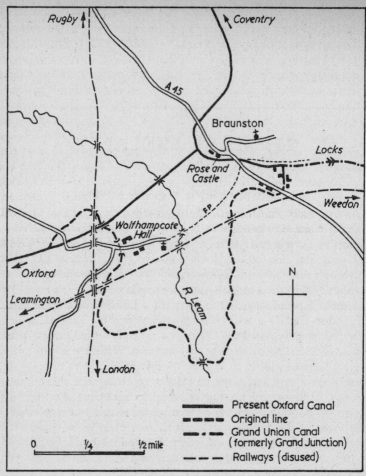

Oxford Canal loops (1)

over ½ mile, heading up the valley of the Leam. Then it turns sharply to the west to cross the valley on an embankment, with two culverts for the river. It made its way along the west side of the valley; much of the line is now obliterated, although its general direction around the hillside is clear. Soon it approaches the embankment of the old Great Central Railway and turns northward across the Weedon line again and around the west side of Wolfhampcote Hall. Beneath a minor road there is a dilapidated short tunnel with a towpath. The final length is watered and used for fishing. If you are exploring this loop it is worth

taking the lane to the restored church of St Peter in the deserted
village of Wolfhampcote. The loop continues for a short distance
on the north side of the present canal. This Wolfhampcote loop is
nearly 3¼ miles long and is replaced by about a mile of straight
canal with a cutting, a large embankment and a three-arch aqueduct over the Leam.

Another sizeable disused loop is at Clifton, on the north-east
side of Rugby. The canal is crossed by the A427 Rugby-Market
Harborough road. If you are on the towpath you will then see the
abutments of a railway bridge and, on the right-hand bank, a
reedy inlet. This is the entrance to the Clifton loop with a brick
bridge a short distance along it. This was the original Bridge 60.
Bridge 59 can be found some 500yd further on at the end of a lane
from Clifton-upon-Dinsmore. The line, barely distinguishable,
continues for a further 500yd before turning sharply north-west
to the site of an aqueduct over the Avon. It then takes up the
contour on the northern side of the valley, is crossed by a railway
embankment and rejoins the canal close to the present Avon

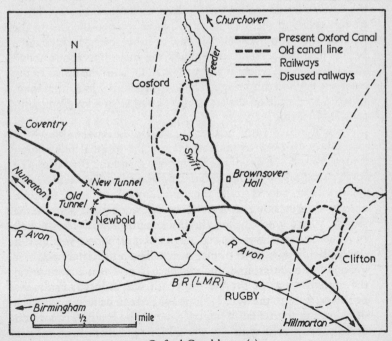

Oxford Canal loops (2)

Aqueduct. The length of the Clifton loop is just over $1\frac{1}{2}$ miles, replaced by 700yd of embanked canal.

On the west side of the A426 road-crossing, a feeder enters the canal from the north, bringing water from the River Swift upstream. This feeder was part of another loop of the original Oxford Canal; it skirts the grounds of Brownsover Hall and is spanned by Bridge 54. In 2 miles the loop line turns sharply west, having reached the point at which James Brindley, the canal's first engineer and surveyor, deemed it expedient to take the canal across the Swift valley and river. The feeder arm is still supplied by a narrower channel running in from the north. The loop is embanked over the valley and a crumbling two-arch aqueduct takes the bed over the Swift. At Cosford there was a wharf, whence the line headed southward keeping close to the Cosford road. Much of this length has been eliminated by ploughing and industrial building. The Cosford loop continues on the south side of the present main line, the first section of it being the arm leading to the Willow Wren cruiser base at Rugby Wharf, which also used to be served by the Midland Counties Railway. There are few traces of the loop once you have reached the end of the watered arm; you may follow some of it by noting hedges and a path in a housing estate. It rejoined the main line about 400yd before Bridge 51. There is another small loop on the north of the canal just beyond this bridge. The Cosford loop was 4 miles long, replaced by $\frac{3}{4}$ mile of almost straight canal with a long embankment and cutting.

A few hundred yards further on, the B4112 Rugby-Newbold road edges up close to the canal. Here the original line swung abruptly south in front of the Barley Mow and the Boat Inn. The north portal of the old Newbold Tunnel was on the north side of the road; the tunnel took the canal under the road and the churchyard emerging in a field on the south-west side of the church, where you can find the brick south portal. The tunnel, some 400ft long, was altered during construction for fear it would affect the stability of the church. The northern section was wider, with a flatter arch; the southern part was made elliptical and the width of the wooden towpath was reduced. From the south portal the depression of the canal bed can be seen making its way through the fields. It ran up close to the Rugby-Nuneaton railway line, was bridged by the minor road from Newbold to Little Lawford and rejoined the present main line on the west side of the B4112 road bridge. On the new main line the tunnel was replaced by one of generous dimensions with a towpath each side of a channel wide enough for two narrow boats to pass.

A mile further westward another loop on the south side of the present line was bypassed between Bridges 43 and 42, near Cathiron. At Brinklow the channel was widened by the construction of an embankment alongside Brindley's eleven-arch aqueduct and, when the line was straightened at Brinklow and Stretton, sections of the loop became short branches leading to wharves. There was another loop just past the M6 motorway-crossing; this skirted Nettle Hill on the south side of the present line and Hopsford Hall on the north. The line was also straightened at Ansty and at the length known as Wyken Straight, but the Wyken arm, now used as moorings, was made in 1840 as a privately built branch to Wyken New Colliery.

The excessively tortuous line of the original North Oxford is not especially characteristic of Brindley and may owe something to his successor, Samuel Simcock. When Brindley died, in 1772, construction had reached only from the junction with the Coventry Canal to Brinklow. Charles Hadfield points out that the extraordinary loop at Wormleighton on the southern section was laid out by Simcock who seemed to have an aversion to locks or major engineering works. The Wormleighton loop was never bypassed and cruising it gives you a taste of the leisurely character of the old canal—and perhaps some idea of the frustration the old boatmen must sometimes have felt.

OS sheet 151

The Grand Union Canal Branches

The Wendover Branch
The Wendover arm of the old Grand Junction Canal was completed four years before the more important branch to Buckingham. Both were authorised by an act passed in 1794, but the short arm to Wendover, whose main purpose was to feed water to the Tring summit, took only a little over two years to complete. Unfortunately, it was not much of an asset to the main line. Throughout the nineteenth century it leaked, losing not only the water it was intended to supply but also draining water from the main canal—eventually a stop-lock had to be built at Tringford

to prevent this. There was some, but not much, commercial traffic on the arm, although the persistent leakage did not encourage carriers to use it. The canal above Tringford was closed to navigation in 1904 and much of it was drained; the top 1½ miles are still open and navigable, but longer boats venturing in may have to come out in reverse as there are no winding holes.

Wendover has a Wharf Road, along which you will find a stream, known as Well Head, and a footpath which leads you to the site of the wharf—the winding hole near the entrance to the wharf is discernible. You can follow the canal, parts of which are watered, out into the country, noting traces of the old branch railway line to Halton. A wide watered stretch is followed by a masonry and iron bridge. The next bridge, at Halton, has been lowered, but a fine iron bridge bearing the monogram of the Rothschilds—the area around Tring was Rothschild country— survives. After passing RAF Halton, the canal skirts the southeast border of the Rothschild estate of Green Park and arrives at Bucklandwharf, a self-explanatory name for this small outpost of Buckland village. Here there are a pub and a few canal cottages as well as the site of the wharf itself.

A short distance further on, the water of the Wendover arm is taken off to feed into Wilstone Reservoir. Between here and the old stop-lock at Tringford, a distance of about 1½ miles, the channel is dry but is easily followed. Tringford Pumping Station, which dates from 1818 and once housed a Boulton & Watt beam-engine, is now electrically operated and stands near the beginning of the navigable section of the arm. On this section you will find New Mill and the site of a firm of boat-builders, Bushell Brothers, which was still building wide boats for the Grand Union Canal Company in the 1930s. The arm meets the main line a few hundred yards to the west of Bulbourne Maintenance Yard. A mile to the west at Marsworth is the junction with the Aylesbury arm, now happily free from the threat of abandonment.

The Newport Pagnell Canal

The Grand Union Canal continues northward through Milton Keynes until at Great Linford it turns to the west to run for some miles along the plain of the Great Ouse. Between 1814 and 1864 there was a connection from here to Newport Pagnell by a canal 1¼ miles long with 7 narrow locks. For a few decades it was a profitable undertaking, carrying several thousand tons of coal a

year and other cargoes at higher than average rates. Trade fell off
after the opening of the London & Birmingham Railway and,
when a Newport Pagnell Railway was mooted, the canal company sold out to it. The railway, long since gone, used the course
of the canal for much of its own line.

Few traces of the Newport Pagnell Canal can now be found.
Walking along the towpath westward from the road bridge by
the Black Horse midway between Wolverton and Newport Pagnell, you soon come to a detached house. This used to be the Old
Wharf Inn and behind it is the lock-keeper's house on the branch.
So much new building is taking place in this area that it would be
misleading to try to describe the remains of the canal, but it runs
parallel to, and within ½ mile of, the road into Newport Pagnell.
The seven locks were all obliterated many years ago. In Newport
Pagnell the railway station and goods yard were built on the site
of the canal basin and public wharf; these in their turn were
replaced in the 1970s by new industrial buildings. The Swan
Revived in the centre of the town is now about the only reminder: here the canal committee held its first meetings in 1814.

The Old Stratford and Buckingham Branch
This branch was opened in 1801. To find the junction with the
main line make for the village of Cosgrove and walk south along
the towpath from the fine stone bridge. The branch swings off
just above Cosgrove Lock; it looks a good, healthy stretch of
water, but not for long. The construction of a new road has
hindered plans for restoration up to Old Stratford.

At Old Stratford on the A5, just south of the traffic lights at the
junction with the A422 Buckingham road, Wharf Lane leads to
the site of Old Stratford Wharf, now private property. You can
trace the outline of the wharf and the channel; there is also a brick
warehouse, now used as a garage. Below ground are large brick-
built vaults, once used for storage. They may be unique; certainly
I have not come across similar underground facilities at any other
disused canal wharf. From 1870 until 1923 this wharf was used by
the boat-building firm of Edward Hayes, the warehouse then
being a workshop. Hayes opened an agricultural engineering
works in Stony Stratford in 1840. Later he turned to boat engines
and then to building the boats themselves. When completed, the
hulls were towed along the main road (Watling Street) by horse
or tractor, edged into Wharf Lane and launched sideways into the

canal, an occasion for public rejoicing and entertainment—especially if things did not go right first time. The boats themselves were built to particular specifications: they had to be able to pass the Grand Junction locks and they could not draw more than 4ft. Boats longer than 70ft were built and moved in sections, to be assembled at their eventual destination. Hayes & Co mainly built tugs and launches, many for overseas buyers. Some were fitted out at Old Stratford, but the superstructures, unable to pass under canal bridges, were added at Brentford. From Brentford they might go down to London Docks or up the Thames and through the Kennet & Avon to Bristol.

The Old Stratford Cut, as this length was called, joined the Buckingham Branch about 100yd from the wharf. The branch passed under Watling Street just north of the traffic lights referred to. This long bridge, sometimes described as a tunnel, is being incorporated into the adjoining property and may in time be transmogrified into a cocktail bar. For the 9 miles to Buckingham, the branch keeps close to the A422. For the first 2 miles it lies on the northern side, crossing fields and circling around the village of Deanshanger, where you may find a wharf house by Bridge 9. South of the village the road crosses the canal, which remains between the road and the Great Ouse for the rest of its course. You can follow it easily on the current OS map, although the sections shown as watered may not be so. By road you can find the sites of Thornton and Leckhampstead wharves. The canal, which runs round the southern border of a lake and past the Old Mill House, coincides briefly with the river. The two waterways then make a U-turn southward and return towards the A422 on the approach to Buckingham. Much of the final length of the canal has been obliterated by new housing, but the basin can be found behind a garage on the south of the road entering the town, with buildings that were once canal warehouses around it. A few yards away is the Grand Junction Inn.

Navigation to Buckingham ended in 1910, although the section of the branch from the main line to Deanshanger was not closed until 1961. Had it lasted a few years longer the canal restoration movement might have been able to ensure its survival—and, indeed, the revivifying of the whole branch. It is now too late, however, and another asset has gone to waste.

OS sheets 152, 165

The Charnwood Forest Branch of the Leicester Navigation

The Forest line of the Leicester Navigation was made up of lengths of both canal and tramroad intended to serve collieries at Coleorton and Swannington. This it did for a couple of years, and that was all. It was opened in 1794 but lacked sufficient water for regular traffic. To remedy this a reservoir was constructed at Blackwood, being completed in 1797. The coal began to move until in February 1799 the reservoir burst under pressure of flood-water, which also destroyed an aqueduct and part of the canal embankment. Repairs were effected, but by the time the line was usable again local interest had waned and further damage led the proprietors to try to abandon the canal. They were unable to do this until 1848 owing to opposition in Parliament.

There were no locks on the line, but some of its bed may still be discerned. There was a tramroad between the Leicester Navigation at Loughborough and the village of Nanpantan, which is 2½ miles south-west of Loughborough on the B5350. A public footpath 300yd east of the cross-roads in the centre of the village is the towpath of the canal and can be followed through a golf course as far as the embankment of the M1. To the west of the motorway it wanders between Shepshed and the A512; Shepshed Cemetery lies on top of it. Five minor roads heading north off the A512 all cross its course; the bridges have been lowered, but the canal is not hard to find. South of Osgathorpe the line divided at a toll-collector's house called Junction House. One branch went north-west for ¾ mile to the foot of Barrow Hill; the other ended by the main road near Thringstone Bridge close to the drive to Cinder Hill Farm.

OS sheet 129

The Melton Mowbray Navigation and the Oakham Canal

For over forty years there was a waterway junction of some importance at the foot of Burton Street, Melton Mowbray. Here was the basin constructed in the 1790s for the Wreak (or Melton Mowbray) Navigation, later shared by the Oakham Canal opened in 1803. The basin was to the north of the river bridge, close to the present Boat Inn. The Wreak connected the town to the Leicester Canal at Cossington, 14¾ miles to the west, while the canal wandered away south-eastward to Oakham, 15¼ miles by water but just over 9 miles by crow. Navigation on the Wreak continued until 1877 when there was insufficient traffic to show a profit; on the canal it ceased in 1846 when it was bought and closed by the Midland Railway.

The Wreak, for the most part, has reverted to natural river, but many of the twelve locks can still be found, their brick chambers crumbling away. There are locks at Ratcliffe, Brooksby and Asfordby, all easy to find as they are situated close to bridges. Many of the navigation bridges also survive, some of them with double arches. Some of the lock cuts, made to bypass mills, are now dry, but mostly they are still traceable. The A607 road from Melton towards Leicester runs on the south side of the river and the minor road from Asfordby to Ratcliffe is close to the northern bank. The Wreak is a good example of a non-tidal inland river navigation, of which there never were many, and has retained more of its structures than one usually finds.

The Oakham Canal is not so accessible and there is not much of it left. It left Melton on the south side of the B676, close to the River Eye. Some of its bed was used by the railway which bought it. By Wyfordby level-crossing some traces may be visible; south of the crossing is the site of a wharf where the canal's only boat-owner used to operate. The canal swings along the eastern side of Stapleford Park, where the too intrepid explorer may find himself confronted with a lion. It is safer to make for Edmondthorpe where there is an embankment south of the village. West of Market Overton on the road to Teigh there is a wharf, its buildings still standing and inhabited, and an attractive length of canal. The line follows the contours southward through fields with the site of Cottesmore Wharf on the Ashwell–Cottesmore road. The next road that crosses it is the Ashwell–Oakham road; look for the kennels of the Cottesmore Hunt and a prison. You can find the canal a short way along the turning to Langham and walk beside it for ½ mile towards Oakham; this stretch is used for angling. On the approach to Oakham the canal lies at the rear of Springfield House and Catmose Vale Hospital. The wharf site is now occupied by Oakham School and a canal warehouse has been converted into the school hall.

On the Oakham Canal there were no fewer than 19 locks, 72ft by 14ft 2in. Although the canal was closed so long ago, I doubt if all the sites have been obliterated entirely. The publication of an up-to-date survey of the remains of this waterway would be welcome.

OS sheets 129, 141

The Grantham Canal

The Grantham Canal, a 33 mile waterway wandering across the Vale of Belvoir from Grantham to the Trent at West Bridgford, was opened in 1797, traded successfully into the mid-nineteenth century and then sold out to a railway company when threatened with competition. Regular trading ended in 1917, but boat movements continued until 1936 when the London & North Eastern Railway refused to meet the cost of new lock gates and abandoned the canal. In fact, the gates survived for some time, but their remnants were removed in the 1950s, the locks were weired and several road bridges levelled. Then the Grantham became one of the first canals to be considered for restoration. The watercourse itself remains open, and there are no tunnels or major aqueducts on the line. The main obstacle is plans for open-cast mining in the vale and the future of the canal is uncertain.

The canal lies south of the A52 Grantham-Nottingham road and is clearly marked on the OS sheets, so finding it is no problem. Grantham Basin has gone and you find the canal on the west side of the town between the hospital and the railway line. You can walk the towpath to the A1 crossing and thence for almost all the length; much of the towpath has been cleared recently by volunteers of the Canal Restoration Society. Many wharves and locks are still shown on the maps. The length by Cropwell Bishop, where the canal was cut across gypsum beds, always leaked and is often dry. The condition deteriorates west of the A46 and a new cut might be necessary if navigation is to return.

The Grantham Canal fits into the landscape more like a river than a canal; in this country of wide fields, gentle hills and little villages it has become an essential feature.

OS sheets 129, 130

The Derby Canal

Today, very little evidence can be found of the existence of the

Derby Canal. It was opened in 1796, connecting Derby to the Erewash Canal, 8 miles east, and the Trent & Mersey, 5 miles south. There was also a short branch from Derby to Little Eaton where there was a tramroad connection for coal traffic. It was quite a prosperous undertaking in its first few decades, but its proprietors, unlike those of other Midland canals, never amalgamated with any other company and never sold out to a railway. They were not moved, it seems, by sentiment or belief in the future of inland navigation but wanted rather to dispose of it for commercial land development. For many years they were frustrated by ICI, who continued to use the canal, but in 1964 the waterway was closed.

In Derby itself, almost all the traces of the canal have now gone. There used to be a special reason for canal historians to visit the city—to see the cast-iron Holmes Aqueduct, designed by Benjamin Outram and completed in 1796, the first to be made in this material, just anticipating the more famous example at Longdon-upon-Tern. It was 45ft long and took the canal over a mill stream. It became incorporated into a road bridge opposite the bus station. During recent reconstruction three panels were removed to be preserved in the Derby Industrial Museum but, owing to an error in the City Engineer's Department, they were sent for scrap. All that is left now is a bridge taking the railway line over the road access to the locomotive works, north of Derby Station. This road used to be a canal and the towpath is visible. The bridge itself was built by Stephenson. Near here is Canal Street and traces of a short arm that served factories in this area. On the London road a mile from the city centre there are signs of the canal near Wilmorton College as well as a bridge. The dedicated enthusiast can try his best with the Little Eaton Branch.

The towpath between Derby and Long Eaton has become a public footpath and the disgraceful rat-infested mess that the canal company left behind is being tidied up with the help of the Ramblers' Association. To the south the canal bed has gone, but it is possible to pick up clues such as the alignments of paths to enable you to follow its course. The junction with the Trent & Mersey at Swarkestone is in water up to the first bridge and used as moorings by a boat club, with the canal cottage as headquarters.

OS sheets 128, 129

The Nutbrook Canal

This short canal was opened in 1796 to carry coal from mines in the Shipley and West Hallam areas to the Erewash Canal and thence throughout the Midlands. Later, it served the iron and steel works that developed in this district for both carriage of goods and water supply. It was bought by the Stanton Ironworks Company in 1946 and traffic ended three years later. Since then, much of the line has been obliterated. It ran in a south-easterly direction from a reservoir at Shipley Hall (now demolished) on the north-west of Ilkeston, was crossed by the A609 by the golf course and by the B6001 between Kirk Hallam and Little Hallam. At New Stanton it swung eastward through the Stanton Works, locking into the Erewash south of Trowell. There were 13 locks in its 4½ miles. A detailed history of the canal, by Peter Stevenson, was published in 1970.

OS sheet 129

The Nottingham Canal

The intention of the promoters of the Nottingham Canal was to provide a direct route into the city for goods originating from the Cromford Canal, which otherwise would follow a circuitous route along the Erewash Canal and the Trent. It was cut from the Trent, to the west of Trent Bridge and nearly opposite the junction of the Grantham Canal with the river, through the centre of Nottingham, joining the Beeston Cut at Lenton; it climbed out of the city on the eastern side and then turned north along the Erewash Valley to the basin it shared with the Cromford Canal at Langley Mill, a total distance of 14¾ miles. Several short branches were also made, some of them private.

The Nottingham Canal enjoyed about fifty years of reasonably profitable life, co-operating usefully with both the Cromford and Grantham Canals. With the Grantham Canal it was transferred to railway ownership in 1855. Trade continued well into the present century, mostly short-haul in the area of Nottingham itself, but by 1928 most of it had ceased. Apart from the length from the Trent to the Beeston Cut, the canal was abandoned in 1937.

From Chain Lane in Lenton the waters of the River Leen have been diverted into the course of the canal for a short distance.

Where the A52 Derby road crosses, the old canal bridge can still be seen. The canal line then enters the Raleigh Works where it may be possible to find the remains of lock chambers. The Nottingham Ring Road crosses the canal at the end of Radford Bridge Road; a public footpath takes you under the bridge where you may see the remains of Lock 6. Housing has obliterated the next length, but at Wollaton on the north side of the A609, about 3 miles from the city centre, you can discover the derelict chambers of the top 7 of the Wollaton flight of 14 locks; not a happy sight, and it is sad that, over the years, neither the local authority nor any private body has thought fit to preserve or tidy up this area. At the top of the flight the canal vanishes again, this time under the Ballon Woods Housing Estate. West of the estate, however, the line is in water and is stocked for fishing.

The A609 takes you across the M1 motorway, beneath which the canal is culverted. It is still watered at Trowell; you can follow it by road through taking a turn northward a few hundred yards after the motorway-crossing. Look out for the junction with the branch to Robbinetts. The canal swings to the west of Cossall, where an aqueduct has been culverted, and is embanked on the west side of Cossall Marsh. Still in water it circles Awsworth and continues as far as Newthorpe where open-cast mining extinguishes it for some distance, although a drainage ditch indicates the line with near accuracy. When it reappears on the south-west side of Eastwood—the birthplace of D. H. Lawrence, who refers to the canal in *Sons and Lovers*—it is in poor condition, but you may find a reconstructed wooden swing-bridge and a brick bridge on the Tinsley road. The final 300yd before the basin have been filled in.

A Nottingham Canal Society was founded in 1976 and achieved some success in preserving a stretch of canal at Trowell. Unfortunately, enough local support has not been forthcoming and what is left of the canal must be considered in jeopardy.

OS sheets 120, 129

The Cromford Canal

Of the East Midlands canals, the Cromford is the most varied and interesting. It was opened in 1794, just over 14½ miles long from Cromford—home of the cotton-mills of Sir Richard

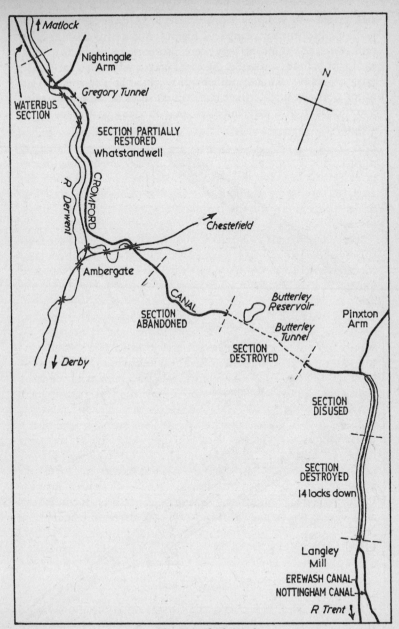

The Cromford Canal

Arkwright—to Langley Mill, where it met the Erewash and, later, the Nottingham canals. William Jessop and Benjamin Outram were the engineers; they were also partners in the Butterley company whose ironworks the canal was to serve. Several mines, quarries, leadworks and another ironworks at Somercotes also lay on or near the line of the canal, which soon became busy with commercial traffic, carrying over 300,000 tons a year in the 1830s and 40s.

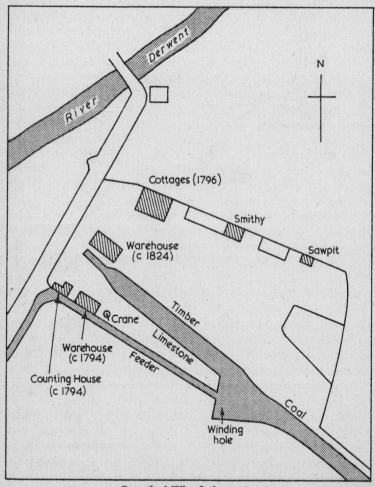

Cromford Wharf, about 1830

A look at a map of the Midlands in the early nineteenth century would show an obvious gap in the transport system between the two basins of the Peak Forest Canal and Cromford. To reach Manchester and Liverpool, goods from the Nottingham and Derby area had to travel a long roundabout route via Stoke on the Trent & Mersey. A canal connection was impractical owing to the hilly countryside, but in 1831 the gap was closed by the building of the Cromford & High Peak Railway, linking with the Peak Forest Canal at Whaley Bridge. The gradients were mastered by stationary steam-engines drawing trucks up the steep inclines. High Peak Wharf, where goods were transferred between the canal and railway, is a mile from the Cromford Canal wharf and opposite the Leawood Pump House. You can see the course of the railway diagonally ascending the hillside.

First, though, there is Cromford Wharf itself. This is opposite the parish church, built by Arkwright. The first of Arkwright's cotton-spinning mills stands by the road and many of the cottages were built to house the mill-workers. Most of the wharf area is now a car park, but you can see two warehouses, the wharfinger's office and a few smaller buildings. The feeder arm runs by the office, with a winding hole for the 70ft boats by its junction with the main canal at the east end of the wharf.

Thanks to the Cromford Canal Society you can travel from the wharf to Leawood Pump House by horse-drawn boat, a service which began in late 1977; or, if the boat is not running, you can appreciate the towpath which the society has cleared. The pump was installed in 1849 to overcome water shortages caused by an altered pattern of land drainage and the diverting of a drain which fed the canal. The pump draws water from the Derwent through a 150yd long tunnel to a reservoir beneath the pump-house, then lifts it 30ft into the canal (the present tense is accurate as the pump was restored in 1979 and can be seen in steam on certain week-ends during the summer). It is, in fact, a beam-engine similar to the much earlier Boulton & Watt pattern; the beam is 33ft long and the plunger weighs 10 tons.

Just past the pump the canal is carried over the Derwent on the Wigwell Aqueduct. This has a single span of 80yd and was designed by Jessop. A crack appeared shortly after it was completed; Jessop acknowledged responsibility for using unsuitable materials and repaired it at his own cost. 'I think it common Justice that no one ought to suffer for the faults of another,' he said, a sentiment that perhaps not every canal engineer shared. It is a splendid masonry structure and in good condition today. On the northern side of the aqueduct, which can be crossed by either of two swing bridges, is the short Nightingale arm which once served Lea Mills.

The towpath can be followed to Ambergate, where the watered section of the canal ends. Canal, river, railway line and the A6 trunk road share the narrow Derwent Valley, with woods rising steeply on either side. Canal Society members are working on the length from the aqueduct to the short Gregory Tunnel and a second boat will be launched here in the near future. The intention is that boat trips will extend to Whatstandwell eventually and the length from Whatstandwell to Ambergate will become an official nature reserve. There are few points of access from the road, but the towpath walk, with Crich Chase on one side and Shining Cliff Woods on the other, is very pleasant.

From Ambergate to Langley Mill only fragments of the canal remain. The line swings eastward to follow the River Amber, but Bull Bridge Aqueduct that took it over this river was demolished in 1968. A gasworks was also built on the canal. For 3 miles the A610 Nottingham road runs very close to the Cromford. By the junction with the B6013 you can find some traces; there used to be a short tunnel by the boundary of a transport-café car park. If you continue into Ripley and take a minor road heading north to Pentrich you come in about ½ mile to a settlement called Hammersmith. A lane beside a playground takes you beneath railway bridges, past a sewage farm and to a path that crosses the top of the west portal of Butterley Tunnel and leads down to the towpath. Note the massive battered stone wall in which the portal is set; the tunnel was extended to this point when the railway above it was built.

Butterley Tunnel, about 3,000yd long, was built to take narrow boats although the locks below it were wide. At its completion, it was the third longest canal tunnel; it was made comparatively speedily and a reservoir was constructed on top of it. Mining under it by the Butterley company caused subsidence; the tunnel was closed between 1889 and 1893 and again in 1900, this time never to reopen.

The tunnel's east portal is midway between Butterley and Ironville. A cross-roads by the Newlands Inn, north-east of Ripley, has the towpath on its northern side. Follow the towpath towards Butterley into what is imaginatively known as the Golden Valley. In about 200yd you come to the portal, a surprisingly insignificant hole in the hill face, with water cascading down the hillside from the reservoir above. The portal is silted up, but all the same the bore was one of the most restricted of all the major canal tunnels.

At Ironville the canal is in evidence and you can see the junction with the short Pinxton Branch. Ironville itself has its own fascination as a relic of Victorian industrial housing; here lived the work-force of the Butterley company, unable to escape the influence of their employers even in the very name of their settlement. There is water in the canal and the wide lock-chambers are in good condition.

After Ironville the Cromford swings south. This last stretch has been almost entirely obliterated. It runs close to the River Erewash and a railway line; if you wish to examine it, take the minor road south from Ironville to Langley Mill and then the left turn to Stoneyford. The Boat Inn is within a few yards of the canal line. The minor road joins the A610; two left turns from this road also take you to the course of the Cromford. At Langley Mill the Great Northern Basin, where the Cromford and Nottingham Canals connected, was cleared out by volunteers and reopened in 1973 to make a new terminal basin for the Erewash Canal.

The restored section of the Cromford Canal is a tribute not only to the canal society but also to Derbyshire County Council which supported and aided the society's work. Some idea of the present amenity value of the canal can be gained from the total of 12,000 people who enjoyed trips on the society's boat between April and September 1980; such is the demand that a second boat has been purchased and is being renovated for service. There are also plans for a museum at Cromford Wharf, which will make a valuable counterpart to the tramway museum at nearby Crich.

OS sheet 119

The Chesterfield Canal above Worksop

The Chesterfield Canal was opened in 1777, 46 miles long from Chesterfield to the Trent at West Stockwith, with 65 locks and a long tunnel. More than half of it, from Worksop to the Trent, is still open. Commercial traffic on this section ended in 1955, but in recent years the canal has become popular with pleasure cruisers and the basin at West Stockwith, once so full with narrow boats that you could walk across it from boat to boat without jumping, is a useful harbour for boats using the Trent. Above Worksop, however, the canal gave trouble for many years owing to subsidence through mining operations and problems with the tunnel. Much of the canal company's revenue was required for tunnel repairs until in 1908 a collapse closed it finally. This put an end to all traffic above Worksop and the upper canal gradually fell into decay. In 1976 the Chesterfield Canal Society was founded and if you visit the upper canal now you will see plenty of evidence of restoration work in progress.

In Chesterfield you can find the canal to the north of the town; take the A619 Staveley road and turn on to the B6050, Lockoford Lane. This takes you to the canal and you can walk along the towpath towards Chesterfield until the canal merges with the River Rother. There were five locks down from Chesterfield, with the descent ending at the entrance to Staveley Ironworks, served by the canal for many years. The line of the Chesterfield–Rotherham railway is close for several miles; this is a rough and desolate stretch, access to which is difficult. You can try searching at Renishaw and on the west side of Killamarsh; fragments of the canal, on which there were fourteen locks lifting it towards its summit, may still survive here and there.

From Killamarsh, the A618 heads north for Rotherham. In less than a mile it crosses the canal at Norwood. Look for a white house on the east side of the road; this was the Boatman Inn and stands at the foot of the Norwood flight of 13 locks, consisting of one four-lock staircase and three triples. The canal society takes a special interest in this area and is clearing and preserving the site. At the top of the flight is the bricked-up portal of Norwood Tunnel, 2,850yd long as built but extended to 3,102yd at the eastern end when the railway was made. The M1 crosses the line of the tunnel close to the western portal and to continue you must drive a further mile north on the A618, turning right on to the B6059 for Kiveton.

The canal lies just to the south of Kiveton Park Station and is easily followed to a deep cutting and the eastern portal of Norwood Tunnel, also bricked up. On this part of the summit pound the canal society, having cleared the towpath, proposes to run a trip boat when dredging of the canal has been completed.

Between Kiveton and Worksop the canal and railway run close together, the canal on the southern side. It is an attractive stretch, much of it through woodland, and there are 30 locks in the 5 miles, bringing the canal down two-thirds of the gradient to the Trent. The only way to explore is to follow the towpath; but if you have no time, take the minor road from Kiveton to Thorpe Salvin and continue for another 1¼ miles until you come to a lane leading to Turner Wood. The village—or settlement, rather—lies alongside a pound which has been cleaned out and the banks planted with flowers. There are ruined locks at each end and you can battle along the towpath in either direction.

The Thorpe Salvin road leads you into Worksop; it crosses the canal at Shireoaks and accompanies it towards the town. Morse Lock marks the beginning of the navigable section of the Chesterfield, which is well worth following through the centre of Worksop. Note the Canal Tavern (once the less euphonious Gas Tavern), a real old canalside pub. A fine warehouse straddles the canal nearby. Twelve hours' walk—or voyage—away is West Stockwith; if you are continuing, note the change in scale when the wide locks begin on the stretch from Retford to the Trent. The Chesterfield was first surveyed by James Brindley, who planned it as a narrow canal—narrower than most, in fact, as the locks were only 6ft 11in wide. The six wide locks were installed while the canal was building and were paid for by nine shareholders and Retford Corporation.

As you examine the Norwood-Worksop section, consider the difficulties that would have to be overcome to make it navigable once again. Here it is not a matter of having to deal with the massive barriers of motorways or the disappearance of major structures, but with the more mundane problems of water supply and heavy lockage. Solutions to these problems would be very welcome.

OS sheets 119, 120

Bibliography

BOOKS
Compton, Hugh, *The Oxford Canal* (David & Charles, 1977)
Faulkner, A. H., *The Grand Junction Canal* (David & Charles, 1973)
Hadfield, C., *Canals of the East Midlands* (David & Charles, 1970)

Hassall, John, *Tour of the Grand Junction Canal* (1819, Cranfield & Bonfiel, rep 1968)

Stevens, Philip, *The Leicester Line* (David & Charles, 1972)

Stevenson, Peter, *The Nutbrook Canal, Derbyshire* (David & Charles, 1970)

Tew, David, *The Oakham Canal* (Brewhouse Press, 1968)

ARTICLES AND BOOKLETS

The Aylesbury and Wendover Canals, Bob and Elizabeth Bush (Aylesbury Canal Society, nd)

'The Oxford Canal', K. G. Parrott, RCHS *Journal*, Vol XVIII, No 4, and Vol XXII, No 2 (1972 and 1976)

SOCIETIES

Aylesbury Canal Society
Chesterfield Canal Society
Cromford Canal Society
Grantham Canal Restoration Society Ltd
Nottingham Canal Society

6

THE EASTERN COUNTIES

The Ipswich & Stowmarket Navigation

The Gipping is a little-known river, overshadowed by its famous and more controversial neighbour the Stour. Three tributaries unite to form the main channel which flows through the busy market town of Stowmarket and thence south-eastward to Ipswich where it widens into its estuary, changing its name to the Orwell. To some extent it was used for navigation in medieval times, but not until the closing years of the eighteenth century was it improved. Both Jessop and Rennie were involved in the planning and in 1793 the Ipswich & Stowmarket Navigation was opened, nearly 17 miles long with 15 locks of similar dimensions to those on another Rennie undertaking nearby, the Chelmer & Blackwater, taking barges 52ft 6in by 13ft 6in. The lock cuts were comparatively short and no major engineering works were needed.

A moderate trade soon developed and the prosperity of Stowmarket increased. A through voyage took 7-10 hours and in the early 1800s there were generally more than 30 passages a week. In 1846 the navigation was leased to the Eastern Union Extension Railway which had opened its Ipswich-Stowmarket line along the Gipping Valley; the Great Eastern Railway (which developed out of the Eastern Union) did not wish to renew the lease and in 1888 the navigation reverted to its own trustees. Trade to Stowmarket, where there was an explosives factory, ended in about 1910 and for the next few years the only traffic was between Ipswich and Bramford. This ended in 1929 and three years later the navigation was officially abandoned.

You can walk the length of the Gipping along the towpath, now a public right-of-way; the only obstacles you are likely to meet are dedicated anglers surrounded by tackle. By car it is not

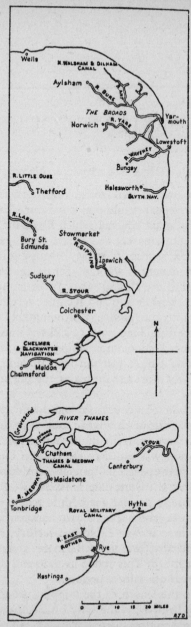

The Eastern Counties (1)

so easy; the recently improved A45 runs close to the navigation for almost all of its length, but once on this road you may find it hard to escape. You need to keep to the minor roads and have a good map-reader.

The head of navigation in Stowmarket was below Stowupland Bridge on the A1120, close to the railway station. There are some fine buildings along the towpath, including a splendid maltings now converted into a pub and restaurant. Except by the bridge, where some attention has been paid to it, the river is shallow and narrow—a sad waste of an amenity in a town which has some interesting things to offer including a museum of rural life and a splendid 1849 railway station. The river takes you through the industrial sector of Stowmarket, which is an experience of a sort.

The lock-chambers on the Gipping have survived and some of them are marked on older editions of the OS maps. You can find two at Needham Market, which lies on the road that used to be the A45 but is so no longer. The first turning left in the village takes you to a fine disused mill, dating from the 1880s, and the site of Needham Mill Lock, now widened out and with a sluice at the lower end. At the southern end of the village the B1078 crosses the Gipping by the restored Bosmere Mill; the gateless lock-chamber is adjacent to the mill and easily accessible. Several lakes are appearing hereabouts and the interests of the anglers are being enthusiastically catered for. Needham Market, its attraction enhanced by the removal of most of the heavy through road-traffic, makes a good centre for an exploration of the Gipping.

There were locks at Pips Farm, Baylham Mill, Shamford and Claydon—the latter overshadowed by the new A45. Bramford Paper Mill Lock is interesting, with the chamber in good condition and a primitive wooden sluice with four descending paddles now installed at the upper end. The handsome mill building has been renovated. Below the lock are the extensive Fisons Works, built on the riverside and served by barges until the closure of the navigation. Bramford Mill Lock is nearly a mile further on at the southern edge of the village. The mill has disappeared and the lock-chamber is messily patched up. Here the river is noticeably wider and heavily fished. There is a convenient car park and you can walk the towpath in either direction.

The next lock south, Sproughton Mill Lock, is in a most attractive setting. The parish church of All Saints stands beside the road; opposite is the mill itself, now an impressive private

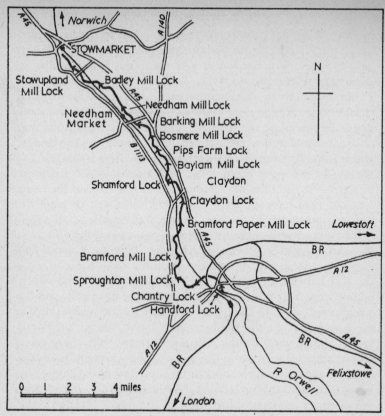

The Ipswich & Stowmarket Navigation

house. You can see the lock-chamber from the road. It is used to help control the water-levels with an adjustable weir at the head, and recently it has been resurfaced. Only the comical concrete road-bridge strikes an incongruous note. Then, after Sproughton, you enter the suburbs of Ipswich. Chantry Lock, on the longest of the Gipping's lock cuts, can be reached from the towpath walk but not from the road. Handford Lock, where the Gipping becomes the Orwell, lies to the south of the A12.

This is a placid, friendly navigation to explore. Compared to the Stour, the Gipping Valley is scenically unexciting, but there is enough evidence from the past—the mills, the riverside buildings in Stowmarket and Ipswich, the works at Bramford—to enable you to visualise the river as a working navigation with horse-drawn lighters or, as in later years, steam barges towing butties.

With many of the lock-chambers in reasonable condition, restoration does not seem impractical; certainly it would improve the water-levels, which in turn would assist both the river's land-drainage function and the fishermen's sport. Although there may be little prospect for commercial use, for recreational purposes the river seems ideal; one day in the future the Gipping may again be transformed into the Ipswich & Stowmarket Navigation.

OS sheet 155

The River Stour

The Stour, which for much of its length forms the boundary between Suffolk and Essex, is as a navigation by no means wholly lost. The legal right to navigate still exists, but a debate on whether powered craft should be allowed to use the river continues to rage. One side is led by the River Stour Trust, formed in 1968; among the Trust's recent achievements are the restoration of the basin at Sudbury and the reclamation of a lighter, raised from Ballingdon Cut in 1972 and again afloat on the river. Opposition is mainly represented by the Country Landowners Association and the Dedham Vale Society. Uneasily in the centre of the controversy is the Anglian Water Authority, which shows willingness to restore the locks but whose proposed by-laws would ban powered vessels.

The Stour was a working river for over 200 years. Locks and staunches were constructed under an act of 1705 and traffic was moving between Manningtree and Sudbury four years later. Even in the early days there were problems with the landowners, resulting in the towpath frequently changing from one bank to the other. Fences between fields were continued to the water's edge and had to be jumped by the barge horses, as demonstrated by Constable's famous 'Leaping Horse'. There were well over 100 jumps on the navigation and 20 places where the horses had to be ferried across.

Trade on the river increased greatly following the appointment of new commissioners in 1781. They included Golding Constable, a Dedham miller and the father of the painter, and two brothers of Thomas Gainsborough, whose own birthplace was Sudbury. The river was dredged and a handsome warehouse, now restored, was opened in 1791 at Sudbury Basin. Later the staunches were dispensed with and the locks rebuilt. These were 95ft long, able to take two barges or lighters end-on, and were originally turf-sided. Later the chambers were lined with timber. The gates were unique, being hung on hinges like field gates. To counteract the strain imposed by the weight of the gates on the gate-posts, the latter were extended high above ground-level with a lintel placed between the top ends. This gives the effect of a massive oak frame at the entrance to the lock, as you can see at the newly restored and operational lock at Flatford.

An important trade in bricks soon developed; these were made in brickfields at Ballingdon to the south of the river at Sudbury and taken to Mistley where they were transhipped for Deptford. In the mid-nineteenth century twenty-two barges were busy with this trade. During the 1860s, however, railway competition began to bite. The traffic in coal to Sudbury fell away in favour of coal brought by rail from the Midlands and the grain traffic also suffered. Bricks and flour were the main cargoes in the later part of the century, but these yielded to railway inducements. In 1892 the River Stour Navigation Company Ltd was set up as successor to the proprietors, but the concern did not prove financially viable. Trade to Sudbury stopped in about 1916; two years later several barges were sunk in the Ballingdon Cut and many of the horses were shot. Some trade to Dedham continued until 1930 and in 1937 the company was dissolved. Ironically, in the 1930s the lower four locks—Stratford St Mary, Dedham, Flatford and Brantham—were rebuilt by the South Essex Waterworks Company in return for leave to abstract water from the river. Commercial craft never used these locks. Brantham Lock has been replaced by a tidal barrage at Cattagate which has rollers for light craft but no means of passage for anything larger.

Ballingdon Bridge is the head of the navigation; it carries the A137 over the river and into Sudbury. The river loops around the south-west of the town. The basin, reached by Quay Lane, is now clean and tidy and the restored warehouse is to become the Quay Theatre. The trust intend to restore a short arm on the backwater close to the basin and the adjacent building, once a granary. A bridge that used to carry the railway crosses the entrance to the basin and the Ballingdon Cut is on the far side of the main river.

Between Sudbury and Bures there are no road bridges; to approach the east bank you take the A133 and for the west the less busy minor road through Henny Street and Lamarsh. Cornard Lock has become an automatic sluice and Henny Lock has gone. It is worth stopping at the Swan at Henny and walking across to see the weir and mill race. Continuing southward for about a mile you come to Daw's Hall; a lane beside the Wildfowl Farm takes you to the remains of Pitmire Lock. The next lock, Bures, has been replaced by a sluice.

You need to cross the Stour at Bures and take the minor road to Nayland. A right turn about 2 miles along takes you towards Wormingford Mill, crossing on the way the derelict lock cut on which are the remnants of Wormingford and Swan locks, $\frac{1}{4}$ mile apart. The river by the mill house is especially beautiful, and can be seen from a footpath.

Back on the Nayland road, in another 2 miles, you come to a turning for Wissington, with its little Norman church. A weir has replaced the lock, but the mill is very handsome. Nayland Lock is also now a weir, but the lock cottage has survived. Nayland is a lovely place, but its attractions are not enhanced by the bridge carrying the A134. This replaced an eighteenth-century hump-backed bridge which succeeded a timber bridge erected by William Abel, a local clothier, in the early sixteenth century. On the bridge is preserved a rebus, a bell with an A on it, commemorating this local benefactor who once lived in Alston Court in the centre of the village. The Anchor Inn, close to the bridge, was a bargeman's pub and its car park is on the site of a wharf. The present late-Victorian building replaced the original 1753 inn, once the headquarters of a press gang but sadly destroyed by fire.

The next lock, Horkesley, has vanished and the locks at Boxted and Langham have gone as well, again replaced by weirs. We are now very much in John Constable's country; his 'Valley of the Stour', painted in about 1805 from Gun Hill, Langham, shows the bridge at Stratford St Mary in the foreground and looks towards Dedham with Harwich in the distance. The rebuilt lock at Stratford is accessible from a path opposite the Swan Inn. The lock-chamber is in good condition and restoration to working order would require only new gates and clearing of the channel. Close to the lock is a pool where barges serving Stratford Mill used to wait. Dedham Lock, a mile further east, is in similar condition. You can walk along the riverside from Stratford to Dedham where the lock is dominated by the massive mill buildings on the site of the mill which Golding Constable bought when his business at Flatford prospered. The river here is busy in summer with rowing boats and sightseers.

Flatford is busier still and more beautiful. The lock is workable and boats have access to 3 miles of river. The Trust's proposal to operate a passenger-trip boat here seems thoroughly reasonable, and if it were horse-drawn it is hard to see any ground for objection. Tourists are going to flock to Flatford anyway; they cannot enter the mill so they might as well have something to do. The scene here has not changed so very much since Constable's time and you may still be able to trace the site of the boatyard owned by his father which is the subject of 'Boat-building at Flatford' painted in 1814. It is a short distance upstream from the lock. You may walk beside the river to Dedham or in the opposite direction to Cattawade Barrage on the northern stream of the river past the remains of Brantham Lock. The southern stream flows into the estuary through Cattawade Sluice, known as 'Fifty-six gates', but this stream was never navigable.

'I associate my "careless boyhood" to all that lies on the banks of the Stour', wrote Constable in 1821. In his day it was a living, working navigation. Judge for yourself whether it would be better so today.

OS sheets 155, 169

The River Blyth (Halesworth Navigation)

The last wherry to use the Blyth, Fred Lambert's *Star*, was beached at Walberswick in 1911 and the navigation, after a life of 150 years, came to an end. The Blyth is a short river; a couple of streams meet just above Halesworth and the river flows 9 miles almost due east to meet the sea between Southwold and Walberswick. It is difficult today to visualise it as a navigation at all, so narrow and shallow does it appear. In its earlier years, however, it was quite a busy little river with up to a dozen wherries trading along it.

Halesworth was a lively market town in the eighteenth century, serving a large area of wealthy farmland. Southwold was a small east-coast port. The river was tidal for about 5 miles to Blythburgh; between Southwold and Blythburgh were several thousand acres of saltings which were covered at every tide. As the tide ebbed the water coming off the saltings scoured the outfall and made it possible for vessels to use Southwold Harbour. In 1757 an Act was obtained to make the river navigable; the money was raised locally, Langley Edwards was appointed surveyor and engineer (although the records show he was generally conspicuous by his absence) and four years later the first boat arrived at Halesworth. Four locks, similar to those on the Stour, were constructed, at Bulcamp, Blyford, Mells and Halesworth; there was also a tidal staunch above Blythburgh. With bridges and associated works the total cost came to a little under £4,000.

The first boat to arrive in Halesworth in July 1761 carried a cargo of coal; coal and corn were the chief goods throughout the life of the navigation. For some years the local landowners had been reclaiming small areas of the saltings near Blythburgh, a process that was accelerated in the early decades of the nineteenth century. Now embankments were put up to keep out the tides; the effect of this was to diminish the scour at Southwold and make it progressively more difficult for the harbour to be used. Capstans were erected to help haul the vessels over the harbour bar, but this gave little encouragement to boat-owners or merchants who wanted to use the Blyth. As the commissioners for the navigation were also the local landowners there was little hope of remedy. The reports of engineers called in to survey the harbour all agreed that, in John Rennie's words, 'for many years past it has been gradually getting more shallow, owing to the embankment of the salt marshes over which the tide used to flow'. Rennie and other experts reported that only the destruction of the embankments would solve the problem, but their words were ignored. A campaign led by Patrick Stead, owner of maltings in Halesworth and a principal user of the navigation, forced a public enquiry in 1839 after several vessels carrying his goods had been unable to leave the harbour. His evidence, followed by the report of another leading engineer, James Walker, proved incontrovertible, but the landowners were saved by the passing of the General Enclosure Act in 1845 which gave them security of tenure of their enclosed—and embanked—lands. Stead left Halesworth a few years later and in 1884 the commissioners declared that the river was no longer used as a navigation and declined responsibility for any repairs. Legal abandonment, however, was delayed until 1934.

Southwold is a pleasant little seaside town. It has escaped the worst horrors of holiday development and is known for its lighthouse, its squares and triangles of grass, its cannons and Adnams' superb beer. A road leads south to the harbour, busy in the summer with yachts and sometimes a few fishing boats. The point where goods used to be transhipped from sea-going ships into wherries was ¾ mile from the harbour mouth on the Southwold side. A rowing-boat ferry may still ply to Walberswick.

Blythburgh is now a small village on the A12, 5 miles inland from Southwold. Its past importance is evident from the superb church, 127ft long and 54ft wide, one of the finest in Suffolk. From here you can see what happend to the Blyth and can discern the embankments that caused the harbour and the navigation to decay.

Between Blythburgh and Halesworth there are only two road bridges over the river. You may be able to walk alongside the river or you can follow the course of the Southwold Railway, a 3ft gauge independent undertaking that operated between 1879 and 1929. Look for evidence of the existence of locks. At Halesworth the basin has been filled in and the maltings demolished. The Wherry Inn, a rebuilding of an old thatched house burnt down early this century, stands close to the sometime head of navigation; it has an especially attractive sign. Unfortunately, I cannot remember if it is served by the excellent Southwold brewers who supply the historically fascinating Harbour Inn at Southwold.

OS sheet 156

The River Waveney above Geldeston

At one time the Waveney was naturally navigable to Bungay, but the condition of the river so deteriorated in the seventeenth century that Beccles became perforce the head of navigation. In 1670 an Act—the first relating to the Norfolk rivers—was obtained to enable the Waveney between Bungay and Beccles to be improved. Three locks were to be built and commissioners were appointed to control the use of the river. This stretch of the river was privately owned by a succession of merchants and maltsters—the last of whom was Watney, Combe, Reid & Co— until 1934 when navigation through the locks was abandoned.

Today, the Waveney is open to craft up to Shipmeadow (or Geldeston) Lock, 2¼ miles above Beccles Town Bridge. From the Norfolk side you can reach it by heading for the village of Geldeston, which lies to the south of the A143 Bungay-Beccles road. At the west end of the village a track, signposted to The Locks, leads across the marshes; it is advisable, and preferable, to leave your car at the top of the track and walk. From Suffolk you take a track northward from Shipmeadow on the A1116. The county boundary is the river and runs through the centre of the lock. Hence the popularity of this place in the days when the constabulary was strictly county controlled. This was where the local prize-fights were held; the crowd had only to nip across the lock to avoid the forces of the law from whichever direction they came. It seems they never came from both directions at once. Smuggling was another popular local activity; in the eighteenth and nineteenth centuries Shipmeadow Lock seems to have been a centre for organised crime.

Approaching from the Norfolk side, you come to The Locks. This used to be the mill house, but the mill disappeared over fifty years ago—it is risky walking here in the dark as you may fall into the mill leat. Until 1973 The Locks was kept by Susan Ellis, an indomitable warrior who ruled the pub and its customers for thirty-five years with no concessions to modernity or commercialism. Under Susan, The Locks had no electricity, no running water and no draught beer; but with its high-backed oak settles, candle-light and Susan's stories of ghosts and telepathy it had character and atmosphere in plenty. When Susan died the river commissioners bought the pub, partly to keep it from 'development'. Walter, who now runs it, has brightened up the interior and made a few minor changes (now you don't have to collect a key to use the Ladies and bang on the door first to frighten the rats away), but this is still one of Britain's most fascinating pubs.

The gates of Shipmeadow Lock are rotting away, but the chamber is in good condition. J. W. Robberds wrote in 1834:

The rudeness of its structure and simplicity of its contrivances contrast strikingly with the more finished labours of modern engineers, but here they are in perfect keeping with the rustic scenery in the midst of which they are embowered, and which is a favourable specimen of the natural beauties adorning the course of this river.

With allowance for the style, this might be said today.

There are two more abandoned locks above Shipmeadow. One is at Ellingham; the road from Geldeston heading west takes you there in a little under two miles. Ellingham Mill has been converted to a gallery; the bridge has been flattened over the river, but you can see the remains of the lock. The second lock is at Wainford by the large Watney's maltings on a minor road joining the A143 and the A1116, a mile east of Bungay. The river here is controlled by a sluice and weir. Try to identify the lock-chamber and to make out the functions of the various water channels. Above Wainford the Waveney was navigable for a further mile to the staithe in Bungay, on the east side of the town centre.

OS sheets 134, 156

The North Walsham & Dilham Canal

Opened in 1826, the North Walsham & Dilham Canal is an improvement of the River Ant from Wayford Bridge to a basin east of Antingham Ponds. Below the bridge the navigation was continued along the Ant, through Barton Broad to the Bure. The canal was no great financial success, but the surplus water at the locks was useful to the adjacent mills. Edward Press of Bacton Wood Mill owned several wherries and hired them out as pleasure craft. He bought the waterway in 1866 for £600; unfortunately, the clerk to the proprietors ran off with most of the purchase price. Some trading continued, although the top 1⅜ miles, including 2 locks, were abandoned in 1893. Press died in 1906; the canal was sold by auction and sold again in 1921 to the North Walsham Canal Company, which still owns it. Trade on the canal ended in 1935.

The canal begins above Wayford Bridge on the A149 2 miles west of Stalham. The navigable cut to Dilham, called Dilham Dyke and owned by the East Anglian Waterways Association, is open, and navigation to the tail of Honing Lock may not be impossible. However, the first bridge, called Tonnage Bridge because tolls were collected at the adjacent wharf, has partly collapsed. At Briggate, west of Honing, there are a lock-chamber, mill and warehouse. Ebridge Lock and Mill are almost 2 miles further north. The canal now becomes considerably narrower. Spa Common is the nearest point to North Walsham; here there is a warehouse by the bridge, and the site of Bacton Wood Lock. The B1150 and B1145 roads from North Walsham cross the canal at Auston Bridge and Swafield Bridge; warehouses stand by both bridges. North-west of Swafield Bridge the canal becomes a small water-channel leading from Antingham Ponds. The site of the basin is in the angle of the two roads to the south-east of the pond; here there were bone-mills and a boat-house.

Restoration of at least part of the canal has been much discussed in recent years and there is no doubt that it would form a useful and attractive extension to the overcrowded Broads. To improve the upper reaches would be very costly, but a reopening to Ebridge, or possibly to Bacton Wood, might not be impractical. Proposals for some limited restoration are being considered by the Broads Authority at this time.

OS sheet 133

Great Ouse Tributaries

The River Ivel Navigation

The Ivel is a quiet little river joining the Great Ouse at Tempsford. Plans to make it navigable to Hitchin, with branches to Baldock and Shefford, were discussed in the mid-eighteenth century; the primary purpose was to cheapen the cost of coal which otherwise had to be carted from Tempsford. A navigation as far as Biggleswade was completed in 1758, where it remained for sixty-five years. Trade was moderate and the fact that the Ivel is a slow-flowing river meant that no major improvements were required during that time. In the early 1820s, however, renewed enthusiasm for extending the navigation became apparent and in 1823 a new line was opened from Biggleswade to Langford and then along the western arm of the river to Shefford. The navigation's useful life continued into the 1850s. Then the Great Northern Railway's main line from London was opened along the Ivel Valley, running close to the river at Biggleswade and Sandy, with the Bedford-Hitchin branch of the Midland Railway reaching Shefford in 1857. Within a few years trade on the river came to an end and the navigation was abandoned in 1876.

On the east side of Shefford the Ivel divides and there were

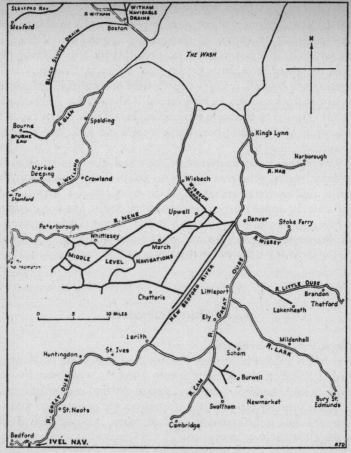

The Eastern Counties (2)

wharves by both the North and South Bridges. From Shefford
you can walk alongside the river to a bridge on the Stanford-
Clifton road. In places it is the navigation cuts that hold water
while the natural bed of the river is dry; elsewhere the reverse has
happened. At Stanford there is a stone lock-chamber, accessible
from a track to the west of the village.

The next access point from the road is at Holme on the B658, a
mile west of Broom, by Jordans Mill. Holme Lock is used as a
sluice, its operation supervised by an enigmatic pedestalled bust.
The walk along the river resumes here beneath the A1 crossing
and on to a footbridge 3 miles further north. The Ivel forms the

western boundary of Biggleswade. On this stretch there were three staunches erected when the navigation was first made and now untraceable. By the mill at Biggleswade there was a wharf, and north of this a large turf-sided lock, no longer visible.

Between Biggleswade and Sandy the river is sandwiched between the railway and the A1. Sandy Wharf was by the mill and the lock has been replaced by a weir overflow. South Mills Lock between Sandy and Blunham has been demolished and replaced by a sluice, but the site of Blunham Wharf to the north-east of the church has been rediscovered. Between Blunham and the Ouse the Ivel mostly takes the course of the navigation, meeting the main river just below Tempsford Lock. On your tour, look out for the navigation bridges built by Moreton & Kinner of Biggleswade and erected in 1823. These bridges have decorative iron railings and are especially attractive.

Now that the navigation of the Great Ouse to Bedford has been reopened there is talk about the restoration of the Ivel Navigation. As a route for smaller craft there is a good case for this, but one hopes that this river would never be made to accommodate the larger gin palaces of the Great Ouse.

OS sheet 153

The Upper Reaches of the Lark and Little Ouse Rivers
Both the Lark and the Little Ouse are open as navigations for part of their length. Scenically, however, it is the less attractive parts that are open: the lower reaches, straightened and embanked where they run through the sinking peatland. For practical purposes they lead nowhere; the Lark Navigation peters out by the tiny village of West Row while the Little Ouse fails to arrive at Brandon. In their time, however, both navigations had important termini: Bury St Edmunds for the Lark, and Thetford for the Little Ouse. The lengths between these towns and the present heads of navigation are well worth taking the time and trouble to explore.

Stone from Barnack for the abbey at Bury St Edmunds came up the River Lark, and one of the oldest bridges in England, dating from the thirteenth century, can be found on the east side of the town where the wall of the abbey precincts crosses the river. The bridge below this, Eastgate Bridge, marks the head of the legal navigation, although boats never came this far up in the recorded history of the river. This legal navigation dates from 1700 when Henry Ashley, whose father (also named Henry) made the Great Ouse navigable to Bedford, was empowered to extend the navigation of the Lark from Mildenhall to Bury. The work, involving making several artificial cuts, locks and staunches, took fifteen years—and even then it was incomplete. Nevertheless, Ashley was receiving tolls and throughout the eighteenth century the river was kept in trade, making a few hundred pounds a year for its owners. Coal for Bury was the major cargo, brought, like most of the goods carried, by lighters from King's Lynn.

Early in the nineteenth century it became clear that unless improvements were made trade was likely to cease. Water levels were not maintained and the channel was often obstructed; at times it took a week for a gang of lighters to be hauled up to Bury from Lynn. The owner of the navigation was now Susanna Palmer, a descendant of the Ashleys. On her death she left the Lark—as well as her share of the Upper Great Ouse—to her nephew, Sir Thomas Geary Cullum. He set about an extensive programme of restoration on both rivers. You can see his initials on some of the surviving navigation works, including the cottage at King's Staunch—'1842 TGC'. There was a brief revival of trade until the railway opened between Ipswich and Bury in 1846. Now goods from Lynn were no longer needed and the fortunes of the navigation rapidly declined. Within a few years, trade on the river had stopped.

Unexpectedly—and certainly optimistically—a company was formed in 1890 under the aristocratic guidance of Lord Francis Hervey and the Marquis of Bristol to purchase and revitalise the Lark Navigation. This, the Eastern Counties Navigation & Transport Company Ltd, bought the river from the confluence of the Lee Brook to Bury, removed three staunches, changed one to a lock and repaired the other locks, dredged the channel and opened the Tuddenham Mill Stream to boats. In 1892 the proprietors, their staff, steam tug and lighters were photographed at St Saviour's Wharf, Bury. Two years later the work was completed. The company's funds, however, were exhausted and the new lock at Tollgate collapsed, cutting off the Bury terminus from the rest of the navigation. In December 1894 a receiver was called in. Trading continued for a few years, but the upper reaches began to decay. A Mildenhall firm, Parker Brothers, bought the navigation rights and a small amount of traffic, mostly in road-building materials, continued into the 1920s.

Bury St Edmunds, which kept the navigation at arm's length until St Saviour's Wharf was built in 1890, shows little regard for its river—in marked contrast to Thetford and the Little Ouse. The site of the wharf is on the north side of the railway, close to the point where the link road joins the A45. Above Tollgate Bridge, where the A134 Thetford road crosses the Lark, is the site of Tollgate Lock. For nearly all of its lifetime the terminal basin of the Lark was at Fornham Wharf. The cut here has been filled in and the wharf area is now a car park. Look for the Kingsbury Furniture Store on the north-east side of the A1101. This has been converted from a maltings and the wharf lay behind it.

For most of its length the river is easy of access and you can follow the towpath. Most of the bridges are modern, but you will find remains of both locks and staunches. If you follow the A1101 to Flempton and turn right for West Stow, you will see the chamber of Flempton Lock upstream of the bridge. Then cross the river and turn immediately right. Soon you come to an art gallery in the mill house of a demolished water-mill and nearby is Chimney Mill Lock, with its chamber in surprisingly good condition. This lock was rebuilt in 1948 by the Great Ouse River Board as part of a restoration scheme that was never completed.

Return through West Stow and continue to the entrance of West Stow Country Park, opened in 1979. Here you can spend a fascinating couple of hours. In the centre of the park is a reconstructed Anglo-Saxon village and to the east is the pump-house of the 1887 sewage works to which coal was brought by the river. Further east is the chamber of Fulling Mill Lock. Walk downstream along the towpath, passing the foundations of Lackford Staunch and the site of a lock-keeper's cottage south of the wooden village. You are walking, in fact, alongside an artificial cut which ends at the chamber of Cherry Ground Lock. It is unwise to say that any lock is 'unique', but this one is out of the ordinary in that one wall is crescent-shaped. At either end the brickwork is crumbling and in the protected environment of a country park it is hoped that conservation of this unusual structure will be a priority. Cherry Ground Lock was a creation of Sir Thomas Cullum and his initials were carved on one of the coping stones.

The main road crosses the river at Lackford, to the west of the country park. Just under ½ mile further on are the remains of Lackford Double Lock, which consisted of a pair of staunches about 100yd apart on a straight artificial cut. At Icklingham, a mile from Lackford Bridge, the road to Cavenham crosses the Lark at Old Hall Staunch. Boats tied up below the staunch to take on gravel dug from pits nearby. William Howlett, a journalist and champion of the Lark Navigation in the later years of the nineteenth century, entertained navvies employed in the 1890s improvements in the Red Lion in the village. Icklingham Lock itself is by the entrance to Marston's Mill; it was rebuilt by the river board in about 1939 but has never been navigated. There are the sites of two more staunches between Icklingham and the entrance to Tuddenham Mill Stream. The stream is no longer navigable, but the mill has been converted into a restaurant with the mill-wheel and some of the machinery restored and retained as a feature of the décor.

At Barton Mills, south of the busy roundabout, the A11 London–Norwich road was realigned in 1962 and the river was culverted beneath it. The old bridge is tucked away on what is now a by-road in front of the Bull Hotel. The two nearby buildings were the water-mills which gave the settlement its name. Continue along the A1101 to Mildenhall and turn on to the B1102 Fordham road. Although Mildenhall has developed a suburban area, especially on its northern side, the centre is especially attractive and the church is superb. This is the Mildenhall of the treasure—the Roman hoard now in the British Museum. The river flows south of the centre. Stop by the Ship Inn, once the house of the adjacent mill. This belonged to the Parkers, who also owned the navigation. The mill-stream enters the river a few yards away; the pool is known as Gaspool and the rebuilt lock, whose guillotine gate you can easily see, is Mildenhall Gas Works Lock. The old brick bridge with roundels each side of the navigation arch takes a heavy load of traffic and the brickwork needs attention. The lock below the bridge was converted from a staunch by the Eastern Counties Company in 1890. Under the Lark Restoration Scheme, currently under discussion by the local authority and other interested groups, this would become the head of the navigation.

King's Staunch is a mile further west and is easiest to reach by walking along the towpath. There is a footbridge across it and a

TGC cottage close by. The initials are also visible on a coping stone on the staunch island, which itself is in good condition. From here it is another mile along the towpath to Judes Ferry, West Row, the present head of navigation. The Lark loses much of its attractiveness below the bridge—or rather below the working lock at Isleham. Thereafter it is embanked and most of its course is artificial.

OS sheets 143, 144, 155

The Little Ouse, or Brandon River as it is sometimes known, was also a transport route for Barnack stone, carried during the twelfth century for the building of Thetford Priory. As a legalised navigation it antedates the Lark, the river between Whitehouse, below Brandon, and Thetford, being covered by an act of 1669-70. Work seems to have been completed by 1677, although in the following decades there was frequent difficulty in maintaining navigable levels. The administration was tightened up in an act of 1751, following which the Corporation of Thetford, the owners of the navigation, built 7 staunches in the $12\frac{1}{2}$ miles of river in their control. No precise details of these staunches appear to exist. Their condition deteriorated over the years until it became obvious that replacements were necessary, and they were rebuilt, presumably on or close to the same sites, between 1827 and 1835. A further staunch was added later at Crosswater, near the entrance of Lakenheath Lode. They were built on the guillotine principle, the operator having to ascend a ladder and turn a large spoked wheel. A barrel was affixed to the shaft of the wheel and the door raised and lowered by a chain attached to the barrel. The framework and door were of oak, the wheels of iron and the structure was built into brick piers, one at the bankside and the other in the stream. Beside the staunch was a 'clough', a device to control the flow by the use of boards and small falling doors, and next to this was the overfall, a miniature dam over the top of which the excess water could flow when the level rose higher than required for navigation.

After the reconstruction of the staunches, commercial navigation prospered moderately for about fifty years. Iron boats were built at Thetford and a small paddle-steamer, *Pride of the Ouse*, took passengers to Cambridge or around the Fens. The firm of Fisons were major users of the river and indeed were subsidising its use in later years. By the beginning of the twentieth century the staunches were in poor repair and by 1914 commercial traffic ceased. When the river came under the aegis of the Great Ouse Catchment Board the remains of the staunches were removed and steel sluices were installed at Thetford and Brandon.

Today, the Little Ouse is navigable to Brandon Staunch. Above Brandon it is used for canoeing and rowing, more easily than many rivers as slipways have been constructed by the sites of the staunches. If you have been exploring the Lark it is a quick and direct journey to Thetford from either Bury St Edmunds or Mildenhall. Turn into the town centre at Thetford and park by the river. Here the contrast with Bury's treatment of its river is obvious. The riverside is tactfully landscaped, the shopping precinct has been built to scale, an intriguing triangular footbridge takes you to the island close to the junction of the Little Ouse and Thet. Upstream is a handsome mill; downstream a fine iron bridge bearing the date 1829 on one side and the Thetford coat-of-arms on the other. A riverside walk takes you out of the town and away towards Thetford Forest.

Between Thetford and Brandon only one road bridge crosses the river. This is at Santon Downham, now the headquarters of Thetford forest. Take the B1107 Brandon road and fork right in 3 miles through a superb avenue of lime trees. Leave your car in a Forestry Commission car park and walk along the towpath upstream. A footbridge crosses the Little Ouse about 1,000yd from Santon Downham Bridge. On the south bank just above the footbridge you will see some brickwork; this is all that is left of Santon Downham Staunch. It may seem a long way to come to see a few bricks, but this is one of the loveliest stretches of river in the eastern half of England and you should walk on at least as far as the little riverside church of All Saints, Santon, built in 1628. To find out more about this fascinating area on the Norfolk-Suffolk border, look for a copy of W. G. Clarke's *In Breckland Wilds*, first published in 1925 and revised by R. Rainbird Clarke in 1937. It contains a beautifully clear photograph of Santon Downham Staunch.

At Brandon the river is tucked away on the north side of the town. It was shifted about 100yd southward when the old bridge—predecessor of the present wide flint-faced structure—was built. The old channel of the river ran under the present Ram Inn. The Little Ouse through Brandon and for several miles either side marks the boundary between Norfolk and Suffolk. Some 8½ miles below Brandon Bridge is the junction with Lakenheath Lode, which was used by lighters until about 1910. Part of its length has been filled in, but its course from Botany Bay around the south-west edge of Shepherds' Fen to the west side of the village of Lakenheath is quite clear.

OS sheet 144

The River Nar

The Nar, tucked away in north-west Norfolk, must be one of the least known of 'lost' navigations. There was a time, before the thirteenth century, when the Great Ouse made its outfall at Wisbech and the King's Lynn estuary was formed by two little rivers, the Nar and the Gay. Following the Ouse's change of outfall, the lower reaches of the Nar were diverted to flow through the centre of Lynn. However, the river was not made navigable until the inhabitants of Lynn and other towns and villages along or near its course submitted a petition to Parliament. With evidence in support that the commerce of the neighbourhood would be greatly increased, an Act was passed in 1751 for the river to be made navigable from Westacre to Lynn, with locks and towing paths to be paid for out of tolls. Progress was not rapid, long periods of inactivity being interrupted by occasional reports, surveys and attempts to raise money. Eventually, with the surveyor Langley Edwards under the threat of a penalty clause, the work was completed in 1759. In the early years, however, little use was made of the navigation; its condition deteriorated, and the commissioners entrusted with its administration quickly lost interest. In 1770 the Reverend Henry Spelman discovered that he was the only subscriber left; he energetically took matters into his own hands, invested more of his own money and obtained a further Act regulating the use of the river and enabling repairs to be made.

The Nar was made navigable by the construction of ten staunches and one pound-lock in the 5 miles downwards from Narborough. According to Langley Edwards's estimate, a new cut was to be made to Westacre Bridge, with two staunches. The fact that the lock at Narborough was a pound-lock would indicate that the river was navigable above that point, but evidence of the two staunches is lacking. Today, the river at Westacre seems about as unlikely a navigation as one could imagine—a narrow, shallow, fast-flowing stream—and the village itself, notable for the remains of an Augustinian priory, is elusive for the motorist and almost invisible behind its hedges.

There are few bridges over the Nar—I counted six from Narborough to the suburbs of Lynn. It is worth stopping at Narborough, keeping a careful eye on the fast-moving traffic on the A47 which bends its way dangerously through the village. At the south end is the church; then comes a handsome mill; and just before a sharp bend the road crosses the lock cut. Turn into the minor road to Pentney and walk back. The lock-chamber is under the main road with the central part of it culverted and the water controlled by sluices at each end. Here 'much business is transacted in coal, timber, corn, malt &c, by Messrs Marriott', says White's *Norfolk*, 1845. On the west side of the lock you can see where the business was transacted, an area of semi-derelict but impressive mills, granaries and warehouses. Marriott's owned the navigation in the mid-nineteenth century and fought on its behalf against a proposed railway from Lynn to Dereham. The fight was lost; in 1848 the line to Dereham was open, with a station at Narborough.

Navigation on the upper reaches ended in 1884 and, apart from the lock and the site at Narborough, it has left few traces behind it. Until 1932, however, the lowest reach of the Nar was in use, with the West Norfolk Farmers Manure Company (now Fisons) being supplied with gas and water from Cambridge Gasworks via the Cam and the Ouse. Doors have been installed by the factory to keep out the tidal waters and to allow flood-water to escape. Below the doors, the river is sometimes used as moorings by fishing boats. Only the most devoted enthusiast would go to King's Lynn merely to see the outfall of the Nar, but the town itself and the extensive docks are well worth a few hours of anyone's time.

OS sheet 132

The Wisbech Canal

The Wisbech Canal, although it made little impact either on waterway history or local trade, has its own particular interest. It was dug along the line of the Well Stream, a river which wound its way roughly diagonally across what later became the Middle Level of the Fens, a natural meandering river in distinction to the straight artificial cuts which Vermuyden and his successors drove across the flat lands. By 1794, when Parliament was petitioned for a canal, the old river had been mostly filled in and houses built close to and in its bed. This river, it was maintained, had been navigable by small craft. The Wisbech Canal Act authorised the demolition of the houses and by the beginning of 1796 the 5¼ mile canal was open with a lock at each end. It drew its water from the River Nene in Wisbech, a procedure known as 'letting the tide in'. The accumulation of silt at the Wisbech lock gates was a continual problem; it kept the water out until only the spring tides raised the river high enough to supply the canal.

The best years for the canal were the 1840s when reduction of tolls led to an increase in the amount of coal carried and even enabled a dividend to be paid. Thereafter the coal traffic moved to the railways. In 1883 the Great Eastern Railway opened the Wisbech & Upwell Tramway virtually parallel to the canal. A year later, according to the *Wisbech Advertiser*, this was carrying 600 tons of goods a week—equal to the highest tonnage recorded by the canal in its peak year of 1848—and 3,000 passengers at 2d a head. Mr Whybrow of Nordelph also charged 2d a head for passengers in his horse-drawn packet boat from Outwell to Wisbech, but he soon gave up in face of this competition. The tramway also carried large quantities of agricultural produce from Upwell and Outwell to Wisbech and took coal to Outwell where it was loaded into lighters to be delivered to the pumping stations in the Fens via the Old Nene or Well Creek. The story of the tramway with details of the locomotives and rolling stock is told in a well-illustrated booklet, *The Wisbech and Upwell Tramway*, by E. J. S. Gadsden and others, reprinted in 1972. The tramway long outlived the canal and was not closed until 1966.

There were moves to close the canal in 1903 as the receipts were insufficient to pay for the maintenance, but the borough of Wisbech and other local authorities succeeded in keeping it open as they were enabled to carry highway materials on it free of charge. It struggled on into the 1920s with the receipts in 1922, the last year of operation, amounting to 12s 6d. In 1926 a warrant of abandonment was issued and in 1944 the ownership of the canal bed was vested in Wisbech Corporation.

The A1101 Wisbech–Bury St Edmunds road closely follows

the line of the canal to Outwell. The site of the entrance lock at Wisbech was just below the A1101 bridge over the Nene and the roundabout and realigned main road lie on the canal course. From the outskirts of Wisbech the canal (or rather its predecessor, the Well Stream) formed the county boundary and, although the canal has disappeared from modern maps, the boundary conveniently gives its line. For almost all its length the road lies on the north-east side of the canal course, with the tramway line alongside the road apart from occasional diversions for depots on the route. By now it is likely that almost all—if not all—of the canal bed has been filled in, although a few years ago there was a well-defined section of its course opposite the Prince of Wales. Approaching Outwell Basin the road looped northward while canal and tramway kept close company. By the basin was the original terminus of the tramway which, when extended to Upwell, crossed the canal just past the basin by an iron bridge. The canal entered Outwell between two roads with rows of houses facing each other across the waterway, reminiscent, on a smaller scale, of the eighteenth-century Brinks in Wisbech. The canal line, however, is now infilled, with bungalows and their gardens on top of it. To the north of the church is the junction of the canal with the Old Nene and with Well Creek, which continues the line of the old Well Stream. The 97ft long Outwell Lock has been obliterated.

OS sheet 143

The Stamford Canal

You will find very few references to the Stamford Canal in waterway histories, and those that you do come across are likely to apply to proposals to link Stamford to various parts of the canal network to the west. There is—or was—an actual Stamford Canal, however, cut from the River Welland near Hudd's Mill on the east side of the town and running roughly parallel to the river on its northern side, rejoining it at Market Deeping. It was opened in the 1660s, although the first act authorising its construction was passed as long before as 1571, only the tenth navigation Act in British history. The Welland itself had been navigable to Stamford in medieval times and had helped to create the prosperity of the town, but by the mid-sixteenth century the condition of the river had deteriorated and navigation was impossible. For a variety of reasons construction of the canal was delayed until, after further legislation, Daniel Wigmore, an alderman of Stamford, took on the undertaking and completed a 9½ mile canal with 12 locks at a cost of approximately £5,000. At this time it was the longest locked canal in Britain. The locks accommodated lighters about 35ft long, usually worked in gangs of four.

Traffic on the Stamford Canal ended in 1863 and within a few years much of the line had been sold off. No records of its trading history have yet been discovered and, apart from the legal documents and a brief account in Samuel Wells's *History of the Drainage of the Great Level*, 1830, there is only the odd mention in Stamford local studies. It was shown in detail on the first edition of the 1in Ordnance Survey map, but it was not until 1958 that two industrial archaeologists, Maurice Berrill and J. M. Palmer, intrigued by a dry channel at Uffington Bridge near Stamford, undertook research which brought at least some of the story of the canal to light.

The Welland was not navigable above Stamford and the canal began at a point very near the head of navigation. Wharf Road is the place to make for; there are some seventeenth-century warehouse buildings which presumably served the canal as the river navigation during that century was very little used. To follow the canal take the A16 Spalding road; the turnings on the south side between Stamford and Market Deeping cross the channel just before the bridges over the Welland. The best-defined stretch is at Uffington, where the dry channel skirts the southern edge of Uffington Park. Look out for evidence of locks, bridges and wharves, but do not expect to find substantial remains. Elsewhere some lengths of the channel have been filled in, or run through private property.

If you continue through Market Deeping for a further mile, taking the B1166, you reach Deeping Gate where the river flows through the centre of the village and you can examine the remains of a lock approximately 60ft by 12ft. This, I assume, marks the end of the canal, but I have not discovered the exact point at which the canal rejoined the river.

It might be argued that the Stamford is not a 'true' canal but only a canalisation of the Welland. In favour of its claim is the fact that it did not draw its water from the Welland but from the

River Gwash via a feeder especially dug for the purpose. It has, I suggest, as much right to be called a canal as the St Helen's, which it antedates by nearly a century. While you are in the area, try to find time to visit the village of Barnack, 1½ miles south of Uffington Bridge over the canal and Welland. Note the splendid honey-coloured building stone, and then make for the 'field of hills and holes' on the south-west side of the village. This is the great medieval stone quarry, the source of 'Barnack rag' used in many major buildings, cathedrals and abbeys, in the southern and eastern parts of England. The Welland was one of the main transport routes for this stone, although the quarries were probably worked out by the time the Stamford Canal was made.

OS sheets 141, 142

The Bourne Eau

Through the settlement that is now Bourne passed the oldest canal in Britain, the Car Dyke, cut by the Romans to link the River Cam with the Witham near Lincoln. Bourne itself grew up around the Well-Head, or St Peter's Pool. This large pool, to the south-west of the cross-roads in the centre of the town, is fed by several springs and is the source of the Bourne Eau, which gave its name to the town. The Car Dyke crossed the eau at Eastgate, ½ mile from the town centre, and although today you will find no trace of the Roman waterway here the eau itself is still a major feature of the town. For a time it was contributory to the town's prosperity; through the eau, the Glen and the Welland goods from Bourne could reach the Wash and the port of Boston and from the sixteenth to the mid-nineteenth century this water route was in regular use.

The first legislation covering the Bourne Eau was an Act of 1781 which referred to the waterway having become almost unnavigable owing to mud and other obstructions and appointed trustees empowered to clean it out and charge tolls. Corn and wool were the main cargoes to Boston and coal and groceries were brought up; there was a coal wharf on the north bank of the eau in Eastgate in the nineteenth century. On market days a passenger boat sailed, or was hauled, when conditions permitted. Frequently, however, it did not, as the Glen, on which the use of the eau depended, flooded often, with the flood-water at times backing up to Bourne. To control this, self-acting doors were installed at the junction, Tongue End, but they did not prevent the breaching of the Glen's banks which happened once every three or four years in the nineteenth century. There were also times when the springs ran dry and there was insufficient water in the eau for navigation.

The Glen joins the Welland below the busy town of Spalding and, when the railway reached Spalding in 1848, the trade of all three navigations began to decline. Then in 1857 Lord Willoughby opened a little railway to the west of Bourne. This line, which reversed the usual order of events by commencing with locomotive traction and ending with horses, ran from Little Bytham, where it collected coal brought by the main line trains, to Edenham, within 3 miles of Bourne. Now it was easier to fetch coal by cart from Edenham than have it come by sea and river. Boats now used the eau only occasionally, until in the 1860s a sluice was erected at Tongue End, cutting off the navigation from the Glen. The Bourne Eau Act, however, was not repealed until 1862.

Cherry Holt Road in Bourne, a turning off the A151 Spalding road, takes you across the eau, which is controlled by a sluice beneath the bridge. It is a narrow watercourse and does not look much like a navigation; but if you peer closely at the northern bank above the bridge you will see a mooring ring. Out of Bourne the eau is embanked and its bed is above the level of the surrounding land. There are no road bridges between the town and Tongue End. (Eau, incidentally, is strictly pronounced 'ee'—tempting though it may be to say 'o'. It derives from the Old English *ea* which meant river or stream.)

The Glen above Tongue End was navigable to the Lincoln–Peterborough road at Kate's Bridge, 3 miles south of Bourne. Light craft may well have used the river for a further 2 miles—there is some evidence of moorings and storage buildings at Greatford Hall—but this would have ceased when Kate's Bridge was lowered. Tongue End is now the highest point on the Glen where boats of any size can turn and so, in practice, it has become the head of navigation.

OS sheet 130

The Sleaford and Horncastle Navigations

Acts were obtained in the same year, 1792, to provide the Lincolnshire market towns of Sleaford and Horncastle with navigable connections with the River Witham. The Sleaford Navigation, involving improvements to the River Slea and its lower reaches known as the Kyme Eau, was opened in 1794, and the Horncastle Navigation, a canalisation of the River Bain, was completed in 1802. Both ceased to be used for commercial traffic in or about 1878 and were legally abandoned a few years later. With both undertakings the famous naturalist Sir Joseph Banks was closely connected and the locks of both were built to the same dimensions.

The A153 connects Sleaford and Horncastle and is seldom more than a mile from the banks of both navigations. Sleaford Wharf is on Carre Street, a turning off the A153 opposite the splendid St Denys Church. The stone entrance to the wharf bears the inscription '1792 Navigation Wharf'. Some of the wharf buildings have been replaced and a warehouse converted to other use, but the navigation office, built in 1838 and with the arms of the navigation company carved above the door, survives and is now a Department of the Environment listed building. The recently formed Sleaford Navigation Society hopes to ensure its preservation and to restore the navigation as well. Continue along Carre Street and turn left along a path to follow the cut to the turn-round point where in 1798 the scene was dominated by a large corn-grinding windmill. From here you can walk the towpath, although a short section has been barred (whether legally or not I cannot say) in the grounds of Haverholme Priory.

In the first 2 miles of the walk you pass three lock-chambers, two with adjacent mill-buildings. By car, the fourth lock is found above the bridge on the road to Evedon, about $2\frac{1}{4}$ miles along the A153. This is Paper Mill Lock which, together with Haverholme and Anwick Locks, was handed over to the care of the owner of the priory when the navigation was closed. The chamber of Haverholme Lock is above the next bridge, rebuilt after the closure of the navigation, a dignified and—to judge from the coats-of-arms it bears—a noble little structure. Anwick Lock was constructed just below the junction of the New and Old rivers—this division pre-dated the navigation as did the divisions of the Slea in Sleaford itself. There is no road approach to this site, which is accessible by walking along the bank from the Ewerby Thorpe road.

For the Kyme Eau length of the navigation take the B1395 to South Kyme with the remains of a priory and the isolated keep of a castle built in the fourteenth century by Gilbert de Umfraville, the first person recorded to have levied tolls on shipping using the Kyme Eau and who may have been responsible for straightening the river between South and North Kyme and Chapel Hill. This part of the river remained navigable until Kyme Lower Lock was converted into a sluice in the 1940s. Indeed, a proposal to convert this sluice into a navigable lock again is now under discussion, which would enable the river to be reopened to boats up to Ewerby Waithe Common. To reach the junction with the Witham take the minor road off the A153 through Dogdyke.

From Dogdyke you can see the outfall of the River Bain on the opposite bank of the Witham. The Horncastle Navigation joined the Witham a couple of miles further upstream. The promoters of the navigation had incorporated in its route the mile long Tattershall (or Gibson's) Canal, cut as a private under-taking across the Earl of Fortescue's land in 1786. This stretch is now dry and an embankment has been made across the site of the entrance lock. Tattershall on the A153 is dominated by the splen-did brick-built keep of Ralph Cromwell's castle, begun in 1433. The main road crosses the navigation between Tattershall and Coningsby and thereafter is not more than ½ mile away from it on its eastern side. It may be more convenient, however, to follow the minor road through Kirkby-on-Bain and Roughton which joins the B1191 to enter Horncastle from the west. The several locks have been weired, but the original brickwork can be found in places. Look for rather larger bricks than usual; these were locally made and their dimensions and quality were speci-fied by the navigation committee. As with the Sleaford Naviga-tion, there are comparatively few bridges.

In Horncastle there were two basins which have been recon-structed as drainage channels. The swimming pool is on the site of the dry dock. There may still be mooring rings on the walls of warehouses by the north basin. Like Sleaford, Horncastle is an attractive town to potter about in with much of interest to be found.

OS sheets 122, 130

The Caistor Canal

The market town of Caistor stands 250ft high on the western edge of the Lincolnshire Wolds. It is of great antiquity; at one time a British hill fort, it became a Roman walled town and was later referred to by the Venerable Bede as a place of some importance. By the closing years of the eighteenth century it was a moderately wealthy small market town whose prosperity, it was thought by several local merchants, could be increased by a canal connection with the River Ancholme. A survey was entrusted to William Jessop and work commenced after an act was obtained in 1793.

Sadly, the canal was a failure. It was cut from the Ancholme about midway between Brigg and Bishopbridge but reached no further eastward than Moortown 4 miles away—half the distance from the river to Caistor. There were 5 locks: Beck End, on the river, Ings, Willow, Hill and Moor, raising the canal 42ft. The road between North and South Kelsey crossed the canal and there was a basin by the bridge. The intention was to bring the canal much closer to Caistor, and Navigation Lane leads from the centre of the town to the proposed site of the basin, near (or beneath) the sewage works. The money to complete the undertaking, however, did not materialise and it appears that no interest on the shares was ever paid. There are no trading records, but it would seem likely that there was some navigation in the first half of the nineteenth century. The canal was abandoned in about 1855.

Moortown is on the crossing of the B1205, a road that potters around Lincolnshire without getting anywhere in particular, and the B1434—which does the same sort of thing at lesser length and heads roughly north–south instead of east–west. The basin is on the north side of the crossing, behind the phone box, although you may need to use some imagination. The bed lies beneath cottage gardens on the north side of the B1205, but it soon becomes discernible as you head westward. The road swings away, but the canal takes up some water from a stream and makes almost due west for South Kelsey Basin. From here to the Ancholme it is a deep, and sometimes damp, ditch. The entrance lock, gateless now, is close to a point where the old course of the Ancholme crosses the new.

Caistor itself is worth a visit if you are in the vicinity, but the canal has little attraction to offer. Why not, though, walk down to the foot of Navigation Lane and try to re-create the planned route of the canal to Moortown? Can you be sure that none of this route was cut?

OS sheet 113

The Louth Canal

The Louth Canal is an isolated navigation tucked away by the north-east coast of Lincolnshire. As with other Lincolnshire towns—Horncastle and Sleaford are examples—Louth's trade suffered in the eighteenth century from poor roads running through marshy country. Louth's river, the Lud, was inadequate for navigation but sufficient for a water supply, and the two engineers consulted by the corporation, John Grundy and John Smeaton, agreed in general on a route to the mouth of the Humber at Tetney Haven, a distance of 11¾ miles, based on the river and including 8 locks. The work was completed throughout by 1770, over 20 years before Sleaford and Horncastle obtained their canals.

For many years the canal was in the hands of the Chaplin family who had managed to negotiate a 99-year lease. They ran it at some profit to themselves with, it is estimated, tolls rising to about £5,000 a year in the late 1820s. In the last period of the lease the Great Northern Railway took over the canal, but it withdrew when the lease ended. The canal continued trading, with a gradual decline in receipts, until World War I. After 1916 it became very little used and it was eventually abandoned in 1924.

Louth is a tidy old market town with a magnificent church and Alfred Tennyson among the grammar school's old boys. The canal basin is on the north-east side of the town; look for River Head Road and the Woolpack Inn. Some of the large warehouses still survive. The lock at the entrance to the basin has been converted to a weir. The canal heads north-eastward past Keddington and Alvingham, then swings north-west across nearly 6 miles of flat and lonely country. It is crossed at Thoresby Bridge by the A1031 a mile to the west of North Coates, then turns north-east again to Tetney Lock and the outfall at Tetney Haven.

Six of the Louth locks were of especially interesting design.

These locks—Top, Keddington Church, Ticklepenny, Willows, Salter Fen and Alvingham—were brick-built with four bays on each side curving in to the land with wooden ties at their intersections. Whatever the purpose of this method of construction, it does not seem to have been particularly successful as there are several reports referring to the poor condition of the locks, one of which comments on an overhang of 2ft at Alvingham. Remains of the locks, all of which were of slightly different dimensions, can be found in the first 4 miles out of Louth; there is one by the bridge south-east of Keddington and another south of Alvingham, also by the bridge. Out Fen Lock, the one below Alvingham, was built with conventional straight sides, and Tetney Lock, below the bridge on the Tetney-North Coates road, was built with two pairs of sea-doors and two pairs of navigation-doors. It is now converted into a sluice.

Exploring the Louth Canal takes you through a part of England into which few people from elsewhere seem to go. It may not be exciting, but it is an experience worth enjoying. There is some slight possibility that the Anglian Water Authority may reopen the canal in the future.

OS sheet 113

Bibliography

BOOKS

Barley, M. W., *Lincolnshire and the Fens* (EP Publishing, 1972)

Boyes, J. and Russell, R., *Canals of Eastern England* (David & Charles, 1977)

Clark, Roy, *Black Sailed Traders* (Putnam, 1961)

Clarke, W. G., *In Breckland Wilds* (W. Heffer, 1937)

Malster, Robert, *Wherries and Waterways* (Terence Dalton, 1971)

Rogers, Alan (ed), *The Making of Stamford* (Leicester University Press, 1965)

ARTICLES AND BOOKLETS

'Flashlocks on English Waterways', M. J. T. Lewis and others, *Industrial Archaeology*, Vol 6, No 3, and Vol 7, No 2, (1969 and 1970)

The Lark Navigation, D. E. Weston (1980)

Stamford, an Industrial History, N. C. Birch (Lincolnshire IA Group, 1972)

'Staunches and Navigation of the Little Ouse River', R. H. Clarke, *Transactions*, Newcomen Society, Vol 30

Stour from Source to Sea, Vernon Clarke (1979)

'Water Transport in Norfolk' information cards (Norfolk Museums Service)

The Wisbech and Upwell Tramway, E. J. S. Gadsden and others (1965, rep 1972)

SOCIETIES

East Anglian Waterways Association Ltd
Great Ouse Restoration Society
River Stour Trust
Sleaford Navigation Society

7

THE NORTH OF ENGLAND

The Mersey & Irwell Navigation

The River Mersey provided an open navigation to Warrington in the Middle Ages. With the growth of Manchester came the demand for an extension of the navigation and in 1736 the Mersey & Irwell Navigation was opened. In later years, following the opening of the competing Bridgewater Canal, improvements were made, the distance being shortened by the construction of several straight cuts. In 1804 the Runcorn & Latchford Canal was opened on the southern side and a new Woolston Cut was made in 1821. When completed, the navigation from Hunt's Bank, Manchester, to Bank Quay, Warrington, was 28¾ miles long. In 1885 it was bought by the Manchester Ship Canal Company which required the navigation for its own line. After the construction of the Ship Canal, most of the Runcorn & Latchford was abandoned together with the cuts above Rixton Junction, leaving only a few short lengths in use, most of which have been abandoned in recent years.

In the city, landing stages on the Irwell survive by Victoria Bridge and there are several old warehouses on Water Street. You may also find the entrance of two canals: the Manchester & Salford Junction, and the Manchester, Bolton & Bury. The Irwell becomes the Ship Canal at Woden Street footbridge, below Hulme Lock at the junction with the Bridgewater Canal. There is no more of the old navigation until Barton, but then you find surviving stretches north of Barton Locks, in the segment between the M63 and A57, between Irlam Ferry and the A57 and at Irlam to the west of the locks. Below Warburton Bridge there is more evidence and from Rixton Junction the river and Ship Canal separate. Woolston New Cut, still holding somewhat polluted water, lies to the south of the A57 between the M6 and A50.

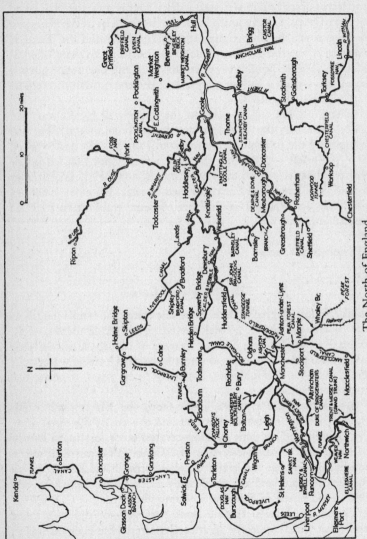

The North of England

The entrance lock of the surviving length of the Runcorn &
Latchford is to the west of the A50 bridge over the Mersey. Bank
Quay, where the navigation began, is on a horseshoe bend; note
the transporter bridge and soap works. This is now the tidal reach
of the Mersey. On the south bank are the remains of the Runcorn
& Latchford, the Ship Canal, the Bridgewater and the Trent &
Mersey at Preston Brook, while to the north is the abandoned St
Helen's. There is much to see in this area; the Ordnance Survey
sheet and Gordon Biddle's *Lancashire Waterways* will prove per-
fectly adequate guides.

The most famous worker on the Mersey & Irwell was Old
Billy, reputedly the world's oldest horse, born in 1760. He was
bought by the navigation company in 1762 or 1763 and worked
as a 'gin horse'—providing the power for a hoist that loaded or
unloaded boats—or on the towpath until 1819. He was retired to
a field near Latchford Lock and died in 1822. His story is told in
Old Billy: 1760–1822, a Manchester Museum publication by E. L.
Seyd.

OS sheets 108, 109

The St Helen's Canal

It takes a high degree of dedication to explore the whole length of
the St Helen's Canal, a total, including all the branches, of 17
miles. It is not that it is difficult to trace or that the traffic hazards
are greater than elsewhere; rather it is that this historic waterway,
pre-dating the Bridgewater Canal by three years, is being destroyed piecemeal.

At Widnes the entrance locks from the Mersey still exist,
though serving no useful purpose, and the site of the canal dock
can be detected. A park is being created incorporating a length
of canal on the south-east side of Widnes. You can follow the
towpath alongside the watered canal through Fiddlers Ferry to
Sankey Bridges and on to Bewsey Lock. The canal has been
dewatered north of Bewsey for some distance.

North of Dallam, Hulme Lock survives—or did two years
ago—but what used to be an attractive stretch has been infilled in
the area south and north of Winwick Quay. The workshops at
Winwick have been converted to other uses. Near Vulcan village
a watered stretch can be found, but by Sankey Viaduct the St

Helen's has been almost obliterated. It becomes a footpath through the Sankey Valley Linear Park.

On the east side of St Helen's there are bits of watered canal, including Engine Lock. The Old Double Lock, the first staircase lock to be built in Britain, has been made into a cascade but at least has not been demolished. Further exploration can be attempted from the A58 crossing of the Gerrard's Bridge Branch and from Corporation Street Bridge and Church Street near St Helen's centre. A detailed itinerary can be found in Gordon Biddle's *Lancashire Waterways*.

OS sheet 108

The Manchester, Bolton & Bury Canal

Like other urban waterways, the Manchester, Bolton & Bury Canal is not very suited to exploration by the motorist. It is best to decide on convenient stopping places and to move thence on foot: Salford, Clifton, Prestolee and Bury are suggested, but perhaps Salford should be essayed only by the really dedicated.

The canal was a coal-carrying venture, opened in 1797 with broad locks, there being an idea that it might eventually make a connection with the Leeds & Liverpool. Apart from the connection with the Irwell at Manchester, the canal was completed by 1796 from Oldfield Road, Salford, to Bolton and Bury. The link with the Irwell, north of Hampson Street, was completed twelve years later, after a proposal to join the canal directly with the Rochdale Canal had failed. The canal continued trading well into the twentieth century, but a breach in 1936 resulted in the abandonment of all except two short sections which endured until 1961. It had two specialities of its own: one was a flourishing passenger service, estimated to have carried about 60,000 people annually in the canal's early years, and the other was the use of containers, as on the Bridgewater, with coal being loaded and carried in boxes.

With determination, some glimpses of what is left of the canal in Salford may be obtained; try Princes Bridge, Canal Street and Upper Wharf Street. There used to be 6 locks and 2 short tunnels hereabouts. Agecroft Road Bridge, towards Pendlebury, gives access to the towpath; note the substantial masonry walls and the evidence of trade in years past alongside the channel. You can

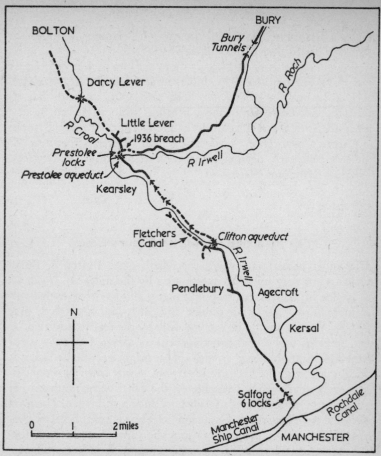

The Manchester, Bolton & Bury Canal

follow the towpath northward to Clifton and see the 3-arched
aqueduct over the Irwell and the 1½ mile long Fletcher's Canal,
cut along the west bank of the river to Wet Earth Colliery.
Access by road to this area is not easy. Continuing along the canal
past Clifton is not very profitable, unless sewage works have
a special attraction for you.

If you have taken the A6 out of Salford, branch on to the A666
and then turn right at Kearsley to the A667. A mile along the
road crosses both Irwell and canal at Ringley. Walk northward
from here, past the seventh milestone and the remains of double
locks. Now the canal is watered and there is a fine view of the

Irwell as you cross it by the workmanlike 4-arch Prestolee Aqueduct built of stone and red brick. The canal turns and widens into a basin, on the north side of which are the remains of the Prestolee flight of 6 locks, lifting the canal 66ft up the valley side. There is another basin at the top, where the canal divides into the Bolton and Bury arms.

There is about a mile of the Bolton arm still in water, wide and well preserved as it is used by an angling club. At Nob End, where the arm begins, there are some interesting old cottages. The stretch ends at Little Lever by the A6053. The canal continued to Bolton above the course of the River Croal. Two aqueducts along here have been destroyed and few traces of anything can be found. The Bolton Basin and terminal buildings were demolished for a feeder road to the nearby motorway.

The Bury arm, nearly 5 miles long, can be followed all the way. First there is a dry stretch, with evidence of the 1936 breach. Then water reappears after a brick dam and you can walk on to Radcliffe, noting the massive $\frac{1}{4}$ mile stones and the original bridges. The canal is blocked at Radcliffe, but it is easy to regain the towpath. Just over a mile further on, Elton Reservoir lies on your left and the Irwell approaches below you on the right. Soon the industrial buildings of Bury close in on you. A few years ago you could have wandered around the terminal basins with their splendid warehouses. It is difficult not to regard their destruction as an act of vandalism; this was a unique canal terminal of the 1790s and its loss, in terms of industrial history, is tragic. You may find it worth while, however, to look for the yard of Renwick's Freight along a turning off Bolton Street. This yard was the top basin and was infilled in about 1958. Look at the old buildings and find a small tunnel coming out from under a warehouse. Here is part of the Weddell Brook Extension cut to meet a feeder from the Irwell close by.

If you happen to be in Bury and wish to spend an hour or so exploring the canal it is worth calling in at the Department of Leisure Services, Textile Hall, Manchester Road, for a copy of *An Intimate Look at Bury's Old Canal*, a booklet by Fred Campbell published by the Bury & District Local History Society. The mixture of information and reminiscence will make your exploration more rewarding.

OS sheet 109

The Manchester & Salford Junction Canal

This impressively named navigation was opened in 1839, a mere $\frac{5}{8}$ mile in length, connecting the River Irwell with a short branch of the Rochdale Canal. Its purpose had been forestalled, however, by the Bridgewater Canal which a year earlier had completed its Hulme Cut, enabling traffic to move between the river navigation and the Rochdale via its own Castlefield Wharves. With its 499yd tunnel, 4 locks (3 of which were duplicated) and 2 pumping engines to lift water from the Irwell, it cost about £60,000 to construct but attracted little trade. Nevertheless, it proved a benefit to the Mersey & Irwell Company, bringing them an additional toll revenue and a reason for building additional wharves, while it was responsible for its own heavy maintenance costs. In 1842 the Mersey & Irwell took it over as the Salford Junction was no longer a viable proposition on its own. Both navigations passed into the Bridgewater empire three years later.

The Junction Canal lasted until 1875 with a small revenue from tolls continuing to accrue. In that year the 2 furlongs nearest the Rochdale Junction, between Mosley Street and Water Street, were filled in for the building of Central Station. In 1899 the Great Northern Goods Station was built nearby over the canal; 2 wells were sunk 25ft down to the canal for the interchange of goods between the railway and the docks of the Ship Canal via the Irwell. This traffic continued along the Salford Junction until 1922. The remaining length of the canal was abandoned in 1936.

If you are examining the Rochdale Canal in central Manchester it is worth continuing to try to discern what is left of the Salford Junction. Look for the entrance to the canal from the Rochdale; you should find it in the area bounded by Oxford Street on the east and Whitworth Street West. You may find a brick bridge on Lower Mosley Street and another bridge of different character on Great Bridgewater Street; both of these crossed the canal. Part of the tunnel, which incorporates a towpath, lies beneath the Granada Television Studios. During World War II it was used as an air-raid shelter. If you are really enthusiastic, it might be possible to obtain permission to view it. From here, make your way to Quay Street from where you should be able to see signs of the canal's entrance to the Irwell. It may be worth mentioning that canal-hunting in Manchester is not particularly easy. A car is an encumbrance, and you may find the exercise impossible without a good street guide. If you have the opportunity to lay on to this the lines of the canals, which you can obtain from early Ordnance Survey maps in the city Reference Library, then you should have little difficulty—and you may well find relics that have not been referred to here.

OS sheet 109

The Rochdale Canal

The Rochdale Canal was a massive and ambitious undertaking. Its engineer, William Jessop, cut it boldly through the centre of Manchester from a junction with the Bridgewater Canal at Castlefield and lifted it over the Pennines to Sowerby Bridge with 92 locks in 33 miles. Unlike the Huddersfield—which terminated almost hesitantly on the outskirts of Manchester—it had no summit tunnel and its locks could take the wide boats off the Calder & Hebble or two narrow boats together. At £600,000 it cost not much less than the Leeds & Liverpool, which had the same number of locks and was nearly four times the length. None of this, however, has saved much of it from an ignominious fate, rescue from which, though not impossible, will prove vastly expensive.

As with the Huddersfield Narrow, the Rochdale Canal is shown throughout on the Ordnance Survey sheets and is accessible almost throughout. Apart from the first 1¼ miles from the Manchester terminus the canal was abandoned in 1952; however, it is still owned by the Rochdale Canal Company and not by the British Waterways Board. This bottom section was saved from abandonment by the strenuous efforts of a few individuals, including Dr David Owen who steered a narrow boat through it in 1964, the journey from Castlefield to the junction with the Ashton taking twelve days. In the early 1970s a great deal of voluntary work was organised on this stretch by the Inland Waterways Association and the Peak Forest Canal Society. With the reopening of the Ashton Canal—and hence the Cheshire Ring—the Rochdale Company has agreed to keep this link, with its nine locks, open, and although navigation may not always be easy, it is possible.

You find the entrance to the Rochdale at Castlefield and you can follow the towpath through the centre of Manchester passing in a tunnel beneath Piccadilly. At Princess Street a bridge takes the towpath across the canal and on to Canal Street. The canal company's offices are in Dale Street, where the basin has become a car park. Rodwell Tower now stands above Dale Street Lock. In the car park are two large warehouses and the impressive gateway arch is a token of the canal company's importance and assurance in the early days.

Having passed the junction with the Ashton, the canal, no longer navigable, markedly deteriorates. The water still flows, but only through rubbish and detritus. Soon you will find that the canal and its immediate surroundings have been 'landscaped'—there is some grass and a few trees, an asphalt towpath and a channel of water a few inches deep with locks filled in to make waterfalls for garden gnomes. Council estates, then factories, lie on either side. Near Newton Heath you will find Rochdale Canal Park, a further example of municipal manicuring. See it for yourself and form your own judgement of this approach to treating an 'abandoned' waterway.

Leaving Manchester, the canal swings northward towards Rochdale. At Failsworth it is culverted beneath a shopping centre, but a victory for restoration was recently won at Chadderton, where a proposal to eliminate 1,000yd of canal by the M66 Manchester Outer Ring Road was defeated in Parliament as a result of a campaign by the Rochdale Canal Society. North of Chadderton the A664 takes you alongside the canal which, however, has been butchered by the M62 crossing near Castleton, close to the junction with the short infilled Heywood Branch.

After Castleton the canal turns north-eastward through industrial Rochdale. On the left of the A664 there is a succession of large spinning-mills; behind them runs the canal. One of the canal's two most interesting bridges—Gorrell's—has unfortunately been demolished for road building. These were both skew bridges; the stones of Gorrell's Bridge were laid in straight courses and this made a fascinating comparison with the construction of its neighbour, March Barns, where winding courses were used to solve the problem of the angled crossing. These bridges date from about 1797. The canal here, although interrupted by culverts, carries a fair depth of water. Continuing through Rochdale, you soon come to a surprising development: as a result of a job-creation scheme a particularly decrepit stretch has been transformed. Four locks have been restored, the channel cleared, trees and shrubs planted, cobbles laid—compare this 'landscaping' with the efforts in Manchester. The canal has been used by trailed boats and the hope is that a narrow boat will be launched before long for passenger trips. The short branch into the centre of Rochdale has been filled in and the terminal warehouses demolished; some of the bridges that spanned the branch, however, can still be found.

From Rochdale the A6033 takes you towards Littleborough and Todmorden; houses cluster close to the road as the scenery becomes wilder. On your right the canal continues its ascent, with the reservoirs constructed to supply it in the hills above. At Smallbridge it is worth taking a lane to Clegg Hall; you will find some interesting buildings lining the canal as well as the derelict hall. North of Littleborough there are several locks close together leading to the short summit level; this, only ¾ mile long, gave the boatmen little respite. Between Castlefield and the summit 56 locks were built; the summit itself is in a cutting 38ft deep. As with the Huddersfield Narrow, however, particularly in the middle decades of the nineteenth century, disappointingly little traffic went over the summit level, more and more of it being restricted to short-haul, especially at the Manchester end.

It is well worth stopping at the summit and the Summit Inn is conveniently placed. Longlees Lock has recently been restored by the canal society. It is in this area that you can best appreciate the skill of the canal's engineers and the craftsmanship of its labourers. Samuel Smiles wrote of it:

> Whoever examines the works at this day, even after all that has been accomplished in canal and railway engineering, will admit that the mark of a master's hand is unmistakably stamped upon them.

Very true, despite the fact that Smiles addressed his words to Rennie and not to Jessop, the canal's engineer to whom the tribute was due.

From Littleborough to Todmorden the A6033 keeps you within a few hundred yards of the canal. At Todmorden you turn eastward on to the A646 along the Calder Valley. The descent is through thirty-six locks; the spectacular scenery is more popular with tourists than the grimmer landscape on the Lancashire side. There are plans for improvements to the canal in Todmorden and Hebden Bridge. It is in Hebden Bridge that you will find the canal's only major aqueduct, of four arches over the Calder. It may be easier to find the post office first; the aqueduct is close to it. Hebden Bridge itself was a weaving town; the industry moved here from the nearby village of Heptonstall when steam power came to the valley and mills were built near the Calder.

The final stretch of the Rochdale runs south of east through Mytholmroyd to Sowerby Bridge, still accompanied by the A646. The junction with the Calder & Hebble in Sowerby Bridge is close to the church; you will find a basin, warehouses and some massive mooring rings. A length of the canal in Sowerby Bridge is culverted under the main road. An inspection of a Calder & Hebble lock will show you another reason why the Rochdale Canal, although for many years a profitable undertaking and the most successful of the trans-Pennine waterways, did not fulfil all its expectations; at 57½ft these locks could not accommodate the 70ft boats mainly used on the Rochdale, and commerce between the canals was thereby impeded.

A tour of the Rochdale is both an exhilarating and a melancholy experience. In conception and execution it was one of Britain's greatest canals and a journey along its route helps you to understand some of the achievements of the Industrial Revolution. Its abandonment as a commercial navigation was, no doubt, inevitable—as can be said of the Huddersfield Narrow—but its subsequent treatment, particularly in the area between Dale Street and the Manchester boundary, says little for the environmental sensitivity of the post-war years. Restoration in this area, should it take place, may well make use of the Hollinwood arm of the Ashton Canal as it might prove more practicable to restore this arm and connect it to the Rochdale than to disinter the Rochdale from its shallow graves. In the meantime, there are hopeful signs that no more of the Rochdale will be destroyed and that the local authorities are becoming aware of the asset that it may prove.

OS sheets 109, 110

The Huddersfield Narrow Canal

There is no difficulty in finding the Huddersfield Narrow Canal, either on the map or on the ground. Although some short stretches have been culverted and most of the locks have been cascaded or capped, the canal is still in water; indeed, it serves a vital purpose as a water-supply channel for industry and other waterways. There is an active restoration society, founded in 1974, which looks hopefully towards bringing back navigation to the Huddersfield Narrow; and although the problems are complex, they may not be insuperable.

The Huddersfield Narrow is the third and shortest of the trans-Pennine routes. It was opened in 1811, joining Sir John Ramsden's Broad Canal in Huddersfield with the Ashton Canal in Manchester. Its seventy-four locks, and the demands of the mill-owners for water, necessitated the construction of ten reservoirs. In Standedge Tunnel it boasts the longest tunnel on the British waterways, and at 656ft above sea-level it is also the highest. Unlike its great neighbour and rival the Rochdale Canal, however, it was never a major commercial success and, owing partly to difficulties and mishaps with the tunnel, most of its traffic was short-haul at either end. Another hindrance was the narrow locks which could not accommodate boats off the broad navigations to the north-east; here the Rochdale with its wide locks had an advantage. The canal company found railway competition too much for it and sold out to the Huddersfield & Manchester Railway in 1844. Three years later the first railway tunnel pierced the hills at Standedge.

Traffic over the summit of the canal had stopped by 1905, by which time the cost of maintenance was exceeding receipts. Some use continued to be made of the navigation for the next few decades but ceased in World War II. Apart from a short section in Huddersfield, the canal was abandoned in 1944; the remaining length followed in 1963. About 10 per cent of the channel has been infilled since abandonment.

As the canal is easy of access and can be followed almost throughout, there is no need to do more than indicate some of the more interesting features. The Narrow and Broad Canals meet in the centre of Huddersfield, but some stretches have been culverted in the town. The A62 Oldham road accompanies the canal for some 7 miles to Marsden; the River Colne is also close to the canal, which crosses it several times by single-arch aqueducts. There is an aqueduct at Golcar and a swing bridge which could be restored to use. The locks, as you may see, have either been cascaded or capped with concrete; in a few instances the chamber has been partly demolished. At Slaithwaite a considerable length has been culverted and a pedestrian walkway built over it; Britannia Bridge has been demolished and the roads realigned. After Slaithwaite the canal continues to climb towards the summit through eighteen more locks; the scenery is impressive, with many massive Victorian mills surviving along the canalside.

For the north portal of Standedge you turn northward to Marsden Station and then left to the Junction Inn. A lane leads to the BWB maintenance yard and from a bridge over the canal you can see the portal with two disused single-track railway tunnels above it and the double-track tunnel still in use. Note the derelict tunnel-keeper's house. Standedge Tunnel, which cost about £160,000 to construct and was the most expensive canal tunnel as well as the longest, was built 9ft wide and 9ft high above water-level. It was cut through gritstone and only part of it was lined. There were three passing places originally. L. T. C. Rolt made one of the last voyages through it in the 1940s, describing it as:

> a unique experience which I shall never forget ... For the greater part of its length the walls and roof are of jagged rock which reveals to this day the shot holes of those intrepid 'navigators' who blasted their way through the Pennines a century and a half ago. In places these rock walls recede and for a short space the narrow cave becomes a roomy cavern where boats were able to pass each other ... There are ventilation shafts at intervals, but these contribute only the faintest glimmer of daylight to the depths, for the shafts are anything up to 600ft deep, while their mouths are protected by stout timber stagings to guard against rock falls. Upon each side at a slightly higher level run the railway tunnels on the line from Manchester to Leeds, and at intervals there are subterranean galleries connecting the tunnels, for the railway engineers made use of the canal tunnel for construction work, drainage and ventilation. At the passage of an express the rocks reverberate with a dull thunder of sound and a sudden blast of air is soon followed by a blinding cloud of acrid smoke which bellies out from the cross galleries. Altogether a closer approximation of the legendary route to the infernal regions by way of the Styx it would be difficult to conceive.

It took Rolt over 2 hours to navigate the tunnel; in earlier years, a time of 3½ hours was allowed for boats to be legged through. As the tunnel is part of the water-supply channel and serves to drain the railway tunnels it has to be kept clear, but it is only open for inspection by BWB engineers.

The south portal is at Diggle, reached by turning left off either the A62 or A670. Make for the railway and you will find access to the portal through a gate beside a phone box. The date 1893 on the keystone is the date when the tunnel was extended by cut-and-cover because of alterations to the nearby railway lay-out.

On this side of the Pennines, the Tame is the river the canal follows. After an attractive stretch at Uppermill, where the canal society has effected some improvements and the lock retains its original paddle gear, the canal crosses the Tame by Saddleworth Aqueduct (irreverently known as 'old sag' for reasons that are apparent when you look at it). This aqueduct has a lock-chamber incorporated into its structure.

After Saddleworth follow the A635 into Manchester. The canal is on the east side of the road; you will see several mills and another aqueduct. On the south side of Mossley is Scout Tunnel, with both portals bricked up. This short tunnel was cut through solid rock and incorporated a towpath. At Stalybridge the canal swings west; here about ½ mile has disappeared beneath road construction and industrial building and, should the canal be restored, the canal society consider it may be necessary to divert it into the Tame at this point.

On the east side of Manchester the Huddersfield Narrow made an end-on junction with the Ashton Canal at Whitelands Bridge. The first lock here is filled in and the adjoining length of the Narrow Canal is in a sorry state. There was no terminal basin for the Huddersfield; the Ashton company, which had encouraged its construction, wanted its traffic to continue on to its own line and use the Ashton Basin at Dukinfield, where the Huddersfield company had a warehouse.

Comparing it with the other Manchester canals, especially the Rochdale, it is easy to see that the Huddersfield Narrow, despite its great tunnel, was built comparatively 'on the cheap'. The workmanship of the lock-chambers in particular is inferior and the narrow locks themselves proved a false economy. With 74 of them in just under 20 miles, no boatman could have looked forward to the through journey with pleasure, especially with the thought of Standedge half-way along. It could never compete successfully with the Rochdale; its most important cargo was general merchandise and the tonnage carried of bulk cargoes—coal, corn and limestone—was small.

Nevertheless, scenically the Huddersfield is a splendid canal. In its present unnavigable state it is a 'missing link' in the Pennine waterways circuit. Of the three trans-Pennine canals, only the Leeds & Liverpool remains open, and this has difficulty in meeting the demands made upon it by increased pleasure traffic. The hope is that the Huddersfield can follow the example of the Ashton and be brought back to full life as a navigable waterway, not merely being prettified into a series of fragments of a 'water park'. Until the finance is available, the aim is to preserve the structures that remain and prevent any further deterioration or infilling.

OS sheets 109, 110

The Dearne & Dove and the Barnsley Canals

These two canals obtained their parliamentary acts on the same day in 1793. Together they formed a connection between the Don Navigation at Swinton and the Aire & Calder at Heath, a line just under 25 miles long with a total of 38 locks. They were opened throughout their length in 1804 with coal carried by Yorkshire keels as the principal cargo.

The Dearne & Dove had two branches, each a little over 2 miles in length, which served collieries at Elsecar and Worsborough. It was an offshoot of the Don Navigation Company and traded profitably into the middle years of the nineteenth century. It underwent various changes of ownership in the second half of the century until in 1894 it was bought by the Sheffield & South Yorkshire Navigation Company as part of a scheme to improve communication between Sheffield and the Humber. Financial control, however, remained with the Manchester, Sheffield & Lincolnshire Railway Company, who were not especially concerned with promoting waterway traffic. The condition of the canal, subject to subsidence in this heavily mined area, deteriorated. The Worsborough Branch closed to boats in 1906; the Elsecar Branch carried on until 1928, and the last through boat reached Barnsley in 1934. The main line was kept open for short-haul traffic to a major colliery until this ended in 1952. Apart from a $\frac{1}{2}$ mile length at Swinton the canal was abandoned in 1961.

This open section of the Dearne & Dove runs by the Canal Tavern on the Swinton–Mexborough road. There are plenty of barges in the lock pounds, owing to the presence of a working boatyard. The line headed north-west, between Wath-upon-

Dearne and Bolton-upon-Dearne, but after the first ½ mile most of it has been infilled, including the 472yd Adwick Tunnel, of which faint traces may still be found on the west side of the railway line shortly after the infilling begins. From Wath to Barnsley the canal line lies between the railway and the A633 Swinton–Barnsley road; most of the bridges that crossed it have gone, but a stone bridge on Wetmoor Lane should still be there. The branch at Elsecar survives; you can find it between Brampton and Wombwell from the B6089, a few hundred yards before the junction with the A633. To follow the branch take the B6097 at Hemingfield to Elsecar Colliery. There were six locks on the branch, now converted to weirs; it terminated just beyond the colliery and was fed from Elsecar Reservoir, which can be found from a minor road.

Nearly all the rest of the main line has vanished in a land-reclamation undertaking. On the approach to Barnsley the line crossed to the south of the main road. Here you may detect it as a weedy ditch, with the junction with the Worsborough Branch still traceable. Worsborough Basin still holds water and its presence is further indicated by the Wharf Inn.

The Barnsley Canal, since its closure in 1953, has fared rather better. It was promoted by the Aire & Calder company, but for the first few years trade failed to come up to expectations, as Barnby Colliery failed and other mines were slow to expand to take advantage of the facilities for transport. In 1809 a tramroad was constructed to connect the collieries at Silkstone with Barnby Basin. The high quality coal produced in these pits was in great demand, and as other local mines built their own connecting tramroad branches, the canal prospered.

Railway competition eventually led the Barnsley company to lease the canal to the Aire & Calder, whose efficient management improved matters. In 1871 the Aire & Calder bought the canal, but within a few years most of the coal traffic had moved to the railway. The length between Barnby and Barugh Locks was abandoned in 1893, but a little traffic lingered on further north until the early 1950s.

Only faint traces of Barnby Basin may be found 3 miles west of Barnsley on the north side of the A635 and west of the motor-way embankment. The canal ran through Barugh and approached the River Dearne which it followed closely around the north of Barnsley. There used to be large warehouses at Barnsley

Basin. The canal turned sharply north-east to cross the Dearne by a five-arch aqueduct, demolished soon after abandonment (SE 356069). It resumed its earlier direction for about ½ mile and then swung north into an area of what are now disused railway lines. It is distinguishable as a ditch from the minor roads running east from Monk Bretton and Carlton, but the bridges have been flattened. There used to be an interesting bridge on the B6428, west of Royston & Notton Station. This had pairs of gates to shut off the road; the bridge was then lifted by electrically powered machinery housed in its four brick columns. It was opened in 1934, but sadly it is no more.

Some sections of the canal are watered and act as reservoirs for the National Coal Board. Rural tranquillity, however, can be found near Cold Hiendley where the canal is preserved for fishing. The Cold Hiendley Cutting is approachable from the minor road heading eastward from Notton; with the mining area left behind us we are now in pleasant, rolling country. By the southern boundary of Haw Park the feeder from Wintersett Reservoir meets the canal which, heading northward, soon resembles an aristocratic ornamental water as it runs alongside the grounds of Walton Hall. To the north of the drive to the hall the canal is infilled as far as Walton Colliery, but a further watered stretch can be found between the colliery and the railway adjoining the A638 Wakefield–Doncaster road, which crosses the canal near the Jolly Sailor.

The Barnsley Canal met the Aire & Calder at Heath, on the south-east side of Wakefield. Now its bed lies beneath Wakefield Power Station. This section of canal, however, was made in 1816 to replace the original cut near Heath village which had proved unsatisfactory as rubbish collected in it when the river rose. The original cut, which took the course of a small stream, may still be traced, and crossing it you can find a stone bridge with grooves made by tow-ropes clearly marked.

As Charles Hadfield says: 'The Barnsley Canal formed part of a transport system that extended from the Trent to Hull, the Yorkshire Ouse and over the Pennines.' As well as coal, cargoes included yarn, oak bark, iron, ironstone, limestone, malt and millstones—raw materials for the industries of the north. With its connecting links destroyed, and with the railway system that replaced it now so attenuated, we are left with our heavy and costly lorries wearing away the roads on which they run. It is something to think of as you explore the few remains of the Barnsley and Dearne & Dove Canals.

OS sheet 110

The Bradford Canal

The Bradford Canal branched off the Leeds & Liverpool at Shipley and ascended to Bradford, $3\frac{3}{8}$ miles away, through 10 locks. It was opened in 1774, coal, iron, stone and, later, wool being the main cargoes. A packet-boat service also developed to Leeds, Selby and Goole, connecting with sailings for London, Newcastle and Hull. As Bradford grew so the canal was almost engulfed with mills, factories and dyeworks built on its banks, drawing off its water and polluting it in return. To maintain its levels the canal company began illegally taking water from Bradford Beck; this was polluted as well. At times the noxious gases in the canal burnt on the surface with a blue flame. Bradford City Council tried, but failed, to close it until in 1866 a court order was obtained prohibiting the canal company from abstracting water from the beck. Having failed to lease their property—not now so profitable owing to the competing Leeds & Bradford Railway—to the Leeds & Liverpool, the Bradford company gave up, closed and drained the canal and sold the top $\frac{1}{4}$ mile for building. This is now Forster Square.

The canal, however, was not yet allowed to die. Other canal companies felt its loss, as did some of the Bradford stone merchants; a new company was set up and by 1873 the canal, now shortened to 3 miles, was reopened. The solution to the problem of water supply was to install pumps at the locks to recirculate the water from the lower pound. Soon the canal was taken over by a joint committee of the Leeds & Liverpool and the Aire & Calder; new warehouses were built in Bradford, but the returns failed to justify the expense. Receipts fell sharply after 1910, trading coming almost to a standstill during World War I. In 1922 the canal was abandoned, drained and the land sold off.

Of the canal today, very little is left. In Shipley the northernmost few hundred yards, below the bottom lock, Windhill, are used as moorings for craft off the Leeds & Liverpool. For the rest of it, you might see something from the train; the railway line from Shipley to Forster Square, Bradford, runs parallel to the line of the canal on its western side. Nearly all the Bradford locks were built in staircase pairs and the remains of one of these were visible a couple of years ago. In Bradford, north of Forster Square there is a Canal Road, now part of a main road, and Wharf Street, a few years ago still cobbled, ran along the back of the warehouses that once lined the canal. There used to be traces of the canal by the gasworks. If there is any more to be found it will be close to Canal Road, but do not be too optimistic.

OS sheet 104

The Market Weighton Canal

No sooner—or so it might seem—does the Market Weighton Canal close than it opens again. An exaggeration perhaps; yet twice this century the canal has been closed, only to be reopened a few years later. The first occasion was in 1917, when the navigation was terminated by the County War Agricultural Committee; three years later control was returned to the canal's trustees who had it dredged and reopened from the entrance lock to Newport. Until 1958 a few vessels used the canal. In 1971 the navigation rights at the sea-lock were rescinded: 'The restoring of navigation on the Market Weighton Canal is not a serious consideration, despite the fact that both North America and the Land of Nod can be found on its banks', I pessimistically wrote in that year. Then in 1972 the sea-lock was scheduled as an ancient monument, thus ensuring its continued existence. The Yorkshire Water Authority soon began restoration work on the lock, the channel was dredged, and in 1978 the lock was back in working order and the navigation of the bottom 6 miles of canal was reopened. Owing to operational problems at the lock only limited use is possible, but it is no longer accurate to describe the Market Weighton, apart from the top 3 miles, as a 'lost canal'.

The main purpose of the canal is, as it always was, drainage of the flat lands between Market Weighton, at the foot of the Yorkshire Wolds, and the Humber. It was opened throughout in 1782, with its terminal basin on a minor road 2 miles south of Market Weighton. In about 1834 a short private branch was built by Sir Edward Vavasour, connecting the canal to the Holme-Market Weighton road; this branch operated for about thirty years and remained in private hands—as it still does.

Although the navigation was bought by the York & North Midland Railway in 1850, it continued to trade reasonably well into the 1880s. Traffic then fell sharply away and the top 3 miles, above Sod House Lock, soon became almost impassable. This section was abandoned in 1900 and remains so today. The rest of the canal was kept going almost entirely by a firm of brick-makers, Williamson & Co, whose works were at Newport, a village that grew up where the Selby–Kingston road crossed the navigation.

The top length of the canal is partly silted up. At River Head, the main line terminal basin, the original building has been incorporated in a farmhouse. Canal Head, at the end of Vavasour's Branch, can be found by the road 2¼ miles south-west of Market Weighton. The next turning left past Canal Head leads to Duck Nest and a bridge over the canal. The lock-chamber north of this bridge has been cleared out by the Market Weighton Canal Society, whose members are hopeful of eventually restoring the whole length of the canal. Near Duck Nest a short length has been infilled, but there are no insuperable difficulties to prevent restoration.

Sod House Lock, about 2¼ miles south of Duck Nest, has also been cleared out and now lacks only gates. From here southward the canal is in water, fed by a drainage channel, and navigable. A mile further on it takes up the water of the River Foulness and continues past North America, Sandholme Landing, beneath the M62 and the bridge at Newport. The bottom 3¼ miles cut across Walling Fen and access from the road is difficult. Weighton Lock on the Humber, nearly opposite Trent Falls, has two pairs of sea gates and two pairs of navigation gates and an inscription: 'Mr Grundy Engineer Mr Allen Surveyor Mr Smith Carpenter Mr Jefferson Mason Anno Domino 1773 Repaired 1826 by Joseph Whitehead.' Entry to the lock from the Humber is not difficult provided the tide and the weather are right.

OS sheet 106

The Pocklington Canal

Allied to the revival of the Yorkshire Derwent is the restoration of the Pocklington Canal, which leaves the river at Cottingwith and wanders generally north-eastward up nine locks in the direction of the pleasant little town of Pocklington. Don't look for it in Pocklington, however, as it gets no nearer than a basin opposite the Wellington Oak on the A1079, a mile south of the town. At the basin—Canal Head—there are an old warehouse and a lock-keeper's cottage, and the towpath is walkable for all of its 9½ mile length. For the first 5 miles of the walk the canal is unnavigable. The remainder of it, including two locks and four swing bridges, has been restored in the last decade by the British Waterways Board and volunteers of the Pocklington Canal Society, and there seems little doubt that eventually the whole waterway will be reopened.

The Pocklington Canal was in operation between 1818 and 1932, when the keel *Ebenezer* made the last commercial voyage. Its engineer was George Leather and, as befits his name, his work was sound and substantial. The bridges in particular are notable, with their strong construction, rounded buttresses and flowing lines. For the most part the canal seems to have had a quiet life with a moderate downward trade of agricultural produce and coal, with building materials, fertilisers and industrial goods coming up in return. Under railway ownership trade gradually declined, but the canal was never legally abandoned. It survived proposals to use it as a linear dump and was classified by the 1968 Transport Act as a remainder waterway. The Canal Amenity Society, founded shortly after the passing of the Act, have been working hard on it ever since.

Although the Pocklington Canal was never a particularly busy waterway, you will realise that the present Canal Head is only the relic of a much larger settlement. There was a Canal Inn close to the Wellington Oak, and a New Inn not far away. At the end of the basin was a coalyard, with another warehouse opposite the one that survives. Other buildings in the vicinity included a maintenance shop, two mills and several dwelling houses.

As you walk from Canal Head notice how the landscape gradually changes, from friendly, hilly countryside to the mysterious ings—wetlands reminiscent of the Fens before they were drained. Within the first 2 miles you pass five lock chambers. Coat's Bridge crosses the canal by the fifth lock; for the next mile, including the short arm to Bielby, the canal is dry. There is a watered section between a fixed swing bridge west of Bielby and Walbut Lock and Bridge: another dry section to Thornton Lock, and the remainder of the canal is in water, including the Melbourne arm where it is possible to launch light craft. Three fixed swing bridges within a mile west of the Melbourne arm prevent navigation and are the next obstacles to be dealt with when funds permit. They are farm accommodation bridges and legally protected; hence they must be replaced, not simply removed, and the cost will be about £50,000.

The lower section of the navigable stretch of canal borders the nature reserve of Wheldrake Ings, especially rich in bird life. The ings have, thanks to the Yorkshire Naturalists' Trust, escaped the draining and ploughing that have so altered the character of the Fens, and well over a hundred different species of birds have been observed there in the past few years, many of them otherwise extremely rare.

OS sheet 106

The North Yorkshire Rivers

Many of the rivers of Yorkshire have been navigable from time to time. The Ouse itself has always been a navigation and today is usable from Widdington Ings to Trent Falls, a distance of 51 miles. In 1767 Acts were obtained to make the Swale navigable to Morton Bridge, near Northallerton, with a branch to Bedale along the Bedale Beck, to make the Cod Beck navigable to Thirsk, and to improve the Ure and make a cut to Ripon. The last of these schemes was the most successful, although the two Ripon Canal locks are currently unusable. On the Swale some work was done and one lock (of five projected) was completed at Topcliffe. The lock was used, but not often, and at the end of 1769, when over £11,000 had been spent, work ceased. Although a new act was obtained and a new company formed, no further progress was made. On the Bedale Beck a wharf was built at Bedale and one lock, at Leeming, seems to have been completed, although it is not known whether it was ever used. At Thirsk on the Cod Beck a basin and wharf were built and one of the proposed five locks. This, it appears, was used once when two 40-ton vessels arrived in York from Thirsk. There is no record that they ever returned. None of these navigations has been abandoned.

More work was done to make the Foss navigable than on any

other of the Ouse tributaries. This was improved, although not very efficiently, between its junction with the Ouse at York and Sheriff Hutton Bridge, 11½ miles north. The top 2 miles were canalised to a basin south of the bridge. Eight locks were built and a moderate trade was carried on until the York–Scarborough Railway was opened in 1845. York Corporation bought the navigation in 1852 and still owns it. Most of it was abandoned in 1859, although the bottom 1¼ miles, including a lock, remain open.

The Foss meets the Ouse near Skeldergate Bridge; follow Blue Bridge Lane, off Fisher Gate, for the junction. About 400yd upstream are the lock and lock house at Castle Mills. Foss Bridge, Foss Islands Road and Foss Bank guide you along its course in the city. To follow the river northward take the minor road through New Earswick, Huntington and Strensall. Between the first two villages there is a lock house and another can be found at Haxby Landing. The canalised section begins a mile north-east of Strensall, to the east of Duncombe Farm. Some 2 miles north of Strensall on the Sheriff Hutton road is the site of the terminal basin, to the south of the bridge over the Foss near the drive to Bridge Farm.

Since 1698 there have been references every now and then to navigation to Tadcaster on the Wharfe and in the mid-eighteenth century keels from Hull were connecting with wagons from Leeds at Tadcaster. There were wharves and warehouses at Tadcaster, but no work seems to have been done on the river until as late as 1890 when the Wharfe River Navigation Company was formed by Tadcaster brewers. Some money was spent on improvements, but the company was wound up in 1898. No locks were constructed on the Wharfe.

The Driffield Navigation (or Canal), an extension of the River Hull, is due for a new lease of life. Commercial traffic ended in 1948 but the navigation was never legally abandoned, although the locks soon became inoperable. Legal problems over its ownership delayed repair work to locks and bridges, but now that new commissioners have been appointed restoration has begun. Driffield Basin, lined by red-brick grain warehouses, some of which have been tactfully converted into flats, has claims to be among the most attractive canal terminals in the country.

There is some hope also for the Leven Canal, a privately built waterway 3¼ miles long from the village of Leven on the A165 to the River Hull. The basin and old warehouses lie behind the New Inn and the canal is popular with anglers and naturalists. A sluice has been inserted at Leven Lock by the entrance to the Hull. There is talk of restoration from time to time, but so far no action has taken place.

OS sheets 99, 100, 104, 105

The Lancaster Canal (Kendal–Tewitfield)

Several canals were destroyed by the building of railways along their route, but the northern section of the Lancaster Canal was a victim of the M6 motorway and its approach roads which have put an end to the prospects of full restoration, at least in the foreseeable future. Limited restoration involving the stretch between Stainton and Tewitfield is a practical proposition—and indeed dinghies and canoes can use much of this length at the moment—but he would be the dizziest idealist who could envisage boats once again voyaging into Kendal, or consent being given to digging a tunnel through the A76.

The topmost stretch of the Lancaster, from Kendal to Stainton, was closed and drained by the British Transport Commission in 1955, trade to Kendal having ended in the early 1930s. Apart from Hincaster Tunnel, the land is now in private ownership. In addition to the tunnel, there are fifty-four bridges and seven aqueducts on the 'remainder' section, many of them substantial and handsome masonry constructions. The towpath, a public right-of-way along the northern section, is walkable throughout.

The canal was opened to Kendal in 1819. There was a sizeable basin, built by the corporation, with several wharves and warehouses. Canal Head is near the gasworks, which was built on land originally owned by the canal company and supplied with coal by canal for over a hundred years. The line of the canal for the first few miles is close to the River Kent; you can find it by turning east off the Natland road and following the right-of-way alongside a clearly defined channel. Note the impressive bridges and the skew aqueduct to the west of Sedgwick.

The major feature on this northern length is Hincaster Tunnel. Shortly after the Levens link road crosses the canal, the latter takes a right-angle turn to the east. There is easy access to the tunnel from a minor road between the Natland road and High

Barns. The tunnel, 378yd long, is open and watered. Along the water-line and for the first 10yd at each end the tunnel is lined with stone; the remainder of it is brick, which the canal committee accepted as a substitute only after lengthy investigations. There is no towpath, but you can follow the narrow old horse-path across the top, passing beneath two footbridges and the railway. Near the east portal the Levens road crosses the canal again. Then comes Stainton; from here on there is water in the channel as far as Tewitfield. Well-made aqueducts take the canal over Stainton Beck and Crooklands Beck, the second of which is the principal feeder channel from Killington Reservoir, supplying water to the whole length of the Lancaster. South of Crooklands the M6 crosses the canal and keeps it close company for the rest of its course to Tewitfield, crossing it twice more *en route*. If you want to see a large number of bridges go to Holme; there are eight within a mile and an aqueduct as well.

At Tewitfield is the flight of eight locks, the only ones on the main line of the canal. The lock-chambers are in good condition, but this is a melancholy place as the extent of the damage done to the canal by the motorway planners is only too clear. To have bridged the canal instead of culverting it would have cost more, of course, but it is hard to believe that in the long run it would not have been worth it. Restoration of the Tewitfield locks would not be a major task, but to restore the navigation to Stainton seems, in present circumstances anyway, an impossibility. The Fraenkel Report (see General Bibliography) recommendation is for amenity development in conjunction with local authorities and, while the towpath is kept clear and the structures maintained, the northern stretch should retain some attractiveness and use. No matter how carefully it is manicured, however, many people will still regard what happened to the Lancaster Canal as a massive example of planners' vandalism.

OS sheet 97

The Carlisle Canal

The Carlisle Canal is one of the least-known inland navigations. It had an active life of only thirty years and its course was almost completely obscured by the Port Carlisle Branch Railway, constructed on the bed of the canal in 1854. There are, however, enough remains to make it worth a visit, although plans to restore or preserve parts of it have not met with any support.

The canal was cut from a basin in Carlisle to Fisher's Cross, renamed Port Carlisle, on the Solway Firth, a distance of $11\frac{1}{4}$ miles. There were eight wide locks, to take coastal vessels, and several drawbridges similar to those on the Forth & Clyde. Trade was mostly in timber, coal and bricks; a packet-boat service was also instituted, with a special passenger jetty being built at Port Carlisle and a hotel for passengers in transit to Liverpool. Originally, the canal company hoped that their waterway would connect with a Newcastle–Carlisle canal; when this project fell through and a railway was proposed, the canal company gave it support in the hope that it would increase their own trade. This it did for a few years, but when the Lancaster and Glasgow rail links with Carlisle were made, the canal's prosperity suffered. Conversion to a railway was supported by the canal company and an Act authorising this was obtained in 1853. The Port Carlisle Branch line closed in 1932.

In Carlisle look for Port Road and Canal Street. The entrance to the basin is by the Jolly Sailor, which replaced a pub of the same name that was contemporary with the canal. The large canal warehouse was demolished in 1974, but you may see a long, low sandstone building; this was the lime and coal vaults. Loads were tipped into the stores from the basin and loaded from there into wagons from the lower level of the building, which can be found down a lane. The 1832 Customs House survives to the west of the basin near the Cumberland Infirmary.

As you head out on the minor road towards Port Carlisle the line of the railway/canal keeps you close company. At Knockupworth, Grinsdale and Kirkandrews there are bridges which originally spanned the canal but were improved to suit the requirements of the railway. There is another bridge at Kirkandrews and a $\frac{1}{2}$ mile loop of canal which the railway avoided. A proposal for an open-air museum on this site was made in 1974 but met with no encouragement locally. Further west there are lock cottages at Beaumont and Burgh-by-Sands as well as two more bridges.

Approaching Port Carlisle you can find another unfilled length of canal bed where the railway diverged. There are substantial remains in Port Carlisle itself, including a lock between the canal and basin, the basin itself with bollards and converted warehouses, the sea-lock, much of it filled in but with the coping still visible, the remains of a timber jetty, and an isolated wharf, built in about 1839, to which for some years the railway used to run across a viaduct supported on wooden trestles. Solway House used to be the Solway Hotel, where packet-boat passengers waited for steamers to Liverpool, and the last house along the sea-front was once the Steam Packet Inn.

An older relic than the Carlisle Canal can be inspected on your journey. This is the western section of Hadrian's Wall which is close to your route and meets the sea at Bowness-on-Solway, a mile west of Port Carlisle.

OS sheet 85

Bibliography

BOOKS

Biddle, G., *Lancashire Waterways* (Dalesman, 1980)

Duckham, B. F., *Navigable Rivers of Yorkshire* (Dalesman, 1964)

— — *The Yorkshire Ouse* (David & Charles, 1967)

Hadfield, C., *Canals of Yorkshire and North East England* (David & Charles, 1972)

— — and Biddle, G., *Canals of North West England* (David & Charles, 1970)

Owen, David, *Canals to Manchester* (Manchester University Press, 1978)

— — *Cheshire Waterways* (Dalesman, 1979)

Smith, P. L., *Yorkshire Waterways* (Dalesman, 1978)

ARTICLES AND BOOKLETS

Canals and Waterways (*It happened round Manchester*), A. H. Body (University of London Press, 1969)

An Intimate Look at Bury's Old Canal, Fred Campbell (Bury & District Local History Society, 1977)

'The Manchester, Bolton and Bury Canal Navigation', V. I. Tomlinson, *Transactions*, Lancashire & Cheshire Antiquarian Society (1965-6)

Old Billy: 1760-1822, E. L. Seyd (Manchester Museum, nd)

SOCIETIES

Huddersfield Canal Society

Lancaster Canal Trust

Market Weighton Canal Society

Pocklington Canal Amenity Society

River Derwent Trust

Rochdale Canal Society

8

SCOTLAND

The Forth & Clyde Canal

Scotland's 'great canal', the Forth & Clyde, striding across the country from estuary to estuary—35 miles with 40 locks—was legally abandoned as a navigation in 1962. By that time commercial traffic had ended and the recreational possibilities of the waterway were hardly recognised. The trunk road between Glasgow and Stirling was being improved and it was estimated that a lifting bridge on the Denny bypass stretch would cost an additional £160,000—so the canal was closed and the extra expense avoided. Since then, some sections have been filled in, many bridges have been lowered and new ones built with no navigational headroom, culverts have been constructed, levels altered, balance beams on lock gates removed and the gates themselves allowed to rot. It is estimated that at 1978 prices it would cost between £20 million and £25 million to restore navigation to the Forth & Clyde throughout. At present, to quote from the Canal Working Party's Local Subject Plan, published in 1980, the Forth & Clyde 'is semi-derelict with some recreational use. There is little prospect of improvement, only of gradual fragmentation.'

Like the Caledonian and Crinan Canals, the Forth & Clyde had no fixed bridges; thus it was possible for sailing ships and steamers to travel from one estuary to the other in a day. The locks were criticised for being too small; they are 19ft 8in wide but 3½ft shorter than the narrow locks on the English canals. The line was laid out by John Smeaton, the canal company's first engineer. He was succeeded by Robert Whitworth who was Chief Engineer when the main line was opened in 1790. The Forth & Clyde drew some of its water supply from the Monkland Canal, the connection being made by a cut of junction between Monkland Basin, near the cathedral, and Port Dundas, at the end of the Forth &

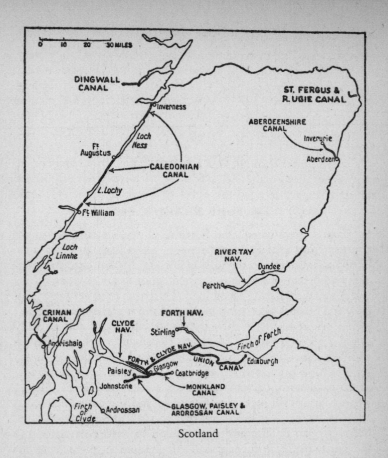

Scotland

Clyde's Glasgow Branch. There was a connection also with the
Union Canal by Lock 16 at Camelon on the outskirts of Falkirk,
opened in 1822.

From central Glasgow the A82 takes you to within a few
hundred yards of the canal's western terminus, Bowling Basin.
Here in July 1790 Archibald Spiers, chairman of the canal's management committee, and the chief engineer, 'launched a hogs-
head of water of the river Forth into the Clyde as a symbol of
joining the eastern and western seas together', as the *Scots Magazine* reported. The basins—there are two of them—are still open
for craft and provide moorings for a motley collection ranging
from weird mis-shapen hulks on which enthusiasts seek to per-
form miracles to smart modern sailing cruisers. Here is the canal's
only remaining bascule-bridge that actually opens, a splendid old

railway swing bridge that no longer swings but whose machinery is open to inspection, one operational and one closed sea-lock, and a shamefully decaying Custom House, urgently needing restoration (and possible conversion to a canalside museum) before it falls down. Bowling Basin is just over a mile below the elegant Erskine Bridge, under which there is a Forth & Clyde lock.

The canal runs through Old Kilpatrick and into Clydebank in close proximity to the A814. Of the seven district authorities through whose territory the Forth & Clyde passes, Clydebank has taken what might be described as the most aggressive line. Between Duntreath Avenue and Kilbowie Road the canal has been partially infilled, with culverts replacing bridges. By some culverts rubbish collects inexorably and duckweed flourishes. Stretches of the towing path have been resurfaced and by the Clyde Shopping Centre the canal manifests itself as an acceptable ornamental waterway where small boys can hopefully fish and tired shoppers can deposit their supermarket trolleys. The fishing, however, is more profitable near the point where the A8014 crosses over; here the principal catch is goldfish, which rise to a variety of bait. Some 2 miles further on a part of the line has been eliminated where it is crossed by the Great Western Road (A82). Two of the Cloberhill locks have been filled in, but recently their coping stones and those of the connecting pound have been excavated and form an attractive and intriguing feature.

The major engineering works on the canal, and the structures of greatest interest to the industrial archaeologist, are at Maryhill, north-west of Glasgow centre: the Kelvin Aqueduct and the five Maryhill locks up to the summit level, with the Kelvin Graving Dock. Access to the top of the locks is from the A81; the Maryhill Aqueduct, taking the canal over this road, is 2 miles north-west from the motorway-crossing. From here you can walk down the flight to the Kelvin Aqueduct, 400ft long with four arches. Substantial though it is, it ranks as only the fourth in dimensions of the Scottish aqueducts: the Avon, Almond and Slateford on the Union Canal are all longer and higher. The Kelvin, nevertheless, was the earliest of these massive and adventurous structures and was apostrophised in the *Glasgow Courier*:

> Tho' spiteful Kelvin threatened to divide
> Forth's tumbling flood from joining with the Clyde,

Thy rising form, Majestic, interpos'd,
Strode o'er the vale, and the wide gap was clos'd ...

The aqueduct, the five locks and the graving dock are now scheduled ancient monuments and the British Waterways Board has outline planning permission for a development scheme for the area, including proposals for housing. Realisation of this project, however, seems a long way off and there will be ample time to sample the atmosphere of desolation alongside the flight and to enjoy a pint or two at the adjacent White House. The locks are inoperable, apart from the bottom gates and one sluice of the top lock. Clearly the area between the Kelvin and Maryhill Aqueducts urgently needs renovation, but, whatever happens to it, one hopes that it will escape the fate of being 'landscaped' out of all recognition. The restoration of navigation would provide the most satisfactory solution.

A short distance east of Maryhill the Glasgow Branch leaves the main line of canal. There were several basins, some of them for timber, along this $2\frac{1}{2}$ mile arm. Beside the Old Basin at Applecross Street is the headquarters of BWB Scotland, a range of white-painted buildings of different ages, some parts of which antedate the canal. There is a timber bascule-bridge, now fixed, at the end of the basin with a derelict bothy, once the bridge-keeper's, next to it.

Port Dundas, named after the first governor of the canal company, Lord Dundas of Kerse, is the nearest point to the city centre reached by the canal. From here it is piped through to Parkston Basin, the terminus of the branch, where Glasgow District Council is proposing the construction of a district park which may incorporate a 'water feature' developed from part of the canal basin. The branch itself now ends in front of a handsome but sadly derelict building, the old canal company offices, dating from about 1812. Here is another possibility for a canalside museum; the building, despite its present condition, is of architectural merit as well as of historical importance and is far too good to be demolished. Next to it is a splendid range of industrial buildings on Spiers Wharf North. Now bonded warehouses, they were originally grain-mills and one was a sugar refinery. They date from the 1850s and loom proudly, if a little grimly, over central Glasgow. Buildings of similar quality and interest used to line much of the Glasgow Branch, but few of them have survived. A grain-mill and two distilleries can be found at Park-ston Basin in the shadow of the motorway which takes the line of the Monkland Canal and the old cut of junction.

From Port Dundas passenger vessels used to ply to Falkirk and Edinburgh, with at one time as many as three sailings a day. From 1893 until 1939 the 'Queen' steamers ran pleasure cruises; the *Gipsy Queen*, the largest and the last to operate, cruised almost the whole length of the summit as far as Craigmarloch. At Port Dundas today this is hard to imagine.

The junction of the branch and main line is at Stockingfield, reached by taking the minor road to the east on the south side of Maryhill Aqueduct. From the junction the main line heads out of Glasgow north-eastward, close to the Antonine Wall; it is feasible to explore both at the same time. In the $3\frac{1}{2}$ miles between the fixed steel bascule-bridge on the A879 at Lambhill and the similar bridge on the A807 the canal is crossed only twice, by fixed concrete bridges at Jellyhill and Cadder. The towpath is pleasant walking through attractive countryside, with Roman forts and the River Kelvin to the north.

Kirkintilloch is the largest settlement on the summit level. This was a station on the Antonine Wall and a twelfth-century royal burgh. Later it developed some industrial importance. There was a boatyard on the canal and the 'Queen' steamers were built here by James Aitken & Company. There was also a busy wharf and good stable buildings survive both here and at Cadder. An aqueduct, 150ft long, takes the canal over the Luggie Water and the track of an old railway.

The A803 and then the B8023 follow the line of the canal out of Kirkintilloch. At Twechar and Auchinstarry steel swing bridges are now fixed. From Auchinstarry the canal continues in almost a straight line within a kind of corridor, with the A803 to the north and the railway line to the south. Wyndford Lock at Banknock marks the end of the summit. A mile further on, the Glasgow-Stirling A80 smashes across the canal.

Castlecary and the two Underwood Locks are accessible from the B816 which runs on the south side of the canal between the A80 and Bonnybridge. The strength of the chamber walls and the massive blocks of facing stone are worth noting. Bonny-bridge has a good stretch of Roman wall nearby and an aqueduct over a stream, road and path. Now the canal runs almost due east for Camelon on the outskirts of Falkirk. Lock 16 by the Union

Inn has given its name to the surrounding area, this being the point where the Union Canal locked into the Forth & Clyde. The inn was built for the boat crews to use while waiting for the locks. The basin here, now filled in and grassed over, was called Port Downie.

The Falkirk section of the canal was improved in 1974 and is now an asset to the town. Only the lock gates are sad and derelict. The banks have been cleaned up and grassed, trees have been planted, there is a good tarmac footpath and some of the canalside buildings have been rehabilitated. A harmonious terrace of cottages with the Canal Inn in the centre is on your left as you look down the canal from Lock 16. The bridge by the lock is impassable, of course, and the A803 bridge is culverted. Below the main road the canal continues past some good industrial buildings; note especially the Rosebank Distillery by the main road and the buildings close to the level-crossing. The last three locks of the Forth & Clyde, as it now is, are on a straight wide stretch of canal below the culverted Bainsford Bridge on the B905. Here one is especially conscious of waste, with this splendid mile of waterway leading nowhere. The pound between Lock 4 at Abbotshaugh and Lock 3 is open, but the rest of the canal to the basin at Grangemouth on the River Carron—and thence into the Forth—has been dewatered.

Even in its present truncated and interrupted state, the Forth & Clyde is used for a variety of recreational activities. Several canoe clubs use its waters and rowing regattas take place on the 2,000m straight stretch to the west of Wyndford. There is an annual race for inflatable craft along the Forth & Clyde and Union Canals, sponsored by the Drambuie company, and rallies for small boats are held from time to time. The canal provides good coarse-fishing and the towpath is sometimes used for pony trekking, as well as for a number of pursuits associated with walking. The canal's own structures also attract plenty of interest. Various volunteer groups have concerned themselves with conservation work on the canal, in particular the Scottish Inland Waterways Association whose members have cleaned out lock-chambers, made landing stages for small craft and undertaken repair work on the banks and towpath. All these activities could be further developed; and all can be impeded by further infilling or by the vandalism which seems to be ineradicable.

Whatever happens to the Forth & Clyde in the near future, the ultimate aim of all those concerned with it must be its reopening to navigation throughout. The cost, as I have indicated, would be enormous; yet compared to the losses which we tolerate from some of our nationalised industries it is really nothing much. There is no doubt that the Forth & Clyde would never have been closed if the values of 1962 in these matters had been the same as those of today. The cost of restoration, moreover, when it does come will be payment, sadly, for what has been described as an 'incredibly stupid and short-sighted move' made by British Transport Waterways—a move that need never have been made. And, despite the recreational activities referred to, there is always the danger that unless the canal is restored to full navigational standards, with consequent obligatory maintenance, shortage of funds at local level will result in further deterioration until the Forth & Clyde becomes on a much larger scale the sort of linear rubbish dump that the Derby Canal was some ten years ago.

OS sheets 64, 65

The Monkland Canal

The Monkland Canal was constructed for the express purpose of supplying Glasgow with cheap coal. It was opened in 1793 from the River Calder near Woodhall, south of Airdrie, to a basin near Glasgow Cathedral. It was connected to the Forth & Clyde at Port Dundas by a 'cut of junction' and supplied water to its larger neighbour. The main line was $12\frac{1}{4}$ miles long and the principal engineering feature consisted of 4 staircase pairs of locks at Blackhill with a 96ft rise. Between 1850 and 1887 the Blackhill locks were supplemented by an inclined plane. The Monkland was profitable, especially in the mid-nineteenth century when a good additional trade in iron developed, mainly to meet the demands of the Clydeside ship-building industry. With falling yields from the mines in the Coatbridge area in the late 1860s, however, trade began to decline. Both the Monkland and the Forth & Clyde were taken over by the Caledonian Railway in 1867 and received little encouragement thenceforth. By the first decade of this century little freight was moving on the canal and the iron trade was finished completely. All traffic ended by 1935.

Although few people had anything to say in its favour, the Monkland was not abandoned until 1950. It was continuing to act as a water-supply channel to the Forth & Clyde and a power station, and there was no question of abandonment unless the owners, at that time the London, Midland & Scottish Railway, agreed to provide piping. Even after the abandonment Act, work on infilling and piping the Monkland was delayed, despite the insalubrious state into which the canal had declined and the frequent drowning incidents in Blackhill locks. Eventually, in 1954, work began on eradicating the canal, and today only fragments of it are left. It is ironical that only a few years after a large section of it was filled in, a few miles away another section is being disinterred, as you can see for yourself.

At Parkston you are close to the M8 motorway and hence close to the corpse of the Monkland Canal, which lies beneath it. The motorway was built on the line of the canal to the outskirts of Glasgow. There is a diversion at Blackhill, just over a mile east of Port Dundas. Here the motorway is elevated above a valley. Standing in the valley with the motorway on the north side about 100yd away, you can see the site of the inclined plane, a grassy slope beside and below Riddrie School. In its time the incline was 1,140ft long, rising 96ft. Hence it was longer and with a greater rise than the far better-known Foxton incline on the Leicester arm of the Grand Junction. The principle of operation of both inclines was the same: boats were floated into caissons which ran on railway lines and were drawn by wire ropes, the power being provided by steam-engines. Between the slope of the incline and the motorway is the site of the Blackhill locks. There is not even a commemorative plaque to record the industrial history of this place, once so important to the commercial prosperity of Glasgow.

The prosperity of Coatbridge, some 6 miles west of the centre of Glasgow, was also largely due to the Monkland Canal. Its coal and iron were conveyed cheaply to Glasgow by water and at one time there were seven blast furnaces in the town. The canal ran through the centre, and a good point to begin exploration is Coatbridge Central Station. Opposite, a walkway is being created by the Scottish Development Association. It takes the course of the old canal, now being excavated. Back to light have come the walls of wharves and the towpath. There is a fascinating collection of railway and other bridges—the first Scottish steam railway passed through Coatbridge in 1826. You can follow the walkway westward, coming before long to a watered stretch of canal and the attractive Blair Bridge. Two short branches to ironworks used to meet the main line in Coatbridge.

The canal terminates south-east of Coatbridge in a bumpy bit of countryside between the B802 and the A8. The bumps indicate coal mines of the late eighteenth and early nineteenth centuries. A track intersects the area, crossing the canal by the Upper and Lower Faskin Bridges. The channel of the Monkland is open but badly silted; the vegetation makes it resemble a placid little lowland river rather than a canal. This is the water that is still piped through Coatbridge and Glasgow and feeds the Forth & Clyde. The Monkland takes off from the North Calder Water at a horseshoe weir a short distance away.

OS sheet 64

The Glasgow, Paisley & Johnstone Canal

Early in the nineteenth century the Earl of Eglinton promoted a canal from Glasgow through Paisley and Johnstone with the intention of terminating it at Ardrossan on the coast where a new harbour would be built and a major port established. This would obviate the necessity of vessels using the difficult Clyde Navigation and also, he hoped, would make him very rich. The canal was completed from Glasgow to Johnstone in 1811 and the basin in Glasgow was named Port Eglinton in honour of the earl. However, the Clyde had been deepened under an act of 1809 and Eglinton was unable to raise enough money to finish his undertaking. In the 1820s a proposal to complete the line by horse railway was made and a length was constructed between Ardrossan and Kilwinning. The canal itself ended at Johnstone.

An unexpected success of the canal company was with passenger traffic. There were no locks on the canal and towpaths were carried through the bridges. The boats used in the 1830s when this traffic was at its busiest were 70ft by 6ft and could hold 90 passengers. They were drawn by 2 horses which were changed every 4 miles; at one time the company owned 78 horses. At their cheapest, fares from Glasgow to Johnstone were 10d cabin and 7d steerage. In the year ending 30 September 1835, 373,290 passengers were carried. In 1843, however, the canal stopped carrying passengers, yielding place to the railways from Glasgow in return for an annual payment of £1,367. The canal's revenues declined and in 1869 it was taken over by the Glasgow & South Western Railway which kept it open after a fashion until 1881. In that year it was closed and a relief railway-line laid over much of its bed.

Nothing remains of Port Eglinton, which was south of the Clyde and to the west of the Gorbals. The best way to trace the canal route is to take the train from Glasgow Central through Crookston. Some 2 miles west of Crookston the line crosses the Cart by the Blackhall Aqueduct, originally part of the canal. Paisley Canal Station is self-explanatory. If you alight here, you may find some of the canal preserved in the grounds of the Ferguslie Thread Works. There were two tunnels in Paisley, one under Causewayside and the other beneath Ralston Square. There is no trace of the Johnstone Basin, but Canal Garage, if it is still there, was built on its site.

OS sheet 64

The Edinburgh & Glasgow Union Canal

This splendid canal was opened in 1822 from Camelon, near Falkirk, to Edinburgh. It connected with the Forth & Clyde at Port Downie, by the Union Inn, and for the first twenty-six years there were regular passenger services between Edinburgh and Glasgow as well as much long- and short-haul goods traffic. The opening of the Edinburgh & Glasgow Railway in 1842 greatly affected the canal's profitability. A few years later the railway company took over the canal, both passing to the North British Railway in 1865 and then to the London & North Eastern in 1923. Commercial traffic on the Union ended in 1933 and the flight of eleven locks at Port Downie was demolished. The navigation was abandoned in 1965. Since then several bridges have been reconstructed, with the canal being culverted beheath them, and some lengths of waterway have been infilled.

More recently, as happened with the Forth & Clyde, attitudes have changed. Proposals to reduce the canal to a water channel have been defeated, as have plans for road building on the canal line and construction of bridges at water-level. The British Waterways Board and the local-government authorities concerned now recognise the recreational possibilities of the canal and are actively promoting them, spurred on by the Linlithgow Union

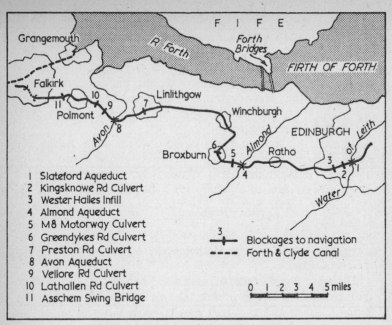

The Edinburgh & Glasgow Union Canal

Canal Society and the Scottish Inland Waterways Association. A Union Canal Project Officer has been appointed to organise and co-ordinate plans and activities. Although the waterway has been chopped up into ten disconnected lengths, some navigation is still possible.

The locks that took the Union Canal up 110ft were to the south of the Union Inn at Port Downie. From the western end of the canal the towpath can be followed throughout, with diversions at the infilled sections. Falkirk Tunnel, 696yd long with the towpath running through it, is a mile from the end; like many other of the canal's structures it is now classified as an ancient monument. Glen High Bridge, near the eastern portal, is worth inspecting with its contrasting carved faces on either side. About 2 miles eastward a swing bridge, now fixed, provides the first obstacle to navigation, but there is a more substantial barrier further along where the bridge carrying the A801 has been re-built without headroom and the canal is culverted through twin pipes. There is another culvert at Vellore Road Bridge. About ½ mile from here is Causewayend, site of a canal/rail interchange. The square basin used for transhipment to the Slamannan Railway survives. The basin, repair dock and the massive Avon Aqueduct to the east are all scheduled as ancient monuments. This 12-arch aqueduct, 810ft long and 86ft high, is the second largest in Britain; like the others on the Union Canal it was designed by the canal's engineer, Hugh Baird, being modelled on Thomas Telford's Chirk Aqueduct and built with his advice. It has recently been restored.

Between the aqueduct and Linlithgow are some stables and canal cottages. In the town the lowered Preston Road Bridge blocks the canal; to the east by Manse Road Basin there is now a canal museum housed in what used to be stables and run by the Linlithgow Canal Society. The canal engineer once lived in Canal House and moored in the basin are two passenger boats, the old horse-drawn barge *Queen of the Union* and the *Victoria*, a reproduction of a nineteenth-century steam-packet boat but diesel-powered.

There are about 8 miles of open water before the next obstruction; part of this length is under the care of the Nature Conservancy Council and part runs past oil-shale bings, from one of which material was extracted to build the nearby motorway. The obstruction is the B8020 road bridge at Broxburn, but this is minor compared with the M8 crossing 1½ miles further on. Here the canal is culverted for 160ft.

There is now a stretch of 8 miles to the outskirts of Edinburgh, cruised by a restaurant boat, *Pride of the Union*, as well as by several privately owned craft. From the Livingston Road Bridge it is a short walk along the towpath to the Almond Aqueduct, 420ft long with 5 arches. A feeder from Cobbinshaw Reservoir joins the canal at the eastern end of the aqueduct. The motorway swings in close to the canal and then turns away; there follows a peaceful stretch with access from the road at Ratho.

After Hermiston Bridge and an aqueduct over the Moray Burn comes the Wester Hailes infill. Following the closure of the canal a housing estate was built here and 1¼ miles of the Union Canal disappeared beneath it. Kingsknowe Bridge to the east of the housing estate has also been culverted. Soon comes the third of the great aqueducts, Slateford, taking the canal over the Water of Leith and a public road. This aqueduct is 500ft long with 8 arches.

The canal continues between sports grounds and alongside Harrison Park and on towards the centre of Edinburgh. Viewforth Bridge is number one on the canal, but between this and the present terminus at Lochrin Basin the vertical lifting bridge that used to stand at Semple Street by the entrance to Port Hopetoun has been inserted at Leamington Road. The basins at Port Hopetoun and Port Hamilton, almost in the shadow of the castle, were closed in 1921 and filled in; the ABC Cinema in Lothian Road commemorates Port Hopetoun on which it was built.

OS sheets 65, 66

The Carlingwark Canal

One of the earliest Scottish canal undertakings to be completed was the Carlingwark Canal on the lower reaches of the River Dee near Kirkcudbright. In 1765 a 1½ mile cut was made from Carlingwark Loch to the river near Threave Castle. This was the work of Sir Alexander Gordon of Culvennan and was known, rather confusingly, as Carlingwark Lane. It reduced the level of the loch by several feet and enabled marl to be dug out of the loch and transported by canal and river to farms in the neighbourhood. The river navigation was improved in or about 1780 by the construction of a second cut, ½ mile long, near Culvennan House on the Dee above Threave Castle. This cut bypassed a swift-running stretch of river and had a lock—possibly two—close to the back of Culvennan House. Then a few years later a much more ambitious scheme was proposed for a 26 mile canal with several locks from Dalry alongside the Ken and Dee to the estuary near Kirkcudbright. This was to be known as the Glenkens Canal and it was authorised by an act of 1802. John Rennie surveyed the route and estimated the cost at rather over £33,000. Sufficient support was not forthcoming, however, and the idea was dropped.

Marl-carrying boats used the Carlingwark Canal until about 1840. As it was a private undertaking there was no official abandonment and it is not possible to say whether it was used at all after that date. Both lengths are still extant and can be explored, although permission and wellington boots are required for certain stretches.

The short northern section can be approached from Glenlochar Bridge, where the B795 crosses the Dee. Above the bridge is the Glenlochar Barrage, part of the Galloway hydro-electric scheme.

Below the bridge is the entrance to the canal, on the left-hand side by an embankment. The site of the lock or locks is near the top of the cut and a line of trees at the back of Culvennan House indicates the course of the canal. This is a marshy area with many drainage channels and several pumping stations to control the levels. The southern entrance to this stretch is near a pumping station and there are indications of an area widened out into a basin.

For Carlingwark Lane take the A75 south-west from Castle Douglas, which crosses the waterway at Buchan. It is possible to battle your way alongside the Lane by swinging from the saplings and leaping the drainage channels. The Castle Douglas-Kirkcudbright Railway crossed the Lane midway; north of the site of the railway bridge the walking becomes easier. You come to a pumping station but may not be able to reach the river because of a wide drainage channel.

The Carlingwark Canal brought a measure of prosperity to the area, especially to Castle Douglas which developed out of a little village called Carlingwark, and, before that, Causewayend. It also has its own personal tragedy: from the parapet of Glenlochar Bridge Sir Alexander Gordon's son fell to an untimely death while still a young man.

OS sheet 84

The Aberdeenshire and St Fergus & River Ugie Canals

Opened in 1805 the Aberdeenshire Canal was cut parallel to the River Don on its southern side from Inverurie to Aberdeen, where in 1834 a sea-lock was constructed to give a direct connection with the harbour. The canal was $18\frac{1}{4}$ miles long with 18 locks, all close to Aberdeen itself. It traded profitably into the 1840s, with a frequent passenger service to Port Elphinstone at Inverurie. In 1845 the canal was bought by the Great North of Scotland Railway and it was closed in 1854, some part of its bed being used for the railway line.

Inverurie is a fine little town. Canal Road indicates the terminal at Port Elphinstone, although the basin has been obliterated. The terminal buildings were to the south and south-west of the road by the present council depot. Aberdeen has a Canal Road, Canal Street and Canal Terrace, although there are no visible remains of the canal itself. For the route the best plan is to take the train; there are stretches of canal bed and embankment to be seen at Brae Farm near Kintore (a milestone here) and at Kinaldie, but no major works. Recently, Holiday Inns have built the new Aberdeen Airport Hotel close to the line of the canal at Bucksburn.

North from Aberdeen a canal was begun by James Ferguson of Pitfour with the intention of connecting his estates at St Fergus with Peterhead. Some 4 miles were cut, but Peterhead was not reached; however, the canal—known as the St Fergus & River Ugie Canal—developed a short branch to Inverquinzie. The intention was to use it for distributing sand to help fertilise the surrounding farmland, but it is unlikely that it was used at all. There is no mention of this canal in Jean Lindsay's *The Canals of Scotland*, but if you wish to explore its remains you will find them described in *The Proceedings of the Society of Antiquaries of Scotland 1967-8*, in an article by Angus Graham called 'Two Canals in Aberdeenshire'. This also gives details of the remains of the Aberdeenshire Canal in the 1960s.

OS sheet 38

The Dingwall Canal

Dingwall is tucked in at the head of the Cromarty Firth and is the administrative headquarters for the Ross & Cromarty District. It lies on the route of the A9, although the centre has recently been bypassed. However, it lacked a harbour and to remedy this a canal about $1\frac{1}{4}$ miles in length was made from the River Conon to a bridge on the Great North Road on the north-west side of the town. It was opened in 1817 and was successful to some extent, although the receipts for tolls seldom exceeded the cost of maintenance and repair. The chief problem was silting. Improvements made in the 1860s enabled larger vessels to use the canal, but the town council, owners of the canal, could not repay the debt incurred nor afford the charges for maintenance. Local trade was being lost to the railway, Dingwall becoming the junction for the Inverness–Kyle of Lochalsh and Wick–Thurso lines. After 1884 the canal ceased to be used. It still exists, holding water, with a footpath along the line of the towing path. Kenneth Clew, who has researched the history of the canal, points out that it is unique in having been constructed under the authority of an Act for building Highland roads and bridges. It is the most northerly canal in Britain.

OS sheet 26

Bibliography

BOOK

Lindsay, Jean, *The Canals of Scotland* (David & Charles, 1968)

ARTICLES AND BOOKLETS

Forth & Clyde Canal Local Subject Plan (Forth & Clyde Canal Working Party Report, 1979)
The Scots Magazine (August 1980)
The Union Canal, BWB Report (1977)
'Two Canals in Aberdeenshire', *The Proceedings of the Society of Antiquaries of Scotland 1967-8*

SOCIETIES

Falkirk Canal Society
Forth & Clyde Canal Society
Linlithgow Union Canal Society
Scottish Inland Waterways Association

OTHER LOST CANALS

BASINGSTOKE CANAL   Almost half the work of restoration is complete and 11 miles should be open by 1982.

KENNET & AVON   After thirty years, reopening is anticipated in 1984. At the time of writing, over two-thirds of the canal is navigable and work is in hand on the Caen Hill flight of twenty-nine locks at Devizes.

ASHBY CANAL   Measham–Moira, the top 6 miles, abandoned 1944. Much is still traceable.

BOTTISHAM LODE   A cut, probably Roman in origin, $2\frac{1}{2}$ miles from the Cam to Lode, near Bottisham. There was one flash-lock. Disused about 1900 but still watered.

BUGSWORTH BASIN   Upper Peak Forest Canal. A complex of terminal basins, tramroads, etc, at the end of a short branch. Being restored by the Inland Waterways Protection Society.

CINDERFORD CANAL   A short lockless canal at Cinderford in the Forest of Dean. Very few traces exist.

COMPSTALL NAVIGATION   Originally a private venture, now in a country park by Compstall, Cheshire. See *Cheshire Waterways* by David Owen.

COOMBE HILL CANAL   Now privately owned, with full restoration planned. Canal Head is close to the Swan Inn by the A38/A4019 junction, 7 miles north of Gloucester. The terminal buildings have been renovated and a museum is proposed.

FOXTON INCLINED PLANE   Used 1900–10, dismantled in 1927. A restoration society has been formed and the site has been cleared. On the Leicester line by the junction to Market Harborough.

MIDDLE LEVEL NAVIGATIONS   Several lengths of abandoned navigable drains. See *Canals of Eastern England* by J. Boyes and R. Russell for these and similar navigable drains in Lincolnshire.

SOUTH WALES Many short canals between Neath and Tenby. See *Canals of South Wales and the Border* by Charles Hadfield.

ULVERSTON CANAL From Ulverston—basin at rear of the Canal Tavern—to Morecambe Bay, $1\frac{1}{2}$ miles. Opened 1796, abandoned 1945 but still in water. A ship canal with entrance lock 27ft wide. Canal Foot worth a visit; the Bay Horse is close by.

There are many more; see Canals of the British Isles Series or *The Complete Book of Canal and River Navigations* by E. Paget-Tomlinson.

GENERAL BIBLIOGRAPHY

In addition to the books and articles mentioned at the end of each section, the following titles are especially useful:

Burton, Antony, *The Canal Builders* (Eyre Methuen, 1972)

Denney, Martin, *London and South East England* (Historic Waterways Scenes, Moorland Publishing, 1980)

Edwards, L. A., *The Inland Waterways of Great Britain* (Imray, Laurie, Norie & Wilson, 5th edition 1972)

Gladwin, D. D., *The Canals of Britain* (Batsford, 1973)

Hadfield, Charles, *British Canals: An Illustrated History* (David & Charles, 6th edition 1979)

— — *The Canal Age* (David & Charles, 2nd edition 1981)

— — *Waterway Sights to See* (David & Charles, 1977)

McKnight, Hugh, *The Shell Book of Inland Waterways* (David & Charles, 1975)

Paget-Tomlinson, Edward, *The Complete Book of Canal and River Navigations* (Waine Research, 1978)

Ransom, P. J. R., *Waterways Restored* (Faber, 1974)

Rodgers, John, *English Rivers* (Batsford, 1948)

Rolt, L. T. C., *Narrow Boat* (Eyre & Spottiswoode, 1948)

— — *The Inland Waterways of England* (Allen & Unwin, 1966)

— — *Navigable Waterways* (Longmans, 1969)

Russell, Ronald, *Rivers* (David & Charles, 1978)

— — *Discovering Lost Canals* (Shire Publications, 2nd edition 1980)

Squires, Roger, *Canals Revived* (Moonraker Press, 1979)

Ware, Michael, *Britain's Lost Waterways*, Vols 1 and 2 (Historic Waterways Scenes, Moorland Publishing, 1980)

Willan, T. S., *River Navigation in England* (Oxford University Press, 1936, reprinted)

Periodicals which often include articles on lost navigations include the *Journal* of the Railway and Canal Historical Society, *Transport History*, *Industrial Archaeology Review*, *Waterways World*, *Waterways News* (the journal of the British Waterways Board) and *Waterways* (magazine of the Inland Waterways Association).

The Fraenkel Report (published 1975) was commissioned by HM Government. It includes a detailed survey of all the nationalised canals, whether navigable or not, with recommendations and costings.

ACKNOWLEDGEMENTS

I am happy to express my thanks to the many people who have helped me with this book.

I am especially grateful to Philip Weaver, discoverer and historian of the Arbury Canals, to Owen Gibbs of Cardiff, to Paul Flarry of the British Waterways Board for the guided tour of Glasgow and its environs, and to Simon Stoker of the Cromford Canal Society. Others who gave much help in many ways include Kenneth R. Clew, Robin Coleman, Mr D. A. E. Cross, Marc Ferdman, Frank Frecknall, John Goodchild (archivist of Wakefield), Michael Handford, Ron Harpham, William M. Hunt, John Marriage, Michael Messenger, Peter Myall, Mr K. G. Parrott, Mr E. G. Porter of the Southern Water Authority, Nicholas Ross, Simon Ross, Adrian Russell, Dr R. R. Sellman, Dr L. E. Smith, Malcolm Smith, David Souden, Dr Roger Squires, Barrie Trinder of the Ironbridge Gorge Museum, and Mary Turner. I am also grateful to the secretaries of the many canal restoration and preservation societies and trusts whom I asked for information and to many librarians and archivists who replied promptly to my enquiries.

Information on the Montgomery, Swansea and Glamorgan Canals is reproduced by permission of the Controller of HMSO and the Royal Commission on Ancient and Historical Monuments in Wales. I have made specific reference to the help of Stephen Hughes and his colleagues in the notes to the appropriate sections.

This is, I hope, a suitable place to pay tribute to the massive achievements of Charles Hadfield, without whom little canal history would have been written. The volumes of his Canals of the British Isles Series are listed in all the sectional bibliographies and it is a source of pride to me that I was privileged to be a co-author of one of them.

Lastly, my thanks to Jill, who once again has given her most generous help and encouragement. The fact that she was undertaking a 600-mile sponsored swim for charity while I was completing this book gave us a double interest. We finished about the same time, despite her breaking a bone in her foot while we still had the Montgomeryshire Canal to visit. Anyway, she is the first person to have examined the Belan Locks in the snow, on crutches and with one foot in a plastic bag. Where a source is given after a picture caption, I am grateful for permission to reproduce the photograph. The rest of the photographs are my own. The ten area maps first appeared in *British Canals: An Illustrated History* by Charles Hadfield. Other maps are reproduced by courtesy of the Cromford Canal Society, Kenneth Clew and K. G. Parrott.

INDEX

A selection of bestsellers from SPHERE

FICTION

PACIFIC VORTEX!	Clive Cussler	£1.95 ☐
REALITIES	Marian Schwartz	£2.25 ☐
CHAMELEON	William Diehl	£2.25 ☐
THE CAMBODIA FILE	J. Anderson &	
	B. Pronzini	£2.25 ☐
THE STONE FLOWER	Alan Scholefield	£1.95 ☐

FILM & TV TIE-INS

E.T. THE EXTRA-TERRESTRIAL	William Kotzwinkle	£1.50 ☐
THE IRISH R.M.	E. E. Somerville	
	& Martin Ross	£1.95 ☐
INCUBUS	Ray Russell	£1.50 ☐
THE GENTLE TOUCH	Terence Feely	£1.50 ☐

NON-FICTION

NELLA LAST'S WAR	Nella Last	£1.95 ☐
THE NUCLEAR BARONS	P. Pringle	
	& J. Spigelman	£3.50 ☐
THE HEALTH & FITNESS		
HANDBOOK	Ed. Miriam Polunin	£5.95 ☐
ONE CHILD	Torey L. Hayden	£1.75 ☐

All Sphere books are available at your local bookshop or newsagent, or can be ordered direct from the publisher. Just tick the titles you want and fill in the form below.

Name _____

Address _____

_____

Write to Sphere Books, Cash Sales Department, P.O. Box 11, Falmouth, Cornwall TR10 9EN

Please enclose a cheque or postal order to the value of the cover price plus:

UK: 45p for the first book, 20p for the second book and 14p for each additional book ordered to a maximum charge of £1.63.

OVERSEAS: 75p for the first book plus 21p per copy for each additional book.

BFPO & EIRE: 45p for the first book, 20p for the second book plus 14p per copy for the next 7 books, thereafter 8p per book.

Sphere Books reserve the right to show new retail prices on covers which may differ from those previously advertised in the text or elsewhere, and to increase postal rates in accordance with the PO.